INTRODUCTION
TO PASCAL
SECOND EDITION

Cover Photo
Courtesy of Laser Fantasy,
Floyd Rollefstad, photographer.

COPYRIGHT© 1980 By WEST PUBLISHING CO.
COPYRIGHT© 1983 By WEST PUBLISHING CO.
50 West Kellogg Boulevard
P.O. Box 3526
St. Paul, Minnesota 55165

Library of Congress Cataloging in Publication Data

Graham, Neill, 1941–
    Introduction to PASCAL.
    Bibliography: p.
    Includes index.
    1. PASCAL (Computer program language)   I. Title.
QA76.73.P2G7 1983   001.64'24   82-21883
ISBN 0-314-69651-2

3rd Reprint—1984

3,289

INTRODUCTION TO PASCAL

SECOND EDITION

NEILL GRAHAM

WEST PUBLISHING COMPANY

St. Paul   New York   Los Angeles   San Francisco

CONTENTS

Preface   ix

Chapter 1
COMPUTERS, PROGRAMS,
AND PROGRAMMING LANGUAGES   1

Information Processing   1
Programming   2
Computer Hardware   4
Computer Software   7

Chapter 2
PASCAL: FIRST STEPS   11

Pascal   11
Data Types   11
The WRITE and WRITELN Statements   16
Identifiers   20
A Sample Program   21
Arithmetic in Pascal   23
Excercises   26

Chapter 3
USING MAIN MEMORY   29

Variables   29
Declarations   30
Assignment   32
Input   37

Interactive and Noninteractive Programs   39
Example Programs   41
Constant Definitions   43
Exercises   46

Chapter 4
MORE ABOUT EXPRESSIONS   49

Operator Priorities   50
Standard Functions   54
Example Programs   56
Boolean Expressions   58
Exercises   64

Chapter 5
REPETITION   67

The FOR Statement   67
Programs Using the FOR Statement   70
Nested FOR Statements   75
The WHILE Statement   76
Reading Data   79
The REPEAT Statement   84
Exercises   87

Chapter 6
SELECTION   91

One-Way Selection   91
Two-Way Selection   92
Multiway Selection   97
Exercises   105

Chapter 7
FUNCTIONS AND PROCEDURES   109

Functions   109
Procedures   115
The Scopes of Identifiers   118
Global Variables   123
Recursion   127
Exercises   132

Chapter 8
THE SIMPLE DATA TYPES   135

Ordinal Data Types   135
Operations on Ordinal Data Types   139
Exercises   143

Chapter 9
STRUCTURED TYPES: ARRAYS   145

One-Dimensional Arrays   145
Using One-Dimensional Arrays   149
Packed Arrays   153
Strings   155
Multidimensional Arrays   165
Exercises   171

Chapter 10
SEARCHING AND SORTING   175

Searching   175
Sorting   183
Exercises   203

Chapter 11
STRUCTURED TYPES: RECORDS   207

Record Definitions   207
Nested Records   210
Record Variants   213
The Scopes of Field Identifiers   216
Pointer Types   218
Exercises   231

Chapter 12
STRUCTURED TYPES: FILES   237

Sequential Access   237
The File-Update Problem   247
Random Access   256
Exercises   269

Chapter 13
STRUCTURED TYPES: SETS   273

Set Declarations   273
Operations on Sets   275
Using Sets   277
Exercises   282

Appendix 1
Pascal Reserved Words   287

Appendix 2
The GOTO Statement   289

Appendix 3
Declarations Assumed in the Text   291

For Further Reading   293

Index   295

PREFACE

The programming language Pascal was originally developed for teaching programming with emphasis on the techniques known as structured programming. More recently, as programmers in business and industry have begun to discover the limitations of traditional programming languages such as COBOL and FORTRAN, interest in putting Pascal to work in the world outside the classroom has increased. An important boost for Pascal has come from its widespread implementation on microcomputers. Pascal is now established as one of the major programming languages that every programmer should know.

This text is suitable for either an introductory course in Pascal or an introduction-to-programming course using Pascal. No previous programming experience on the part of the students is assumed. Students who *have* had previous programming experience should be able to cover the first four chapters quite rapidly.

The book starts out with an introductory chapter on information processing, computers, programs, programming languages, hardware, and software. The study of Pascal itself begins with the second chapter, which introduces the standard data types, the WRITE and WRITELN statements, and simple arithmetic expressions. Complete (although simple) Pascal programs are introduced at this point.

The next two chapters focus on subjects that are often troublesome to beginners—variables, assignment, arithmetic, Boolean expressions, and standard functions. All too many texts pass over these matters so quickly as to confuse beginners, particularly those without extensive mathematical backgrounds.

In Chapter 5 we turn to the control mechanisms of Pascal—repetition, selection, functions, and procedures. Repetition is taken up before selection, so as to get into realistic examples as soon as possible. Without repetition, it is difficult to find examples for which the use of the computer is justified.

Beginning with Chapter 8 the emphasis shifts from control structures to data structures. Enumerated and subrange types are taken up first, followed by arrays, records, pointers, files, and sets. A chapter on searching and sorting illustrates two important applications of arrays. Pointers are illustrated by an in-memory information storage and retrieval program based on a binary search tree. The linked lists discussed in the first edition of this book are now relegated to exercises.

The infamous GOTO statement is not covered in the body of the text. A brief introduction to the GOTO statement, together with warnings against its use, can be found in Appendix 2. The purpose of the Appendix is to tell readers what the GOTO statement and label declarations are without in any way encouraging their use.

In contrast to the first edition, which used the boldface-and-italics publication form for Pascal programs, this edition uses a form similar to actual computer printout. Only uppercase letters are used, partly because of the hardware used to print the program examples and partly because the uppercase-only items stand out well in running text, clearly distinguishing, for example, the general term "integer" from the data type INTEGER.

Pascal syntax is presented through explanations and illustrations instead of syntax diagrams. As useful as the latter are to accomplished programmers, they are apt to be more confusing than helpful to beginners, who have enough trouble learning a programming language without having to learn a metalanguage as well.

The principles of program design, such as stepwise refinement and the use of functions and procedures as modules, are presented mainly by example. Students need much practical experience with these techniques before theoretical discussions of them can be meaningful. Instructors who wish to discuss these design techniques more thoroughly will find that the text presents many opportunities to do so.

The programs in this book are written in UCSD Pascal, the version of Pascal developed at the University of California at San Diego and widely used on microcomputers and minicomputers. The discussions in the text, however, are not limited to UCSD Pascal. The idiosyncracies of UCSD Pascal are carefully pointed out, and the alternatives found in versions of Pascal adhering to one of the standards (Jensen and Wirth or proposed ISO) are discussed.

Three nonstandard features of UCSD Pascal are discussed in some detail: variable-length strings, obtaining external file names interactively, and random access to files. Because of the importance of these features in real-world programming, they are found in a number of versions of Pascal, often with implementations similar to the ones in UCSD Pascal.

For their helpful reviews of the first edition of this book, I wish to thank Gabriel Barta, Philip J. Drummond, and Bill Mitchell. My special appreciation goes to Gabriel Barta, who contributed many of the new exercises for this edition.

Chapter 1

COMPUTERS, PROGRAMS, AND PROGRAMMING LANGUAGES

Information Processing

A computer is a machine for processing information. It accepts information as input and produces information as output. A computer can also store information. In producing its output, it can draw on the stored information as well as its current input. To get a better idea of the kinds of jobs computers can do, let's look at three examples of information processing by computer.

Word Processing.   In word processing the computer serves as an electronic typewriter. Text to be processed is typed on a typewriter-like keyboard and stored in the computer's memory. Any part of the stored text can be displayed on a television-like screen. By entering the appropriate commands, the user can make insertions, deletions, and changes. The computer rearranges text as necessary to make room for insertions or to close up the space left by deletions. When satisfied with the results, the user orders the computer to print out a clean copy of the stored text.

The text being manipulated is stored in the computer's *main memory*. Data stored in main memory is retained only while the computer is in operation. When the computer is switched off (or if the electricity goes off!), the contents of main memory are lost.

For permanent storage, text is recorded on *diskettes*, which look something like 45 RPM phonograph records enclosed in protective jackets. To save the text stored in main memory, a diskette is inserted into a slot in the computer, and the computer is ordered to record the text on the diskette. When the text has been recorded, the diskette can be removed from the computer and stored in a filing cabinet. To retrieve the stored text, the diskette is inserted into the computer, and the computer is ordered to transfer the desired text from the diskette to the computer's main memory. Word processing operators frequently save their work on diskettes to guard against losing text due to power failures or computer malfunctions.

The input to a word processor consists of not only the text that is typed in but also the commands that direct the computer to do such things as make changes or store the text on a diskette. The output is the clean copy of the text that is printed out after the user has finished making changes. Text is stored temporarily in main memory and permanently on diskettes. The information processing consists of manipulating the stored text in accordance with the user's commands.

Computer Portraits.   Computer portrait stands are frequently encountered in shopping malls or on boardwalks. The subject sits in front of a television camera, which is connected to a computer, and observes his or her picture on a television monitor. When the subject is satisfied with the pose, the operator presses a button, and the computer prints out the customer's portrait. The portraits are quite good, with just enough of a ''computer quality'' to make them interesting.

The input to the computer is the picture picked up by the television camera. An electronic device called a *digitizer*, which is connected between the camera and the computer, encodes the picture as a series of numbers that the computer can manipulate. These numbers are stored in the computer's main memory for further processing. The output from the computer is, of course, the printed portrait. The printer merely prints dots in positions dictated by the computer. The dots are close together for dark areas of the picture and farther apart for lighter areas. The computer's job is to analyze the picture received from the camera and tell the printer where each dot is to be printed.

Video Games.   The most obvious feature of a video game is its output: a television display depicting the current game situation accompanied by sound effects from a loudspeaker. The input to the game is the player's manipulations of the various controls.

The computer must respond to the player's input by updating the display and producing the accompanying sound effects as called for by the rules of the game. The player who fires a missile in a certain direction, for instance, expects to see the missile move across the screen in that direction. And if the missile strikes an enemy spaceship, the player expects to see and hear the resulting explosion. The computer also keeps track of and displays the player's score.

Programming

All the information processing that a computer does is controlled by a set of detailed, step-by-step instructions called a *program*. Since the program determines what job the computer does, we can make a single computer do many different jobs by providing it with different programs. On the other hand, a computer will do nothing useful until it has been supplied with a program for the job to be done.

This doesn't mean, however, that a person who uses a computer has to supply the program or even be aware that the program exists. Some computers, such as those in arcade video games and computer portrait equipment, have their programs built in. The user need only provide the program with the information it needs to do its job. The operator of a computer portrait stand, for example, has only to focus the TV camera on the subject and press a button to "take" the picture. A video game player just drops in a quarter and starts playing.

Computers are classified as *special purpose* or *general purpose.* A special purpose computer is dedicated to a particular job (the adjective *dedicated* is often used to designate a special purpose computer). The program for a special purpose computer is often permanently built into the machine. A general purpose computer, on the other hand, is designed to do as many different jobs as possible. Since each job calls for a different program, general purpose computers are designed to make it as simple as possible for the user to change from one program to another.

Any particular job can be done by either type of computer. For example, you can purchase a *dedicated word processor,* a special purpose computer that can be used only for word processing. Or, you can purchase a word processing program that enables a general purpose computer to be used as a word processor. Programs are also available that let general purpose computers serve as video games and make computer portraits, jobs more frequently done by special purpose computers.

Some special purpose computers allow the user limited flexibility in changing the computer's behavior. For example, home video games take plug-in cartridges, each of which enables the machine to play a different game. In fact, each cartridge contains a program that tells the machine how to play the game in question. On the other hand, most such machines are limited to game playing; no cartridges are available to enable the machine to be used as a word processor, say, or for making computer portraits.

The programs that a computer executes are known as *software;* the computing equipment itself is the *hardware.* Programs that are permanently built into a computer are sometimes referred to as *firmware.*

Where does the software for a general purpose computer come from? Some software may come with the computer and additional software can usually be purchased from the computer manufacturer. As a result of the widespread use of small computers, software publishing has become a substantial industry. Software publishers sell their wares by mail order and through computer stores. Recently, retail stores devoted entirely to computer software have appeared. Video game cartridges are sold in record stores, and plans are underway to sell software in book stores.

If no published program meets your needs, you can write your own or hire a professional programmer to write one to your specifications. If the resulting program meets other people's needs as well, you may be able to publish and sell it, in addition to having it for your own use.

An enormous number of computers are now in use and more are being put to work each day. A program is needed for every single job that each of these computers does. Most people who use these computers will not want to bother learning how to write programs. Yet the programs must come from somewhere. Society is faced with an ever increasing need for people who can write computer programs, either for their own use, for publication, or as professional programmers.

Computer Hardware

We refer to the combination of hardware and software as a *computer system*. The hardware of a computer system consists of four major components: the *central processing unit, main memory, auxiliary memory,* and *input and output devices*. These components communicate with one another over a group of wires known as a *bus*.

Main Memory. Main memory holds the program that the computer is currently executing and the data that it is currently manipulating. As far as the data is concerned, main memory plays the role of a scratchpad or blackboard — it provides temporary storage for the information that is being processed.

Main memory is divided into individual *memory locations*, each of which can hold a fixed amount of data. We can visualize main memory as a set of post office boxes, each box corresponding to a memory location. Corresponding to the post office box numbers, each memory location has a unique *address*, which designates that location for storing data in it or retrieving data from it.

Main memory comes in two forms, known as ROM and RAM. ROM, or *read-only memory*, is used for information that is permanently built into the computer. The information stored in ROM is placed there when the ROM is manufactured and cannot be changed by the computer. The programs for special purpose computers, such as video games, are usually stored in ROM.

RAM, or *random-access memory*, can be used for both storing and retrieving data. ROM is like a printed book whose contents are permanent. RAM is like a blackboard that can be erased and reused again and again. In fact, the computer doesn't even have to bother erasing RAM; any data stored in a RAM location automatically replaces whatever data was previously stored there.

The main drawback of RAM is that it is *volatile*; when the computer is turned off, the contents of RAM are lost. Any information that is not to be lost when the computer is turned off must be permanently built into ROM or stored in auxiliary memory.

The term *random access* means that memory locations can be accessed in any order whatever. We neet not first retrieve the contents of location 1, say, then the contents of location 2, then the contents of location 3, and so on. Both ROM and RAM allow random access, so RAM is a poor term for designating memory that allows data to be both read and written. *Read-write memory* is a better term for the latter; the reason it is not more widely used is that it abbreviates to the unpronounceable RWM.

Information is represented inside a computer using only two symbols, 0 and 1. These two symbols are particularly easy to represent inside the computer because 1 can be represented by an electric circuit in which current is flowing, and 0 can be represented by a circuit in which no current is flowing. The symbols 0 and 1 are known as *binary digits* or *bits.* Each memory location holds a fixed number of bits. On many computers the smallest memory location holds eight bits, which are collectively referred to as one *byte.* The size of main memory is frequently given in bytes. Small computers usually have thousands or tens of thousands of bytes of main memory; large computers have millions or tens of millions.

A method of representing information by means of combinations of bits is known as a *binary code.* For example, the letters of the alphabet and the other symbols on the computer keyboard are often represented using the American Standard Code for Information Interchange (ASCII). In ASCII the letter A is represented by 1000001, the letter B by 1000010, and the letter C by 1000011. All the information stored in a computer's memory or otherwise manipulated by the computer is represented by binary codes.

The Central Processing Unit. The central processing unit (CPU) has two functions: it carries out all data manipulations, and it controls the operation of the rest of the computer.

The CPU fetches program instructions from main memory, one after the other, and sees that each instruction is carried out. The CPU itself carries out any data manipulations, such as arithmetic operations, called for by the instructions. When an instruction calls for the use of main memory, auxiliary memory, or an input or output device, the CPU sends control signals to the designated component, causing it to perform the function requested by the instruction.

In the early 1970s engineers learned how to construct a central processing unit on a tiny chip of silicon. Such a CPU-on-a-chip is called a *microprocessor.* Other important computer components, such as those making up main memory, can also be constructed on silicon chips. Low cost microprocessors and main memory chips now make it possible to use computers in games, household appliances, and office equipment, applications that would once have been out of the question. The enormous increase in computer use made possible by microprocessors is known as the *microprocessor revolution.*

Input and Output Devices. Input and output devices convert information between forms that are convenient for humans, such as printed text, and the binary codes that a computer requires. There are many different types of input and output devices, including such diverse equipment as the television camera in a computer portrait setup and the controls and display of a video game. The input and output devices that programming students are most likely to encounter in their assignments are *card readers, printers,* and *computer terminals.*

A card reader accepts information that has been punched on computer cards. The cards are prepared using a device called a *keypunch*, which is operated by means of a typewriter-like keyboard. When a key is struck, a particular combination of holes is punched into the card. The card reader senses these punched holes and sends the corresponding codes to the computer.

Printers vary in the speed with which they produce printed output. The slowest print character by character, like a typewriter. Faster printers, known as *line printers*, print an entire line in a single operation. There are even *page printers* that print an entire page in a single operation. The more advanced printers print tens of thousands of lines per minute and use exotic technologies such as laser beams and electrically directed ink jets.

A computer terminal is a combination input and output device. It consists of a typewriter-like keyboard coupled with either a typewriter-like printer or a television-like display. Information typed on the keyboard is transmitted to the computer. Information received from the computer is (depending on the type of terminal) typed out by the printer or displayed on the screen.

A *microcomputer* or *personal computer* is a desktop computer built around a microprocessor. A microcomputer looks very much like a computer terminal, with a keyboard, a video display, and perhaps a printer. A microcomputer is a complete computer, however, whereas a terminal is just a device for communicating with a computer located elsewhere.

Auxiliary Memory.   Auxiliary memory is used to store permanent data files and program libraries. Information can be stored in larger amounts and at lower cost than is possible in main memory. What's more, information stored in auxiliary memory can be retained for long periods of time, whereas data stored in main memory is lost when the computer is turned off.

On the other hand, a much longer time is required to access information stored in auxiliary memory than is required for information stored in main memory. For this reason, information is usually transferred between main memory and auxiliary memory in large blocks. A block of information is retained in main memory while it is being processed. When it is no longer needed, it is transferred back to auxiliary memory.

The two most widely used forms of auxiliary memory are *magnetic tape* and *magnetic disks*.

The magnetic tape used by computers is similar to that used for sound and video recording, and it suffers from one of the same problems. If you have ever tried to locate a particular section on a tape recording, you know how much time you waste winding and rewinding the tape until you find the part you want. To locate a particular data item on a computer tape also requires time-consuming winding and rewinding. For this reason, computer tapes are usually processed *sequentially* — we start at the beginning of the tape and process the items in the order in which they were recorded. Because of this, magnetic tape is called a *sequential access* medium.

A magnetic disk looks something like a phonograph record but it works on the same principle as magnetic tape — information is stored as magnetic patterns rather than in grooves. Disks (which include the diskettes mentioned earlier) vary greatly in such details as size, composition, and the containers in which they are mounted. In use the disk rotates like a phonograph record. A *read-write head* — analogous to a phonograph needle — is positioned over the part of the disk where information is to be recorded or played back.

The advantage of disk over tape is that, just as a phonograph needle can be put down on any part of a record, the read-write head can be quickly positioned over any part of the disk. Thus, regardless of where the information is stored on the disk, it can be accessed rapidly without the winding and rewinding that would be needed for tape. Thus disk, like main memory, is said to be a *random access medium.*

Auxiliary memory is also known as *auxiliary storage, mass memory, mass storage,* and *secondary storage.*

Computer Software

There are two kinds of software: *applications software* and *system software.* Applications software consists of the programs that do the various jobs the computer was purchased to do in the first place. Programs that make up payrolls, play games, design electronic components, or compute the orbits of spacecraft are examples of applications software. System software, on the other hand, consists of programs that help people write and execute other programs. This section is devoted to system software; we will see many examples of applications programs later in the book.

Programming Languages.   We need some language in which to state the instructions we want a computer to follow. Unfortunately, natural languages such as English are insufficiently precise for giving instructions to computers. Instead, we must use special purpose languages called *programming languages.*

The central processing unit is designed to execute programs coded in *machine language.* Machine language represents instructions and memory locations by binary codes that are convenient for the CPU but not for humans. The following short sample of machine language consists of instructions for getting two numbers from main memory, adding them, and storing the sum back in memory:

Machine Code	Explanation
00100000	Get the first number
00100001	Get the second number
10100010	Add the two numbers
11000100	Store the sum...
00000000	...back in main memory

A program may consist of thousands, tens of thousands, hundreds of thousands, or even millions of such codes. A machine language programmer has to know the codes for the operations the computer can carry out as well as the coded addresses of the locations in main memory where various data items are stored. Keeping track of all these codes is tedious and error prone, as you can well imagine, so programmers avoid machine language whenever possible.

The next step up from machine language is *assembly language*. Assembly language is similar to machine language, except that easy-to-remember abbreviations are used in place of obscure codes. Thus our sample of machine language might look like this in assembly language:

```
RCL    TOTAL
RCL    VALUE
ADD
STO    TOTAL
```

The abbreviations RCL, ADD, and STO stand for the instructions RECALL (get a value from memory), ADD (add two values), and STORE (store a value in memory). TOTAL and VALUE refer to memory locations from which data is obtained and in which the result is stored. These names are chosen to suggest the nature of the data stored in the corresponding locations.

Assembly language is a step beyond machine language, but not a very big step. The instructions still call for very simple operations, such as fetching a value from memory, so that many thousands of instructions are needed to do any job that isn't utterly trivial. And assembly language programs are still dominated by machine oriented concepts, such as machine instructions and memory locations.

To avoid the difficulties of machine language and assembly language, programmers have devised a number of *higher level languages*. A higher level language allows the programmer to instruct the computer in much the same terms that might be used to tell a human being how to do the same job. The concepts and notation of the higher level language are those appropriate for the kinds of problems being solved rather than those dictated by the internal workings of the computer.

A large number of higher level languages have been devised; at last count around 170 were in use. Fortunately for students of programming, the number in *widespread* use is much smaller — around ten. The following are a few programming languages and their areas of application:

BASIC   Personal computing, education, science, business

COBOL   Business data processing

FORTRAN   Science, mathematics, engineering

LISP   Artificial intelligence, robotics

Logo   Education

Pascal   Education and general purpose computing

The following shows how the addition we looked at in machine language and assembly language would be expressed in each of the higher level languages just mentioned:

BASIC   `LET T = T + V`

COBOL   `ADD VALUE TO TOTAL.`

FORTRAN `TOTAL = TOTAL + VALUE`

LISP   `(SETQ TOTAL (PLUS TOTAL VALUE))`

Logo   `MAKE "TOTAL :TOTAL + :VALUE`

Pascal   `TOTAL := TOTAL + VALUE`

Language Processors.   The only language that the CPU can accept directly is machine language. Under the control of an appropriate program, however, the computer will accept and carry out instructions in other languages. A program that makes it possible for a computer to execute programs written in some language other than machine language is called a *language processor*. There are two kinds of language processors: *translators* (also called *compilers*) and *interpreters.*

A translator translates a program from a higher level language into a code that is easier to execute than the original program. (When we say that a program, such as a translator, does a particular job, we mean, of course, that the computer does the job under the direction of the program.) In some cases the program in the higher level language is translated into machine language, which can then be executed directly by the CPU. In other cases the program in the higher level language is translated into an intermediate code that must be further processed by an interpreter program.

An interpreter executes a program by fetching and executing the instructions one by one. An interpreter does for a higher-level-language program what the CPU does for a machine language program. (Looked at another way, the CPU is an interpreter that is implemented by means of hardware rather than software.) An interpreter can execute a higher-level-language program directly, or it can execute the intermediate code produced by a translator.

Thus, there are three ways we can get a computer to execute a program written in a higher level language: (1) We can use a translator to translate the program into machine language, which is then executed by the CPU. (2) We can use an interpreter program to execute the higher-level-language program. (3) We can use a combination of a translator and an interpreter, the interpreter executing the code produced by the translator. This alternative is frequently used for Pascal.

The Operating System.   Getting a computer to execute a program in a higher level language involves a number of steps. Suppose the program is to be translated into machine language. First, the translator program has to be loaded into main memory and given control of the computer. Under the control of the translator, the computer reads the program from auxiliary memory, translates it, and stores the translated program back in auxiliary memory. For certain functions, such as input and output of data, the translated program calls on previously translated *subprograms* stored in a program library. The translated program, then, has to be processed by a *linker* program that combines it with the necessary library subprograms. Finally, the translated and linked program is loaded into main memory, given control of the computer, and given access to the data it is to process.

To prevent the user from having to worry about all these steps, translation, linking, and execution are done under the supervision of a control program known as the *operating system*. Ideally, the entire process should be carried out in response to a single command from the user. For example, in one popular Pascal system, the user need only type the letter R (for "run") in order to get a program translated, linked, and executed.

The operating system is also responsible for keeping track of the programs and data files stored in auxiliary memory. On each disk, for example, the operating system maintains a directory of all the programs and data files stored on that disk. Each directory entry contains a name that was assigned to the program or data file by the user. When the user requests a program or data file by name, the operating system looks up the name in the disk directory, finds where the program or data file is stored on the disk, and transfers it to main memory.

Chapter 2

PASCAL: FIRST STEPS

Pascal

In this chapter we begin the study of Pascal, a popular programming language named after the seventeenth century French philosopher and mathematician, Blaise Pascal.

Like most other programming languages, Pascal exists in more than one version. The programs in this book are written in UCSD Pascal, a widely used version of the language developed at the University of California at San Diego. I will point out the few idiosyncrasies of UCSD Pascal as we come to them. Your instructor can point out the idiosyncrasies of the version of Pascal you are using.

Data Types

A Pascal program can process many different kinds of data. The different kinds of data are represented differently inside the computer and manipulated using different operations. For example, we might want to do arithmetic on a set of numbers and arrange a list of names in alphabetical order. Attempting to do arithmetic on people's names is clearly inappropriate, and although we can arrange numerical data in alphabetical order, there is usually no point in doing so.

To help us deal with the diversity of data and avoid silly mistakes like trying to multiply or divide letters of the alphabet, Pascal classifies data into different *data types*. Items belonging to the same data type can be manipulated using the same operations and represented in similar ways both in Pascal programs and inside the computer.

The data items belonging to a particular data type are said to be *values* of that type. For example, one data type consists of integers (whole numbers), so ten, twelve, and fifteen are values of type INTEGER.

Symbols used to represent specific values in a Pascal program are called *constants*. For example, the integer values ten, twelve, and fifteen would be represented as

10   12   15

Therefore, 10, 12, and 15 are *integer constants*.

We will find it convenient to describe a data type by describing the constants used to represent values of that type. But we should bear in mind that data types are abstractions independent of the particular symbols used to represent the values.

Pascal has four standard data types: INTEGER, REAL, BOOLEAN, and CHAR (CHAR is an abbreviation for "character.") The programmer does not have to define these types; their definitions are built into Pascal.

The Type INTEGER.   Integers are whole numbers that do not contain decimal points. The following are examples of integer constants:

25   100   75   1000   523

An integer constant may be preceded by a + or a – sign:

+24   –100   +75   –1000   +523

When the sign is omitted, a plus sign is assumed. Thus +25 and 25 represent the same value.

Commas are *not* allowed in writing integers (or any other kinds of numbers, for that matter). Pascal uses commas only to separate items in lists, so using them in numbers would confuse the Pascal language processor. Thus the following are *not* valid integer constants:

1,000   12,340   2,500

Pascal allows constant values to be given names and referred to by name throughout a program. For now, we will look at only one example of this. In every version of Pascal there is a constant, MAXINT, whose value is the largest value of type INTEGER allowed for that particular version of Pascal. All values of type INTEGER must lie in the range

–MAXINT   through   MAXINT

In UCSD Pascal, for example, the value of MAXINT is 32767. Therefore, in USCD Pascal, all values of type INTEGER must lie in the range

–32767   through   32767

The value of MAXINT may be different, of course, in other versions of Pascal.

The Type REAL.   For historical reasons numbers that can have fractional parts (that is, whose constants can contain decimal points) are called *real numbers*. The following are examples of *real constants:*

3.5   −2.75   7.943   8.25

A real constant in Pascal may *not* begin or end with the decimal point. Therefore, the following are *not* valid real constants in Pascal:

235.   .53

Instead we must write

235.0   0.53

As was the case with integer constants, commas may *not* be used in real constants.

Pascal allows another way of expressing real values known as *floating-point notation*. Floating-point notation is convenient when we wish to express very large values (such as 1250000000.0) or very small values (such as 0.000000175) without having to write down large numbers of zeros. You may already be familiar with this notation; some calculators use a variation of it.

Let's look at the following examples:

1.25E+9

The letter E stands for "exponent" and the number to the right of the E (9, in this case) is called the *exponent*. (In fact, floating-point notation is sometimes called *exponential notation*.) The exponent specifies the number of places the decimal point is to be moved to the left or right. If the exponent is positive, the decimal point is moved to the right. If the exponent is negative, the decimal point is moved to the left.

To express 1.25E+9 in conventional notation, we start with 1.25 and move the decimal point nine places to the right. We immediately see a problem: there are only two digits to the right of the decimal point. How can we move the decimal point nine places to the right? The answer is that we add as many zeros to the right of the number as are necessary to move the decimal point the number of places specified by the exponent. If we write down seven zeros after the 5 in 1.25, we can then move the decimal point nine places to the right, getting

1250000000.

Therefore, 1.25E+9 represents the same real number as 1250000000.0. Plus signs in front of exponents can be omitted, so the same value can also be written as 1.25E9.

When the exponent is negative, the decimal point is moved to the left. Taking 1.75E−7 as an example, we start with 1.75 and move the decimal point seven places to the left. To accomplish this, we must first place six zeros to the left of the 1. After doing this and moving the decimal point, we get

.000000175

Therefore, 1.75E–7 represents the same real number as 0.000000175.
    The following are a few more examples of floating-point notation:

Floating-Point Notation	Conventional Notation
1.5E3	1500.0
3.1416E2	314.16
2.79E–2	0.0279
475.0E–1	47.5

Floating-point constants always represent real numbers, even if the decimal point is omitted. When the decimal point is omitted, it is assumed to occur immediately to the left of the E. In the following example, the three constants on each line all represent the same real value:

475E–1 .	475.0E–1	47.5
1E3	1.0E3	1000.0
1E–4	1.0E–4	0.0001

There are limitations on the range of real values that can be represented inside the computer and on the accuracy with which the values are represented. As was the case for integers, these limitations vary from one version of Pascal to another. Unfortunately, there is no constant that summarizes the limitations on real numbers in the same way that MAXINT summarizes the limitations on integers.
    Notice that although 235 and 235.0 represent the same value in ordinary arithmetic, the values they represent in Pascal belong to different data types. The two values are represented differently inside the computer, and some of the operations that can be carried out on them are different. They cannot be used interchangeably in Pascal programs.
    Why does Pascal require both real numbers and integers? There are two reasons:

1. All operations on real numbers have to keep track of the position of the decimal point, a problem that does not arise with integers. Therefore, arithmetic operations on real numbers are usually more time-consuming than the corresponding operations on integers.

2. Arithmetic operations on integers always yield exact results. This is not always possible for real numbers. For example, 10.0 divided by 3.0 equals

3.3333333333333...

where the dots stand for an infinite number of additional 3s. Since a computer's memory can only hold a finite number of digits, this value cannot be stored accurately. Even if a large number of digits is stored, such as

3.333333333333333

the stored value is still not exact.

The Type BOOLEAN. An important feature of computers is their decision-making ability, the ability to take different actions depending on the conditions that hold true when a program is executed. This ability allows us to program the computer to respond flexibly to its input.

In support of the decision-making ability, we need to distinguish between conditions that are true and conditions that are false. For this purpose, we use a data type that has exactly two values, represented by the constants

TRUE   FALSE

These are often called *truth values* or *logical values*, but in Pascal they are called *Boolean values*, in honor of the nineteenth century English mathematician George Boole, who was the first to develop an algebra of logic.

The Type CHAR. Characters consist of the letters of the alphabet, the numbers 0 through 9, the usual punctuation marks, and a small number of special signs such as @, $, +, and –. The available characters can vary from one computer system to another and hence can be different for versions of Pascal running on different computer systems.

A *character constant* consists of a character enclosed in single quote marks (apostrophes):

'A'   'a'   '5'   '@'   '+'   '–'

The quote marks are necessary so that the Pascal language processor will know, for example, that + is a character constant and not an addition sign, or that 5 is a character constant and not the integer five.

The character constant whose value is the single quote mark itself is represented by *two* single quote marks in succession, enclosed in quotes:

''''

Note that all four quote marks are single quotes — that is, the single quote key is struck four times. The double quote is an entirely different character and has nothing to do with the single quote.

String Constants. A series of characters, such as a word or a sentence, is known as a *string*. A *string constant* consists of a series of characters enclosed in single quote marks:

```
'Computer programming is fun'
'ENTER YOUR MOVE, PLEASE'
'23549'
'!#@$%&*'
```

As with character constants, a single quote, or apostrophe, must be represented by two single quotes in succession:

```
'Don''t go near the water'
'Why aren''t you in school today?'
```

The WRITE and WRITELN Statements

The parts of a Pascal program that specify the operations the computer is to carry out are known as *statements*. These are *imperative* statements — each one directs the computer to take one or more actions. Some other term, such as "command" or "instruction" or "order" would probably be better than "statement," but "statement" is traditional.

A program is of little use if it does not direct the computer to produce output that people can use. For this reason, the statements that cause the computer to produce printed output are among the most important ones in any programming language. In Pascal, these are the WRITE and WRITELN statements. (WRITELN is an abbreviation of "write line.")

(In this book, we will use the terms "printed output" and "printout," even though in many cases the output will be displayed on a screen instead of printed on paper.)

The WRITELN Statement.   We can print integers, real numbers, and strings with the WRITELN statement. The values to be printed are listed in parentheses following the word WRITELN. Thus the statements

```
WRITELN(250);
WRITELN(3.14159);
WRITELN('HELLO!')
```

cause the computer to print

```
250
 3.14159
HELLO!
```

Note that the three statements in the example are separated by semicolons. We can see this more clearly if we write all three statements on the same line:

```
WRITELN(250); WRITELN(3.14159); WRITELN('HELLO!')
```

The semicolons separate the statements; there is no semicolon before the first statement nor following the final one. Although it's permissible to write several statements on the same line, for ease in reading we usually write each statement on a separate line.

When the word WRITELN is used by itself, it causes the output device to go to a new line. When used immediately after another WRITELN statement, it causes the output device to skip a line. Thus

```
WRITELN('GOOD MORNING');
WRITELN;
WRITELN('HOW ARE YOU TODAY?')
```

cause the computer to print

```
GOOD MORNING

HOW ARE YOU TODAY?
```

We can provide the WRITELN statement with a list of values to be printed. For example, the statements

```
WRITELN(10, 20, -30, -40, 50);
WRITELN(1.1, 2.2, -3.3, -4.4, 5.5);
WRITELN('ONE', 'TWO', 'THREE', 'FOUR', 'FIVE')
```

cause the computer to print

```
1020-30-4050
1.10000 2.20000-3.30000-4.40000 5.50000
ONETWOTHREEFOURFIVE
```

Unfortunately, the spacing of the items (or the lack of it) leaves much to be desired. What's more, the details of the spacing vary from one version of Pascal to another. The printed output shown is for UCSD Pascal, but if you execute the same WRITELN statements in another version of Pascal, the printed items may be spaced differently. (Also, the real values may be printed in floating-point notation.)

Field-Width Parameters. Fortunately, Pascal provides a mechanism, known as *field-width parameters*, for controlling the spacing of printed items. When the spacing is specified by field-width parameters, it will be the same regardless of the version of Pascal that is being used.

Consider the statement

```
WRITELN(250:10)
```

The value to be printed is 250; the field-width parameter is 10. The latter specifies that the value 250 will be printed in a field ten characters wide. That is, ten character positions on the printed line will be reserved for the value 250. The printed value will be preceded by seven blank spaces, so that the blank spaces together with the three digits of 250 will together occupy ten character positions.

To illustrate in more detail, we need some way of making blank spaces visible, so you can see exactly how many blank spaces separate printed items. We can do this by using a small b to represent a blank space. With this convention, we can say that WRITELN(250:10) causes the computer to print

bbbbbbb250

Now consider the statement

WRITELN(10:5, 20:5, -30:5, -40:5, 50:5)

Each of the integers is printed in a field five characters wide:

bbb10bbb20bb-30bb-40bbb50

To make up the five-character fields, 10, 20, and 50 are each preceded by three blank spaces, and -30 and -40 are each preceded by two blank spaces. Replacing the b's by the blank spaces they represent, we see the actual printout looks like this:

    10   20   -30   -40   50

We can use field-width parameters with strings as well as integers. For example,

WRITELN('ONE':6, 'TWO':6, 'THREE':6, 'FOUR':6, 'FIVE':6)

produces

bbbONEbbbTWObTHREEbbFOURbbFIVE

or, as the line would actually look in the printout

    ONE   TWO THREE   FOUR   FIVE

For real numbers, if we provide only one field-width parameter for each value, the values are printed in floating-point notation. Thus, the statement

WRITELN(105.25:15, -73.5:15, 1000.0:15)

causes the computer to print

bbbbbbb1.05250E2bbbbb-7.35000E1bbbbbbb1.00000E3

or, as it would actually look

    1.05250E2   -7.35000E1   1.00000E3

(The number of digits printed may be greater in other versions of Pascal.)

To get a real value printed in conventional notation, we must follow it with two field-width parameters. The first of these, as usual, gives the width of the field in which the real number is to be printed. The second specifies the number of decimal places that will be printed.

Thus the statement

```
WRITELN(2.67:7:3)
```

prints the value 2.67 in a field seven characters wide and with three digits to the right of the decimal point:

```
bb2.670
```

The statement

```
WRITELN(105.25:15:2, -73.5:15:2, 1000.0:15:2)
```

causes the computer to print

```
bbbbbbbbb105.25bbbbbbbbb-73.50bbbbbbbbb1000.00
```

or, as it would actually appear

```
        105.25          -73.50         1000.00
```

The WRITE Statement. The WRITE statement differs from WRITELN in that WRITE does not cause the output device to go to a new line after it has finished printing. Thus,

```
WRITE(10:4, 20:4, 30:4);
WRITE(40:4, 50:4);
WRITE(60:4, 70:4, 80:4)
```

cause the computer to print

```
10  20  30  40  50  60  70  80
```

Since the final statement is a WRITE statement, the output device remains on the same line and the next WRITE or WRITELN statement to be executed continues printing on the same line.

On the other hand, if we use WRITELN statements instead of WRITE statements

```
WRITELN(10:4, 20:4, 30:4);
WRITELN(40:4, 50:4);
WRITELN(60:4, 70:4, 80:4)
```

the computer prints

```
10   20   30
40   50
60   70   80
```

and the next WRITE or WRITELN statement begins printing on a new line.

    We will use WRITELN more frequently than WRITE, since ordinarily we want each output statement to produce a single line of output. Sometimes, however, it comes in handy to have several different output statements print on the same line, and in those situations we can put the WRITE statement to good use.

Identifiers

In everyday life, we are only rarely called upon to make up a name for something. Either we use existing names ("Jack," "Sue," "Baltimore") or we refer to objects descriptively ("the small brown table in the living room," "the green chair in the corner of the den").

    In computer programming, however, we must frequently make up names for such things as data types, constant values, memory locations, data files, the programs themselves, and certain parts of programs. These made-up names are called *identifiers*. Identifiers must be formed according to certain rules, so the language processor can distinguish them from other parts of the program. If, for example, we allowed 25, 5E3, and 'COMPUTER' as identifiers, the Pascal language processor would confuse the first with an integer, the second with a real number, and third with a string.

    The following are the rules for constructing Pascal identifiers:

1. An identifier must begin with a letter of the alphabet.

2. After the first character the remaining characters of the identifier may be either letters or digits. No other characters (such as spaces or punctuation marks) may be used. Some versions of Pascal allow the underscore character, __, to be used in identifiers. The underscore can be used to separate words in multiword identifiers such as

SALES_TAX_RATE

3. An identifier must not be one of the *reserved words* listed in Appendix 1. The reserved words have already been assigned meanings in Pascal and cannot be redefined by the programmer.

4. Identifiers may be of any length, but only the first eight characters of an identifier are significant. Two identifiers whose first eight characters are the same are considered to be identical. Thus, Pascal considers SALESTAX and SALESTAXRATE to be the same identifier, although the programmer probably intended them to be different. (The number of significant characters varies from one version of Pascal to another.)

The following are some examples of valid identifiers:

```
MESSAGE      ARITHMETIC      AMOUNT    TAXRATE    MAKECHANGE
HALFDOLLAR   LENGTH          DIAMETER  HEIGHT     X25
```

X25, though valid, is a bad choice because it gives no clue as to the nature of the object named.

The following identifiers are invalid:

```
3D              Begins with a digit
CUSTOMER#       # not allowed
YEARLY-RATE     Hyphen not allowed
MONTHLY RATE    Space not allowed
PROGRAM         PROGRAM is a reserved word
```

A Sample Program

At this point we are ready to look at a complete Pascal program. The example program, shown in Figure 2–1, causes the computer to print the following message:

```
WELCOME TO COMPUTER PROGRAMMING IN PASCAL!

THIS MESSAGE WAS BROUGHT TO YOU BY YOUR LOCAL
COMPUTER, OPERATING UNDER THE CONTROL OF A
NINE-LINE PASCAL PROGRAM.
```

This program has three distinct parts: a *program heading*, a *comment*, and a *statement part*. Let's look at each part individually.

```
PROGRAM MESSAGE;
(* DISPLAY A MESSAGE TO THE USER *)
BEGIN
    WRITELN('WELCOME TO COMPUTER PROGRAMMING IN PASCAL!');
    WRITELN;
    WRITELN('THIS MESSAGE WAS BROUGHT TO YOU BY YOUR LOCAL');
    WRITELN('COMPUTER, OPERATING UNDER THE CONTROL OF A');
    WRITELN('NINE-LINE PASCAL PROGRAM.')
END.
```

FIGURE 2–1. This program, which displays a message to the user, illustrates the basic structure of a Pascal program. Note the use of semicolons, single quote marks, and the period at the end of the program. As explained in the text, the program heading will be slightly more complicated in non-UCSD versions of Pascal.

The program heading consists of the line

```
PROGRAM MESSAGE;
```

PROGRAM is a reserved word that identifies the line as a program heading. MESSAGE is the name of the program. The program name is an identifier made up by the programmer. We could have called the program GREETING or EXAMPLE or LISA or any other name satisfying the rules for forming identifiers. The program heading is terminated by a semicolon, which you must be careful to include. Omitting semicolons is probably the most common error in Pascal programming.

Many versions of Pascal require a slightly more complicated program heading than UCSD Pascal does. The program heading is required to specify the *files* that the program will use. In computer programming, a file is any source from which data can be obtained or any destination to which data can be sent. Thus, keyboards and display screens qualify as files, as do sets of data stored on disk or tape. There are two standard files, INPUT and OUTPUT, which most programs use. For example, unless we specify otherwise, a WRITELN statement writes to the standard file OUTPUT.

The file names are listed in parentheses following the name of the program. For example, our program MESSAGE sends data to the standard file OUTPUT (via the WRITELN statement). In a version of Pascal that requires files to be listed our program heading would look like this:

```
PROGRAM MESSAGE(OUTPUT);
```

A program that accepts data from the user as well as sends data to the user must list both INPUT and OUTPUT:

```
PROGRAM CONVERSATION(INPUT, OUTPUT);
```

In this example CONVERSATION is the program name, and INPUT and OUTPUT are the file names. Notice the use of the parentheses, the comma, and the semicolon.

Comments.   The line

```
(* DISPLAY A MESSAGE TO THE USER *)
```

is a *comment*. A comment can be enclosed in either the curly brackets { cnd } or the symbols (* and *). Comments are intended for people and are ignored by the computer.

Comments can be placed anywhere in the program. Normally, comments are written in one of two ways:

1. The comment is written on a line by itself, as in the example program. This is usually done when the comment applies to the entire program or to a substantial section of the program.

2. The comment is written on the same line as another statement:

```
WRITELN      (* SKIP A LINE *)
```

This method is usually used when the comment applies to only one statement, the statement that is on the same line as the comment.

The line following the program heading is a good place for a comment that briefly describes the purpose of a program. Note that a comment is often phrased as a command:

```
(* DISPLAY A MESSAGE TO THE USER *)
(* SKIP A LINE *)
(* COMPUTE AVERAGE *)
```

The comment is the command that we would give to the computer if it were able to understand English.

Enough comments should be used in a program so that a person not familiar with the program can understand it. ("A person not familiar with the program" includes the programmer six months after the program was written.) The examples in this book are, for the most part, somewhat undercommented, since the workings of each program are described thoroughly in the surrounding text.

The number of comments needed can be greatly reduced by using meaningful identifiers— that is, by using MESSAGE instead of M35.

The Statement Part. The statement part of a program contains the imperative statements the computer will execute.

The statements are bracketed by the reserved words BEGIN and END. A group of statements bracketed by BEGIN and END are said to form a *compound statement*. The statement part of a program is always a compound statement.

The statements making up the compound statement are separated by semicolons. Regardless of whether the statements are written on the same line or on different lines, the semicolons are used only between statements. There is no semicolon between BEGIN and the first statement or between the last statement and END.

The statements making up a compound statement are usually indented with respect to BEGIN and END. This makes it easy to see at a glance which statements make up the compound statement, saving us from having to hunt through a complicated program to find which END goes with a particular BEGIN. (Although there is only one BEGIN–END pair in the simple program given here, a complicated program will have many.)

The period following END indicates the end of the program.

Arithmetic in Pascal

In Pascal, any combination of symbols that can represent a value is known as an *expression*. Thus the various kinds of constants are examples of expressions:

```
25        -2.5        TRUE        'A'
```

Another way to represent a value is to show how it can be computed from other values. For example, 3 + 5 and 9 – 7 represent the values 8 and 2, respectively. Thus combinations such as 3 + 5 and 9 – 7 also qualify as expressions.

In an expression such as 3 + 5, + is called the *operator*, and 3 and 5 are the *operands*. Since we are interested in arithmetic for the moment, we will concentrate on *arithmetic expressions* — expressions whose values are integers or real numbers. Consequently, we are interested in *arithmetic operators* — those operators that operate on integer or real operands to yield integer or real results.

The arithmetic operators for addition and subtraction are, as you might suspect, + and –. Unfortunately, we cannot use the familiar signs for multiplication and division, since most computer displays and printers do not provide × and ÷. Therefore, we use an asterisk, *, for multiplication. For reasons that we will look at in a moment, three division operators are necessary. They are /, DIV, and MOD. The following table summarizes the arithmetic operators in Pascal:

+	addition
–	subtraction
*	multiplication
/, DIV, MOD	division

The operators +, –, *, and / apply to both real numbers and integers. For +, –, and *, if both operands are integers, then the result is an integer. But if either or both of the operands are real numbers, the result is a real number. The following expressions illustrate this for +

Expression	Value
3 + 5	8
3 + 5.0	8.0
3.0 + 5	8.0
3.0 + 5.0	8.0

This scheme is not satisfactory for division, however. Even when both operands are integers, division may yield a result with a fractional part, as when we divide 3 by 2 and get 1.5. For this reason, the division operator gives a real result regardless of whether the operands are integers or real numbers:

Expression	Value
3 / 2	1.5
3 / 2.0	1.5
3.0 / 2	1.5
3.0 / 2.0	1.5

Pascal does, however, provide a way of dividing two integers and obtaining integer results. This is *quotient-remainder division*, which most of us learned in grade school before taking up fractions and decimals. With quotient-remainder division, we compute an integer quotient and an integer remainder instead of a single real-number quotient:

$$\begin{array}{r} 4 \\ 3\overline{\smash{\big)}14} \\ 12 \\ \hline 2 \end{array}$$ (quotient)

(remainder)

Pascal provides two operators for quotient-remainder division. The operator that computes the quotient is named DIV, and the operator that computes the remainder is (for historical reasons) named MOD:

Expression	Value
14 DIV 3	4
14 MOD 3	2

The WRITE and WRITELN statements can be used to print the values of any expressions, not just the values of constants. For example, the program in Figure 2–2 produces the following printout:

```
23 + 48 = 71
8.5 - 14.3 = -5.80000
1.37 * 4.63 = 6.34310
72.5 / 50 = 1.45000
68 DIV 9 = 7
68 MOD 9 = 5
```

Since no field-width parameters were used, the appearance of the printout may be different for other versions of Pascal.

```
PROGRAM ARITHMETIC;
BEGIN
   WRITELN('23 + 48 = ', 23 + 48);
   WRITELN('8.5 - 14.3 = ', 8.5 - 14.3);
   WRITELN('1.37 * 4.63 = ', 1.37 * 4.63);
   WRITELN('72.5 / 50 = ', 72.5 / 50);
   WRITELN('68 DIV 9 = ', 68 DIV 9);
   WRITELN('68 MOD 9 = ', 68 MOD 9)
END.
```

FIGURE 2–2. **This program illustrates arithmetic in Pascal. Since field-width parameters are not used, the appearance of the printout can vary from one version of Pascal to another.**

Exercises

1. Express each of the following values in floating-point notation:

(a) 2600.0   (b) 9845.6
(c) 758.35   (d) −0.0003
(e) 0.0000285

2. Express each of the following values in conventional notation:

(a) 3.5E7   (b) 1.25E−5
(c) 150E−2   (d) 1E3
(e) 1E−4

3. Why is each of the following identifiers invalid?

(a) FINAL SCORE   (b) R2-D2
(c) 4THDIVISION   (d) BEGIN
(e) %INTEREST

4. Write a Pascal program to print your name and address in the three-line format used to address an envelope.

5. Write a program to print out the top few lines of a letter addressed to the President at the White House. The printout should include the president's address, your address, the date, and the greeting "Dear Mr. President:".

6. Write a program to print the following price list:

```
Item No.     Price

    2974      4.29
    6098     15.95
    8347      1.19
    9841     25.40
```

(*Hint:* To make the column headings and columns line up, use the same field width for a column as was used for the column heading.) Make sure you skip a line between the column headings and the columns.

7. Write a program to print the following diamond pattern:

```
   *
  ***
 *****
*******
 *****
  ***
   *
```

8. Write a program to demonstrate how your system prints integers, real numbers, and strings when no field-width parameters are used.

9. Give the data type of the value computed by each of the following expressions:

(a) 7 - 4   (b) 6 / 3
(c) 3.0 * 9   (d) 25 DIV 9
(e) 17 MOD 7   (f) 9.0 / 3.0

10. Write a program that will work out the following arithmetic problems and print the answers. Each answer should be printed on a separate line and identified with printed text:

(a) 125 + 379
(b) 325 - 150
(c) 65 × 45
(d) 27 ÷ 8 (real number quotient)
(e) 27 ÷ 8 (integer quotient and remainder)

Chapter 3

USING MAIN MEMORY

In the previous chapter, we saw that by using statements such as

```
WRITELN(2543 + 7641)
```

we could cause the computer to carry out a calculation and print the result. What we did not see was how to save the result of a calculation so that it could be used later in the program. Saving results for later use is one function of the computer's main memory.

Variables

Named Memory Locations. Main memory, you recall, is divided up into many separate memory locations, each of which can hold a certain amount of data. Each memory location has a unique address that can be used to designate the location for storing or retrieving data.

We could refer to memory locations by their addresses, as machine language programmers do. But it doesn't take much time wondering whether a result was stored in location 1101100101111011 or location 1101100101011011 to drive a person mad. Fortunately, higher level languages such as Pascal offer a better alternative.

In Pascal, we can use identifiers as the names of memory locations. We can refer to the locations by their names instead of by their addresses. The Pascal language processor keeps track of the address corresponding to each name. It is as if we could just put names on our letters and the post office would look up the addresses for us.

For instance, suppose we have a program that is working with items of merchandise that are taxed at different rates. We might want to keep track of the identification number of the item the program is currently working with, as well as the tax rate for that item. We could use two identifiers, IDNUMBER and TAXRATE, to name the memory locations holding the identification number and the tax rate.

Suppose the identification number of a certain item is 12543 and tax rate is 0.035. We can visualize the part of main memory holding these items as follows:

IDNUMBER | 12543 |

TAXRATE | 0.035 |

By using the names of these locations in the program, we can direct the computer to use the stored values and to store new values in these locations.

Because the contents of a memory location vary as the program is executed and new values are stored in the location, we refer to a named memory location as a *variable*. The name of the location is called the *variable name* and the value stored in the location is called the *value of the variable*. Instead of drawing pictures of memory locations as we just did, we can just list the values of the variables IDNUMBER and TAXRATE:

Variable	Value
IDNUMBER	12542
TAXRATE	0.035

We always refer to variables by their names, just as we refer to people and places by *their* names. Thus, we say that IDNUMBER has the value 12543 and that TAXRATE has the value 0.035. Sometimes we abbreviate this even further and say that IDNUMBER equals 12543 or that IDNUMBER *is* 12543. All these are shorthand ways of saying that the value of the variable IDNUMBER is 12543, and this itself is a shorthand way of saying that the value stored in the memory location named IDNUMBER is 12543.

Declarations

In Pascal the values that any particular variable can have are restricted to a single data type. The *type of the variable* is the data type of the possible values of the variable. For example, a *real variable*—a variable of type REAL—can only have real values; an *integer variable*—a variable of type INTEGER—can only have integer values, and so on.

We must declare the type of every variable appearing in a Pascal program. There are several reasons for this. Values of different types need memory locations of different sizes; the language processor needs to know the type of a variable in order to choose the corresponding memory location. Some operators can be applied to values of more than one type; +, for example, can be applied to both integers and real numbers. The language processor must know the types of the values to which an operator is applied in order to translate or interpret the operator correctly. Finally, by keeping track of the types of all the values in a program, the language processor can catch silly mistakes such as attempting to multiply and divide people's names.

Every Pascal program has a *variable declaration part* that lists each variable to be used in the program and declares its type. The four standard data types are represented by the following identifiers:

```
INTEGER     REAL     BOOLEAN     CHAR
```

The variable declaration part of a program comes between the program heading and the statement part.

For example, consider the following variable declaration part:

```
VAR
    X: REAL;
    I: INTEGER;
```

The variable declaration part is introduced by the reserved word VAR. Following VAR are a number of declarations; each declaration ends with a semicolon. A colon separates each variable name from the following type identifier.

The declarations in the example are

```
X: REAL;
```

and

```
I: INTEGER;
```

According to these declarations, the program of which they are a part uses only two variables, X and I. X is a real variable; its values can only be real numbers. I is an integer variable; its values can only be integers.

When several variables are declared to be the same type, we can combine their declarations as follows:

```
VAR
    X, Y, Z: REAL;
    I, J, K: INTEGER;
```

As is always the case in Pascal we can arrange the program text into lines in any way we find convenient. In the variable declaration part, it is sometimes convenient to list each variable on a separate line together with a comment describing the role the variable plays in the program:

```
VAR
    EMPLNO: INTEGER;        (* EMPLOYEE NUMBER *)
    HOURS,                  (* HOURS WORKED *)
    RATE: REAL;             (* HOURLY PAY RATE *)
```

If we don't want to include the comments, we can write the declarations like this:

```
VAR
    EMPLNO: INTEGER;
    HOURS, RATE: REAL;
```

In the rest of this book we will often discuss examples that are not parts of complete programs. To keep from having to give a declaration part for each example, we will assume the following declarations apply:

```
VAR
    X, Y, Z: REAL;
    I, J, K: INTEGER;
    P, Q: BOOLEAN;
    C: CHAR;
```

That is, without explicitly stating so each time, we will assume that X, Y, and Z are real variables; I, J, and K are integer variables; and so on. The declarations just given are repeated in Appendix 3 for easy reference.

Assignment

Assignment is the operation that stores a value in a memory location. Since the value stored in a memory location is the value of the corresponding variable, the assignment operation gives a variable a new value. We say that it *assigns* a new value to the variable, hence the name "assignment."

The *assignment operator* in Pascal is :=, and the *assignment statement* has the following form:

variable := *expression*

When the computer executes an assignment statement, it evaluates the expression and assigns the resulting value to the variable. The assignment operator can be read as "becomes," meaning that the value of the variable becomes the value of the expression.

The simplest kind of expression is a constant. In each of the following assignments, the expression is a constant:

```
I := 1000;
X := 3.5;
P := TRUE;
C := 'A'
```

After the computer has executed these assignments statements, the variables I, X, P, and C have the following values:

Variable	Value
I	1000
X	3.5
P	TRUE
C	'A'

Further assignment statements can change these values, of course. For example, if the assignments

```
X := 4.8;
P := FALSE
```

are carried out, the values of the variables become:

Variable	Value
I	1000
X	4.8
P	FALSE
C	'A'

The only variables with new values are those whose values were explictly changed by the assignment statements. The other variables retain their old values.

Normally, the values assigned to a variable must have the same type as the variable. Only Boolean values can be assigned to Boolean variables, for example, and only character values can be assigned to character variables.

There is one exception to this rule, however. For every integer value there is a corresponding real value. For example, the real value corresponding to 25 is 25.0, the real value corresponding to 150 is 150.0, and so on. Pascal allows us to assign an integer value to a real variable. When the assignment is executed, the integer value is automatically converted to the corresponding real value. Thus,

```
X := 25;
Y := 150;
Z := 0
```

are permitted. After the assignments have taken place, the values of X, Y, and Z are

Variable	Value
X	25.0
Y	150.0
Z	0.0

The reverse is *not* permitted; we cannot assign real values to integer variables. This is because there are no integer values corresponding to many real values, such as 3.5 and 4.8.

Expressions containing operators can be used in assignment statements, of course. Each expression is evaluated, and its value is assigned to the variable on the left-hand side of the assignment operator. The following statements illustrate this:

```
I := 7 + 5;
J := 9 - 4;
K := 8 * 3;
X := 30 / 8
```

After these assignments have been carried out, the values of the variables are

Variable	Value
I	12
J	5
K	24
X	3.75

Variables in Expressions. We have seen that an expression is any combination of symbols that represents a value. A variable represents a value, namely, the value stored in the corresponding memory location. Therefore, variables, like constants, can serve as expressions, either by themselves or as parts of more complex expressions. For example, the following are all valid expressions:

```
I     J     I + 5     10 - J     I + J     I / J
```

When the computer encounters a variable in an expression, it obtains the value of the variable from memory and uses that value in evaluating the expression. For instance, suppose the values of I and J are

Variable	Value
I	9
J	6

With these values for I and J, the values of the expressions just given are:

Expression	Value
I	9
J	6
I + 5	14
10 - J	4
I + J	15
I / J	1.5

Expressions containing variables can be used anywhere that expressions are permitted. For example, they can be used in WRITE and WRITELN statements. The statement

```
WRITELN(I + 5);
```

causes the computer to print

```
14
```

Expressions containing variables can also be used in assignment statements. For example, the statements

```
K := I + J;
X := I / J
```

assign the following values to K and X:

Variable	Value
K	15
X	1.5

A few kinds of assignment statements should be looked at in more detail, since they sometimes confuse beginners. For example, consider the statement

```
K := I
```

The variable I represents its value, since the variable appears in the expression part of the assignment statement. If the value of I is 9, this assignment is equivalent to

```
K := 9
```

and K is assigned the value 9. The value of I remains unchanged, of course.

We can think of this kind of assignment statement as specifying a copying operation. The value stored in memory location I is copied in memory location K. Figure 3–1 illustrates this kind of assignment.

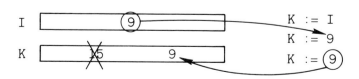

FIGURE 3–1. The assignment K := I can be understood as a copying operation; the contents of memory location I are copied into memory location K.

In executing the assignment

```
K := I + J
```

the computer first replaces the variables in the expression by their values:

```
K := 9 + 6
```

Then the addition is carried out

```
K := 15
```

and the result is assigned to the variable K. Figure 3–2 illustrates this kind of assignment.

Beginners sometimes have trouble with assignment statements such as

```
I := I + J
```

where the same variable appears on both sides of the assignment operator. But this statement is executed just like the previous one. The values of I and J are obtained from memory and substituted for the variables:

```
I := 9 + 6
```

The result of evaluating the expression is assigned to I

```
I := 15
```

Thus 6, the "old value" of I, is used in evaluating the expression. The value of the expression, 15, becomes the new value of I when the assignment takes place. Note that the overall effect of the statement is to increase the value of I by an amount equal to the value of J.

Two important applications of this kind of statement are *counting* and *accumulating totals*. Suppose, for example, that we want to count the ocurrences of some event, using the integer variable I as our counter. We start by "clearing" the counter—we set the value of I to 0:

```
I := 0
```

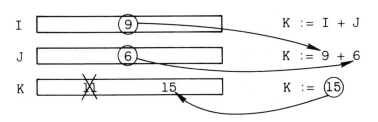

FIGURE 3–2. To execute the assignment K := I + J, the computer first obtains the values of I and J from memory. It then adds the two values and stores the result in memory location K.

Every time we want to count an event we execute

```
I := I + 1
```

which increases the value of I by 1. The following statements and comments show how the value of I changes:

```
I := 0;              (* THE VALUE OF I IS 0 *)
I := I + 1;          (* THE VALUE OF I IS 1 *)
I := I + 1;          (* THE VALUE OF I IS 2 *)
I := I + 1;          (* THE VALUE OF I IS 3 *)
```

Accumulating totals works in much the same way. Suppose we want to use X as the *accumulator*—the memory location in which the running total will be stored. The accumulator plays somewhat the same role as the display on a calculator.

Suppose that we wish to add the values 3.5, 2.7, 1.9, and 6.3. We begin by "clearing" the accumulator

```
X := 0.0
```

and then proceed to add each value to the contents of the accumulator. The following statements and comments illustrate the process:

```
X := 0.0;            (* THE VALUE OF X IS 0.0 *)
X := X + 3.5;        (* THE VALUE OF X IS 3.5 *)
X := X + 2.7;        (* THE VALUE OF X IS 6.2 *)
X := X + 1.9;        (* THE VALUE OF X IS 8.1 *)
X := X + 6.3;        (* THE VALUE OF X IS 14.4 *)
```

Input

Two statements, READ and READLN, are used to input values from the standard input file. For example, the statement

```
READ(I, J, K)
```

causes three values to be read and assigned to the variables I, J, and K. Suppose the input data is

```
25   6   -100
```

After the READ statement has been executed, the variables I, J, and K have the following values:

Variable	Value
I	25
J	6
K	-100

Successive READ statements input successive data items, regardless of how the data items have been arranged on punched cards or typed lines. For example, consider the statements:

```
READ(I, J);
READ(K, X);
READ(Y, Z)
```

If the data entered is

```
25   40   500
3.5   7.9
2.0
```

the variables receive the following values:

Variable	Value
I	25
J	40
K	500
X	3.5
Y	7.9
Z	2.0

The READLN statement reads values for the specified variables and then goes on to the next card or line. Any further data on the current card or line is ignored. For example, suppose that

```
READLN(I, J);
READLN(X, Y)
```

are executed, and the input data is

```
10   20   4.5   19
6.9   8.5   17   3.5
```

The values assigned to the variables are

Variable	Value
I	10
J	20
X	6.9
Y	8.5

On the first line of input, only the first two values, 10 and 20, are used; the values 4.5 and 19 are skipped. On the second line of input, only the first two values, 6.9 and 8.5, are used; the values 17 and 3.5 are skipped. The next READ or READLN statement in the program will commence reading on a new line.

Interactive and Noninteractive Programs

There are two ways of supplying a program with the data it is to process. For an *interactive program*, the user uses a computer terminal to enter each data item at the program's request. The program might request some data, calculate and display some results, request more data, display more results, and so on. The user and the program engage in a two-way exchange of information. For this reason, an interactive program is sometimes said to be *conversational*.

A *noninteractive program*, on the other hand, does not communicate with the user while it is executing. All the program's input must be prepared in advance, either by punching it on cards or storing it in a disk file. When the program is executed, it processes the previously prepared input. Its output is either printed on paper or stored in a disk file. After the program has been executed the user can examine the output to determine if the program worked properly.

Both interactive and noninteractive programs have their places. For such applications as games and computer assisted instruction, the two-way interaction between the program and the user is essential. On the other hand, if our program is to print paychecks for 10,000 employees, we don't want to have a conversation with the computer about each employee. Instead, we need a noninteractive program that takes the employee file as input and produces as output the paychecks, a payroll report, and perhaps an updated employee file.

The choice of interactive or noninteractive programming is not always left up to the programmer. Some computer systems only support interactive programming, and some only support noninteractive programming. Some systems can process noninteractive programs more rapidly and at lower cost than interactive ones. For the sake of economy, some users, such as students, may be restricted to noninteractive programming.

UCSD Pascal, the version of Pascal used to write the programs in this book, is oriented toward interactive programming, so most of the example programs are interactive. The modifications needed for noninteractive programming are discussed where appropriate. In general, interactive programs are slightly more complex than noninteractive ones, so if you are using a noninteractive system you will find that your programs can be slightly simpler than the ones given in the text.

Prompts. An interactive program must ask the user to enter each item of input. The requests for input are called *prompts*. Each prompt must make clear what data item the user is to enter.

For example, suppose a program needs a person's account number and the amount of the person's purchases. The program can use the following statements to obtain this data from the user:

```
WRITELN('ENTER ACCOUNT NUMBER');
READLN(ACCTNO);
WRITELN('ENTER AMOUNT OF PURCHASE');
READLN(AMOUNT)
```

The first and third statements print prompts; the second and fourth statements input the data. When these statements are executed, a dialog similar to the following takes place as the user responds to the prompts:

```
ENTER ACCOUNT NUMBER
1937
ENTER AMOUNT OF PURCHASE
182.75
```

The first and third lines are the prompts printed by the program. The second and fourth lines are the responses typed by the user. ACCTNO receives the value 1937, and AMOUNT receives the value 182.75.

Some systems allow the prompt and response to appear on the same line. In UCSD Pascal we specify this form of dialog by using WRITE for the prompts instead of WRITELN:

```
WRITE('ENTER ACCOUNT NUMBER: ');
READLN(ACCTNO);
WRITE('ENTER AMOUNT OF PURCHASE: ');
READLN(AMOUNT)
```

The dialog now goes like this:

```
ENTER ACCOUNT NUMBER: 1937
ENTER AMOUNT OF PURCHASE: 182.75
```

As before, the program printed the prompts, and the user typed the input data. The statements

```
WRITE('ACCOUNT NUMBER? ');
READLN(ACCTNO);
WRITE('AMOUNT OF PURCHASE? ');
READLN(AMOUNT)
```

give a slightly terser dialog:

```
ACCOUNT NUMBER? 1937
AMOUNT OF PURCHASE? 182.75
```

Not all Pascal systems will allow the prompt and response to appear on the same line, and some that do may use different Pascal statements for this purpose. For example, one system has a special PROMPT statement that must be used in place of WRITE or WRITELN for a prompt that is to appear on the same line with its response.

Noninteractive Programs. Noninteractive programs differ from interactive programs in two ways. First, no prompts are needed because all the input data is prepared before the program is executed. Second, the program should print out the input data as well as the results of its calculations.

Why should the input data be printed by a noninteractive program but not by an interactive one? The input that the user enters for an interactive program will probably still be on the screen when the program prints its results. On the other hand, the input data for a noninteractive program may not be readily available when the user is examining the output.

For example, a noninteractive program that needs a person's account number and the amount the person purchased would simply read them with

```
READ(ACCTNO, AMOUNT)
```

or

```
READLN(ACCTNO, AMOUNT)
```

The input data, punched on a card or stored in a disk file, would have the following form:

```
1937    182.75
```

Before printing the results of its calculations, the program would print the data it had read:

```
WRITELN('ACCOUNT NUMBER: ', ACCTNO);
WRITELN('AMOUNT: ', AMOUNT:8:2)
```

Example Programs

Computing Sales Tax.   Figure 3–3 shows a program, TAX, for computing the sales tax on a purchase and the total amount that the customer must pay. In the variable declaration part, the program declares five real variables AMOUNT, TAXRATE, DCMLRATE, SALESTAX, and TOTAL. Each variable appears on a separate line so that its use can be described by a comment. Note, however, that the punctuation is the same as if the entire declaration had been written on one line:

```
AMOUNT, TAXRATE, DCMLRATE, SALESTAX, TOTAL: REAL;
```

The program begins requesting the amount of the purchase and the sales tax rate from the user:

```
WRITE('AMOUNT OF PURCHASE? ');
READLN(AMOUNT);
WRITE('SALES TAX RATE (IN PERCENT)? ');
READLN(TAXRATE);
```

The value entered for TAXRATE is expressed as a percentage; for example, 3 would be entered for a 3% tax rate, 4.5 would be entered for

```
PROGRAM TAX;
(* GIVEN THE COST OF A PURCHASE AND THE SALES TAX RATE,
   COMPUTE THE SALES TAX AND THE TOTAL AMOUNT TO BE PAID *)
VAR
    AMOUNT,                (* AMOUNT OF PURCHASE *)
    TAXRATE,               (* TAX RATE AS PERCENT *)
    DCMLRATE,              (* TAX RATE AS DECIMAL *)
    SALESTAX,              (* SALES TAX ON AMOUNT OF PURCHASE *)
    TOTAL: REAL;           (* TOTAL AMOUNT TO BE PAID *)
BEGIN
    WRITE('AMOUNT OF PURCHASE? ');
    READLN(AMOUNT);
    WRITE('SALES TAX RATE (IN PERCENT)? ');
    READLN(TAXRATE);
    DCMLRATE := TAXRATE / 100.0;        (* CONVERT TO DECIMAL *)
    SALESTAX := AMOUNT * DCMLRATE;
    TOTAL := AMOUNT + SALESTAX;
    WRITELN('THE SALES TAX IS ', SALESTAX:5:2);
    WRITELN('THE TOTAL AMOUNT TO BE PAID IS ', TOTAL:8:2)
END.
```

FIGURE 3-3. This program computes the sales tax on a purchase and the total amount that the customer must pay. The first four statements of the program obtain the amount of the purchase and the sales tax rate via an interactive dialog with the user. These statements may have to be modified slightly for some versions of Pascal.

a 4.5% tax rate, and so on. Before the tax rate can be used in our calculations, the percent must be converted to a decimal, which we do by dividing the percent by 100.0:

```
DCMLRATE := TAXRATE / 100.0;
```

We compute the sales tax on a purchase by multiplying the amount of the purchase by the sales tax rate expressed as a decimal. We then add the sales tax to the amount of the purchase to get the total amount that the customer must pay:

```
SALESTAX := AMOUNT * DCMLRATE;
TOTAL := AMOUNT + SALESTAX
```

The two WRITELN statements print the results of the calculations. A typical dialog with the user goes like this:

```
AMOUNT OF PURCHASE? 200
SALES TAX RATE (IN PERCENT)? 4
THE SALES TAX IS  8.00
THE TOTAL AMOUNT TO BE PAID IS   208.00
```

Note that we can enter integer values for real variables; Pascal will convert the integers to real numbers. Aside from this, the values entered must always have the same type as the corresponding variables in the READ or READLN statements.

A Noninteractive Version of TAX. Figure 3-4 shows a noninteractive version of the sales tax program. Note that:

1. there are no prompts.

2. the two data values are read with a single READ statement. (A READLN statement could also have been used.)

3. the program prints its input data as well as the results that it calculates.

Constant Definitions

A Pascal program can have a *constant definition part* in which we can define identifiers to represent constant values:

```
CONST
    DISCOUNTRATE = 0.12;
```

```
PROGRAM TAX;
(* A NONINTERACTIVE VERSION OF THE SALES-TAX PROGRAM *)
VAR
    AMOUNT,              (* AMOUNT OF PURCHASE *)
    TAXRATE,             (* TAX RATE AS PERCENT *)
    DCMLRATE,            (* TAX RATE AS DECIMAL *)
    SALESTAX,            (* SALES TAX ON AMOUNT OF PURCHASE *)
    TOTAL: REAL;         (* TOTAL AMOUNT TO BE PAID *)
BEGIN
    READ(AMOUNT, TAXRATE);
    DCMLRATE := TAXRATE / 100.0;
    SALESTAX := AMOUNT * DCMLRATE;
    TOTAL := AMOUNT + SALESTAX;
    WRITELN('AMOUNT OF PURCHASE: ', AMOUNT:8:2);
    WRITELN('SALES TAX RATE: ', TAXRATE:4:1);
    WRITELN('SALES TAX: ', SALESTAX:5:2);
    WRITELN('TOTAL AMOUNT TO BE PAID: ', TOTAL:8:2)
END.
```

FIGURE 3-4. A noninteractive version of the sales tax program. Note that (a) no prompts are printed, and (b) the program prints its input data as well as the results of its calculations.

The constant definition part is introduced by the reserved word CONST. Each definition has the form

identifier = constant;

When present, the constant definition part immediately precedes the variable declaration part.

In the example, the definition

DISCOUNTRATE = 0.12;

defines DISCOUNTRATE as another way of representing the real constant 0.12. Wherever DISCOUNTRATE appears in the program, the effect will be the same as if 0.12 had been written.

Note that, unlike a variable, a constant identifier cannot be assigned new values during the execution of the program. DISCOUNTRATE is just a synonym for 0.12, and a statement such as

DISCOUNTRATE := 0.15

is just as meaningless as

0.12 := 0.15

Only a variable name, the name of a memory location, can be used on the left-hand side of the assignment operator.

Why use constant definitions? First, they make the program easier to understand. DISCOUNTRATE is more meaningful than 0.12, making it easier to follow the statements that carry out the discount calculation. Second, if the value of a constant must be changed, we can just change the constant definition and not have to locate every place in the program where the constant is used. For example, if the discount rate is reduced from 12% to 9%, we need only change the constant definition part of our program to read:

CONST
    DISCOUNTRATE = 0.09;

The Change-Making Program.   As an illustration of constant definitions, Figure 3–5 shows a program for making change. Such a program might be used in a computerized vending machine.

Making change is based on quotient-remainder division. For example, suppose we owe a customer 71 cents in change and need to know how many half dollars to return. Since a half dollar is worth 50 cents, we divide 71 by 50 using quotient-remainder division:

$$
\begin{array}{r}
1 \\
50\overline{)71} \\
\underline{50} \\
21
\end{array}
$$

```
PROGRAM MAKECHANGE;
(* GIVEN AMOUNT OF CHANGE, COMPUTE NUMBER OF HALF
   DOLLARS, QUARTERS, DIMES, NICKELS, AND PENNIES
   TO BE RETURNED *)
CONST
   (* VALUES OF COINS IN CENTS *)
   HALFDOLLAR = 50;
   QUARTER = 25;
   DIME = 10;
   NICKEL = 5;
VAR
   CHANGE: INTEGER;        (* AMOUNT REMAINING TO BE RETURNED *)
BEGIN
   WRITE('AMOUNT OF CHANGE IN CENTS? ');
   READLN(CHANGE);
   WRITELN;
   WRITELN('HALVES   ', CHANGE DIV HALFDOLLAR);
   CHANGE := CHANGE MOD HALFDOLLAR;
   WRITELN('QUARTERS ', CHANGE DIV QUARTER);
   CHANGE := CHANGE MOD QUARTER;
   WRITELN('DIMES    ', CHANGE DIV DIME);
   CHANGE := CHANGE MOD DIME;
   WRITELN('NICKELS  ', CHANGE DIV NICKEL);
   CHANGE := CHANGE MOD NICKEL;
   WRITELN('PENNIES  ', CHANGE)
END.
```

FIGURE 3-5. A program for making change is a classic exercise in computer programming. The Pascal DIV and MOD operators make the exercise easy. In the constant definition part of the program, identifiers are defined to represent the values of all the coins except the penny.

Dividing 71 by 50 gives us a quotient of 1 and a remainder of 21. Therefore, we hand back one half dollar. After the half dollar has been handed back, we still have 21 cents left to return.

In Pascal we use DIV to compute the integer quotient and MOD to compute the remainder. Suppose that CHANGE is an integer variable whose value is the number of cents to be handed back. The number of half dollars to be returned is the value of

```
CHANGE DIV 50
```

and the amount of change remaining to be returned (after handing back the half dollars) is the value of

```
CHANGE MOD 50
```

The program in Figure 3-5 uses constant identifiers to represent the values of the half dollar, quarter, dime, and nickel:

```
CONST
   HALFDOLLAR = 50;
   QUARTER = 25;
   DIME = 10;
   NICKEL = 5;
```

With these definitions, the number of half dollars to be handed back is the value of

```
CHANGE DIV HALFDOLLAR
```

and the amount remaining after the half dollars have been handed back is the value of

```
CHANGE MOD HALFDOLLAR
```

We can assign the latter value to CHANGE, so that the value of CHANGE will always be the amount still remaining to be handed back:

```
CHANGE := CHANGE MOD HALFDOLLAR
```

Having disposed of half dollars, we can go on to quarters. The number of quarters to be handed back is the value of

```
CHANGE DIV QUARTER
```

and we update the value of CHANGE by executing:

```
CHANGE := CHANGE MOD QUARTER
```

We proceed in the same way for dimes and nickels. The final value of CHANGE is the number of pennies to be handed back.

Exercises

1. Suppose that I, J, and K have the following values

Variable	Value
I	10
J	20
K	40

and the following statements are executed, one after another:

```
I := I + J;
J := I MOD J;
K := K - J;
J := 3 * J
```

Give the values of the three variables after each of the statements has been executed.

2. If I, J, and K are integer variables, and X is a real variable, which of the following statements are incorrect, and why?

```
(a) I := J / K          (b) X := I
(c) I := X              (d) X := J DIV K
(e) X := X MOD I
```

3. Write a program to input a length expressed in feet and inches, and output the same length expressed in centimeters. There are 2.54 centimeters to an inch.

4. Write a program to input a length expressed in inches and output the length expressed in yards, feet, and inches. For example, a length of 65 inches would be expressed as 1 yard, 2 feet, and 5 inches. *Hint:* Compare this problem with that of making change.

5. Salespeople at a certain company get an 8% commission on their sales. Write a program to input the amount that a person sold and print both the salesperson's commission and the amount the company receives after the salesperson's commission has been deducted. Use a constant definition for the 8% commission rate.

6. Write a program to input five real numbers and output their sum.

7. Write a program to estimate the world population a year from now. The program should input the current world population, the predicted birth rate, and the predicted death rate. The birth and death rates are given as percentages of the current population. For example, if the birth rate is 1.5%, then the number of people born over the next year is expected to be 1.5% of the current population.

8. Assume (for the sake of argument) that the weight of one kind of organic molecule is 0.00000006397 gm and weight of another kind is 0.00000006327 gm. A biologist with some strange preoccupations wants to know, for various mammals, (a) how many of each kind of molecule the animal would contain if it contained only that one kind (calculate the result as a real number), and (b) what percentage of the animal's body weight one molecule of each kind represents. The sample weights of the mammals the biologist is interested in are: mouse 53.413 gm; dog 15209.0 gm; man 63250.0 gm; and elephant 1193027.0 gm. Do not use CONST in this exercise. Express the weights of the molecules in floating-point notation.

9. Update your program from Exercise 3.8 with new information from the biologist. The first kind of molecule turns out to weigh 0.00000006822 gm, and the elephant has gone on a diet and lost 21010.0 gm.

10. Modify your program from Exercise 3.8 to use CONST, and then make the changes requested in Exercise 3.9.

MORE ABOUT EXPRESSIONS

In the previous chapters we saw how to do calculations with expressions containing one operator, such as

```
3 + 5    7 * I    I - J    K + 5
```

By using enough of these simple expressions, we can do any calculation, no matter how complex. But restricting ourselves to these kinds of expressions may not be very convenient. For example, suppose we want to add the values of I, J, and K, and assign the result to the integer variable SUM. We *could* do this with the following two statements:

```
SUM := I + J;
SUM := SUM + K
```

But how much more natural it is to write

```
SUM := I + J + K
```

and get the same result with one statement instead of two.
  An expression such as

```
I + J + K
```

can hardly be misinterpreted. It's obvious that the values of the three variables are to be added, and we will get the same result regardless of the order in which the values are added.
  On the other hand, with an expression such as

```
I + J * K
```

we must be more careful. We will get different results depending on whether the addition or the multiplication is done first. For example, suppose the values of I, J, and K are 2, 3, and 4. The following are two ways we might evaluate the expression:

Addition First	*Multiplication First*
I + J * K	I + J * K
2 + 3 * 4	2 + 3 * 4
5 * 4	2 + 12
20	14

Obviously, we are in trouble if we don't know whether an expression will evaluate to 20 or 14. We need some rules for determining the order in which arithmetical operations will be carried out in evaluating an expression. Fortunately, the necessary rules are not complicated.

Operator Priorities

To specify the order in which operations are to be carried out in evaluating an expression, we assign *priorities* to the operators. For the arithmetic operators there are only two priorities, *high* and *low*. The high priority operators are applied first, followed by the low priority operators. Operators with the same priority are evaluated in left-to-right order as they occur in the expression.

The priorities of the arithmetic operators in Pascal are:

```
*, /, DIV, MOD      high priority
+, -                low priority
```

Thus, multiplications and divisions are done before additions and subtractions. In our previous example, the evaluation labeled "multiplication first" is correct and the one labeled "addition first" is wrong.

The following examples illustrate the use of operator priorities:

Example 1:

```
5 + 7 * 4              multiplication first
5 + 28                 then addition
   33
```

Example 2:

```
9 * 8 - 4 * 3          multiplication first
   72 - 12             then subtraction
      60
```

Example 3:

```
9 * 5 + 7 DIV 3          multiplication and division first
   45 + 2                then addition
      47
```

Example 4:

```
1.5 * 1.1 + 4.5 / 9.0 - 0.1    multiplication and division first
1.65 + 0.5 - 0.1               then addition and subtraction
          2.05
```

Example 5:

```
3.6 / 1.2 * 3.0          operators are applied in
      3.0 * 3.0          left-to-right order
          9.0
```

Expressions like the one in Example 5 sometimes cause problems. The reason is that we confuse the expression with the built-up fraction:

$$\frac{3.6}{1.2 \times 3.0} = \frac{3.6}{3.6} = 1.0$$

But the expression in Example 5 is *not* a built-up fraction and is not evaluated like one. Instead, the operators are applied in left-to-right order, since they have the same priority. Hence the division is done before the multiplication.

Using Parentheses. Suppose we want to write an expression that *is* equivalent to the built-up fraction, one in which the multiplication will be done before the division. The expression

```
3.6 / (1.2 * 3.0)
```

will do the job. The parentheses override the operator priorities and the left-to-right evaluation rule, causing the multiplication to be done before the division. We use parentheses whenever we want an expression evaluated in some way other than the one dictated by the operator priorities and the left-to-right evaluation rule.

The rule for parentheses is simply this: Any part of an expression enclosed in parentheses must be evaluated before the operators on either side of the parentheses can be applied. For example, in the expression

```
3 * (4 + 5) * 6
```

the addition must be carried out before either of the multiplications can be done. The following examples illustrate the use of parentheses:

Example 6:

```
3.6 / (1.2 * 3.0)          parenthesized part first
3.6 / 3.6                  then division
      1.0
```

Example 7:

```
3 * (4 + 5) * 6            parenthesized part first
    3 * 9 * 6              then multiplication
          162
```

Example 8:

```
3 * (5 * 3 - 9) + 7        multiplication inside parentheses
3 * (15 - 9) + 7           subtraction inside parentheses
3 * 6 + 7                  multiplication
   18 + 7                  addition
       25
```

Sets of parentheses can be nested one inside the other, as in:

```
3 * (5 + 2 * (6 - 2))
```

We begin with the innermost set of parentheses and work outwards:

Example 9:

```
3 * (5 + 2 * (6 - 2))      innermost parenthesized part first
3 * (5 + 2 * 4)            multiplication inside parentheses
3 * (5 + 8)                addition inside parentheses
3 * 13                     multiplication
   39
```

Temperature Conversion.   Figure 4–1 shows a program for converting temperatures from the Fahrenheit scale to the Celsius scale. Science books give the formula for this conversion as

$$C = \frac{5}{9}(F - 32)$$

where F is the Fahrenheit temperature and C is the Celsius temperature.

Usually, no problems are encountered in translating algebraic formulas into Pascal assignment statements. The main difference between the two is that multiplication operators are omitted in algebraic formulas but are required in Pascal.

Let's look at some possible translations of the temperature formula, beginning with

```
C := 5 / 9 * (F - 32)
```

```
PROGRAM CONVERT;
(* CONVERT FAHRENHEIT TO CELSIUS *)
VAR
   FAHRENHEIT, CELSIUS: REAL;
BEGIN
   WRITE('FAHRENHEIT TEMPERATURE? ');
   READLN(FAHRENHEIT);
   CELSIUS := (5.0 / 9.0) * (FAHRENHEIT - 32.0);
   WRITELN('CELSIUS TEMPERATURE IS ', CELSIUS:6:1)
END.
```

FIGURE 4–1. A program for converting temperatures from the Fahrenheit scale to the Celsius scale. The parentheses around 5.0 / 9.0 are not required (why?) but may improve the readability of the expression. The parentheses around FAHRENHEIT − 32.0 are required (why?).

where C and F are real variables. The division will take place before the multiplication since the division and multiplication operators will be applied in left-to-right order. Thus, the value of 5/9 will be multiplied by the rest of the expression, as desired. As in the original formula, the subtraction must be enclosed in parentheses so it will be done before the multiplication.

Parentheses can make an expression more readable even if the expression would be evaluated the same way without the parentheses. For example,

```
C := (5 / 9) * (F - 32)
```

is evaluated the same as the previous statement, but it is easier to read. The parentheses emphasize that the value of 5/9 is to be multiplied by the rest of the expression.

The numbers 5, 9, and 32 are integer constants. The program will automatically convert 5 and 9 to real numbers before dividing them, and it will convert 32 to a real number before subtracting it from the real variable F. We can save the program the trouble of doing this by using real constants in the first place:

```
C := (5.0 / 9.0) * (F - 32.0)
```

The convention in algebra is to use single letters, such as C and F, for variables. In programming we usually find it clearer to use words instead:

```
CELSIUS := (5.0 / 9.0) * (FAHRENHEIT - 32.0)
```

This is the assignment statement actually used in the program of Figure 4–1.

Standard Functions

Only a few of the operations that we might want to carry out are represented by widely accepted operators, such as + and −. For the rest, we use *functions*, which provide a uniform way of representing an operation by an identifier. Pascal has a number of standard functions that we can use without having to define them. In Chapter 7 we will see how to define our own functions. But for now we will stick to the predefined standard functions.

To see how a function works, let's look at a simple example, the function SQR. SQR computes the *square* of a number—the result of multiplying the number by itself.

To use a function we write a *function designator*, which consists of the name of the function followed by the value to be operated on, the lettar enclosed in parentheses. Thus,

```
SQR(5)
```

indicates that the function SQR is to be applied to the value 5. The value in parentheses is called the *actual parameter* or the *argument* of the function.

The function designator, considered as an expression, represents the value that results when the function is applied to the actual parameter. Thus SQR(5) represents 25, the square of 5, in the same way that 3 + 5 represents 8 and 3 * 5 represents 15. The following are some function designators constructed with SQR, along with their values:

Expression	Value
SQR(1)	1
SQR(2)	4
SQR(3)	9
SQR(4)	16

Function designators can be used as parts of larger expressions. The values of the function designators are worked out before any of the other operators are applied:

Expression	Value
SQR(2) + 3	7
2 * SQR(3)	18
2 * SQR(4) + 3	35

The last example is evaluated as follows:

2 * SQR(4) + 3	*apply function*
2 * 16 + 3	*multiplication first*
32 + 3	*then addition*
35	

The actual parameter of a function can itself be an expression. In that case the value of the actual parameter is worked out before applying the function:

Expression	Value
SQR(3 + 5)	64
SQR(2 * 3 - 2)	16
2 * SQR (4 * 3 - 7) + 1	51

The last example is worked out as follows:

2 * SQR(4 * 3 - 7) + 1	*evaluate parameter: multiplication*
2 * SQR(12 - 7) + 1	*evaluate parameter: subtraction*
2 * SQR(5) + 1	*apply function*
2 * 25 + 1	*multiplication first*
50 + 1	*then addition*
51	

Pascal has a number of standard functions. We will look at five of the most useful ones here. Some of the others will be taken up in later chapters.

Function	Definition
ABS	computes the absolute value of its actual parameter—if the actual parameter is negative the corresponding positive value is returned; if the actual parameter is positive, its value is returned unchanged. Thus, the value of both ABS(-5) and ABS(5) is 5.
SQR	computes the square of the actual parameter. Thus the value of SQR(3) is 9, and the value of SQR(1.5) is 2.25.
SQRT	computes the square root of its actual parameter—the value that, when multiplied by itself, is equal to the value of the actual parameter. Thus the value of SQRT(9) is 3.0 and the value of SQRT(2.25) is 1.5.
TRUNC	converts a real number to an integer by discarding everything to the right of the decimal point. Thus, the value of both TRUNC(3.25) and TRUNC(3.75) is 3.
ROUND	converts a real number to an integer by rounding the real value to the nearest integer. Thus, the value of ROUND(3.25) is 3, and the value of both ROUND(3.5) and ROUND(3.75) is 4.

The actual parameters of SQR and ABS can be either integers or real numbers. The result has the same type as the actual parameter. For

SQRT, the actual parameter can be either an integer or a real number, but the result is always a real number. For TRUNC and ROUND, the actual parameter is always a real number and the result is an integer.

We can say more about the functions TRUNC and ROUND. In the previous chapter we saw that Pascal allows integers to be assigned to real variables, since every integer can be converted to a corresponding real number. On the other hand, assignments of real numbers to integer variables is forbidden because many real numbers (such as 1.5) have no corresponding integers.

There are two standard ways of converting a real number to an integer. One, known as *truncation*, consists of simply discarding everything to the right of the decimal point, so that 6.72 becomes 6. The other is *rounding*, which changes the real value to the nearest integer, with a value such as 6.5 rounding up to 7. Thus, rounding 6.72 gives 7.

The functions TRUNC and ROUND carry out the truncation and rounding operations. Thus the statements

```
I := TRUNC(6.72);
J := ROUND(6.72)
```

are both valid. The value of I becomes 6 and the value of J becomes 7.

Example Programs

Figure 4–2 shows a program for computing the volume of a cylinder. The formula for the volume of a cylinder is

$$V = \frac{\pi d^2 h}{4}$$

```
PROGRAM CYLINDER;
(* COMPUTE VOLUME OF CYLINDRICAL CONTAINER *)
CONST
    PI = 3.141593;
VAR
    DIAMETER, HEIGHT, VOLUME: REAL;
BEGIN
    WRITE('DIAMETER? ');
    READLN(DIAMETER);
    WRITE('HEIGHT? ');
    READLN(HEIGHT);
    VOLUME := PI * SQR(DIAMETER) * HEIGHT / 4.0;
    WRITELN('VOLUME IS ', VOLUME:8:3)
END.
```

FIGURE 4–2. This program computes the volume of a cylinder. Note the use of the SQR function to compute the square of the diameter.

where V is the volume of the cylinder, d is its diameter, and h is its height. The Greek letter π represents the mathematical constant pi whose approximate value is 3.141593. The raised 2 following the d indicates that the diameter is to be squared.

To translate this formula into Pascal, we use the variables VOLUME, DIAMETER, and HEIGHT. The constant identifier PI is defined to represent the approximate value of pi. We use the SQR function to square the diameter and, as always, supply the multiplication signs that are omitted in algebraic formulas:

```
VOLUME := PI * SQR(DIAMETER) * HEIGHT / 4.0
```

Figure 4-3 shows a program for computing the area of a rectangle and the length of its diagonal. The formulas for area and diagonal are

$$A = lw$$

$$d = \sqrt{l^2 + w^2}$$

where l and w are the length and width of the rectangle, d is the length of its diagonal, and A is its area.

In Pascal we use the variables LENGTH, WIDTH, DIAGONAL, and AREA. Translating the formula for area is simplicity itself, since all we have to supply is a multiplication sign:

```
AREA := LENGTH * WIDTH
```

```
PROGRAM RECTANGLE;
(* COMPUTE AREA AND LENGTH OF DIAGONAL OF RECTANGLE *)
VAR
    LENGTH, WIDTH, AREA, DIAGONAL: REAL;
BEGIN
    WRITE('LENGTH OF RECTANGLE? ');
    READLN(LENGTH);
    WRITE('WIDTH OF RECTANGLE? ');
    READLN(WIDTH);
    AREA := LENGTH * WIDTH;
    DIAGONAL := SQRT(SQR(LENGTH) + SQR(WIDTH));
    WRITELN('AREA:', AREA:8:3);
    WRITELN('LENGTH OF DIAGONAL:', DIAGONAL:8:3)
END.
```

FIGURE 4-3. **This program computes the area of a rectangle and the length of its diagonal. Note that the actual parameter for SQRT contains two function designators, SQR(LENGTH) and SQR(WIDTH). These two function designators must be evaluated and the addition done before SQRT can be applied.**

To compute the length of the diagonal of a rectangle, we use SQR to square the length and the width of the rectangle

```
SQR(LENGTH)
SQR(WIDTH)
```

add the squares of the length and the width

```
SQR(LENGTH) + SQR(WIDTH)
```

and take the square root of the result:

```
DIAGONAL := SQRT(SQR(LENGTH) + SQR(WIDTH))
```

If the values of LENGTH and WIDTH are 4.0 and 3.0, the expression for the length of the diagonal is evaluated as follows:

```
SQRT(SQR(LENGTH) + SQR(WIDTH))
SQRT(SQR(4.0) + SQR(3.0))
SQRT(16.0 + 9.0)
SQRT(25.0)
5.0
```

Notice that the actual parameter of SQRT contains the function designators SQR(LENGTH) and SQR(WIDTH). This is allowed, and our usual rule holds: The actual parameter of a function must be evaluated before the function can be applied. Therefore, SQR(LENGTH) and SQR(WIDTH) must be evaluated first, so their values can be added together to get the actual parameter for SQRT.

Boolean Expressions

Beginning with the next chapter, much of our attention will be focused on methods for controlling the execution of a program—getting the computer to take the appropriate actions under the conditions that exist when the program is executed.

By a *condition* we mean a declarative statement that can be either true or false. For example, the statement

The value of I is equal to the value of J

is true if the value of both I and J is 5. On the other hand, the statement is false if the value of I is 4 and the value of J is 3. To determine whether the statement is true or false, the computer must obtain the current values of I and J from memory and compare them.

In Pascal we represent a condition by a Boolean expression—an expression that yields one of the two Boolean values, TRUE and FALSE.

As you might expect, the expression yields the value TRUE if the corresponding condition is true and the value FALSE if the corresponding condition is false.

Relational Operators.   Let's return to the condition

The value of I is equal to the value of J

In symbols, we can write this as:

```
I = J
```

We want to consider this as an expression that will have the value TRUE if the values of I and J are equal and the value FALSE otherwise.

The best way to do this is to think of = as an operator that takes integer operands (in this case) and yields a Boolean result. Thus = is on the same footing with operators such as + and −, except that it yields a Boolean result instead of an integer or real one. We refer to = as a *relational operator* since the value of I = J is true only when the relationship of equality holds between the values of I and J.

To illustrate further, the following are the values of some expressions involving the = operator:

Expression	Value
3 = 5	FALSE
8 = 8	TRUE
4 = 5	FALSE
0 = 0	TRUE

Pascal has seven relational operators, of which we will consider six here. (The seventh is used in connection with *sets*, a data type we will not take up until the last chapter of the book.) For each operator, the following table gives a Boolean expression and the corresponding condition. The Boolean expression yields the value TRUE if the corresponding condition is true and the value FALSE if the corresponding condition is false:

Expression	Condition
I = J	the value of I is equal to the value of J
I < J	the value of I precedes the value of J
I > J	the value of I follows the value of J
I <= J	the value of I precedes or is equal to the value of J
I >= J	the value of I follows or is equal to the value of J
I <> J	the value of I is not equal to the value of J

The relational operators can be applied to all four standard data types: INTEGER, REAL, BOOLEAN, and CHAR. Before we can make

use of the definitions just given, however, we must say what the words "precedes" and "follows" mean for values of each type.

For integers and real numbers, "precedes" and "follows" refer to ordinary numerical order. We say that one number precedes another when the first number is less than the second; we say that one number follows another when the first number is greater than the second. For integers and real numbers, we could substitute "is less than" for "precedes" and "is greater than" for "follows" in the conditions defining the relational operators.

The following expressions illustrate the use of the relational operators with integers and real numbers:

Expression	Value
3 < 5	TRUE
7 <> 7	FALSE
9 > 8	TRUE
3.5 < 6.8	TRUE
7.4 > 9.2	FALSE
4.2 <= 8.3	TRUE

The relational operators are rarely applied to Boolean values. For the record, however, the value FALSE precedes the value TRUE:

Expression	Value
FALSE < TRUE	TRUE
FALSE > TRUE	FALSE

For each computer system there is a *collating sequence* that gives the order for characters. In every case we can expect to find the letters in alphabetical order and the numerals in numerical order. Beyond that, however, the collating sequence can differ from one computer system to another.

Many computer systems use the American Standard Code for Information Interchange (ASCII) to represent characters. The following is the collating sequence for the ASCII character set:

```
 !"#$%&'()*+,-./0123456789:;<=>?
@ABCDEFGHIJKLMNOPQRSTUVWXYZ[\]^_
`abcdefghijklmnopqrstuvwxyz{|}~
```

The blank space immediately precedes the exclamation point. The following shows the values of some expressions using the ASCII character set:

Expression	Value
`' ' < 'A'`	TRUE
`'0' > 'Z'`	FALSE
`'C' < 'c'`	TRUE
`'A' < 'Z'`	TRUE
`'0' > '9'`	FALSE

In practice you will usually be dealing with either the letters or the numerals, and so ordinary alphabetical order can be assumed. But occasionally you will have to worry about the relative order of the blank space, the letters, and the numerals. And if your computer allows both uppercase and lowercase letters, the order of the uppercase letters relative to the lowercase letters becomes important.

The relational operators are given a lower priority than any of the arithmetic operators, so in any expression involving both relational and arithmetic operators, the arithmetic will be carried out before the relational operators are applied. The following is the extended priority scheme:

`*, /, DIV, MOD`	*high priority*
`+, -`	
`=, <, >, <=, >=, <>`	*low priority*

The following examples illustrate the evaluation of expressions involving both arithmetic and relational operators:

Example 10:

`3 + 5 < 4 * 2 - 1`	*multiplication first*
`3 + 5 < 8 - 1`	*addition and subtraction next*
`8 < 7`	*relational operator last*
`FALSE`	

Example 11:

`13 DIV 3 = 3 + 1`	*division first*
`4 = 3 + 1`	*addition next*
`4 = 4`	*relational operator last*
`TRUE`	

The Boolean Operators.   The Boolean operators NOT, OR, and AND take Boolean values as operands and yield Boolean values as results.

The operator NOT changes TRUE into FALSE and FALSE into TRUE. That is, the value of NOT P is TRUE if the value of P is FALSE and FALSE if the value of P is TRUE. The following table defines the NOT operator:

Expression	Value
NOT TRUE	FALSE
NOT FALSE	TRUE

The value of P OR Q is TRUE if the value of P is TRUE, the value of Q is TRUE, or both. We can define the OR operator using the following table:

Expression	Value
TRUE OR TRUE	TRUE
TRUE OR FALSE	TRUE
FALSE OR TRUE	TRUE
FALSE OR FALSE	FALSE

The only situation in which the value of P OR Q is FALSE is when the values of both P and Q are FALSE.

The expression P AND Q has the value TRUE only when the values of both P and Q are TRUE. The following table defines AND:

Expression	Value
TRUE AND TRUE	TRUE
TRUE AND FALSE	FALSE
FALSE AND TRUE	FALSE
FALSE AND FALSE	FALSE

Before we can evaluate expressions involving Boolean operators, we have to incorporate these operators into the priority scheme. The priority of NOT is higher than that of any other operator. The priorities of AND and OR are the same as those of * and +, respectively. The following table shows the priorities of the arithmetic, Boolean, and relational operators:

```
NOT                                      high priority
/, *, DIV, MOD, AND
+, -, OR
=, <, >, <=, >=, <>                      low priority
```

There is no general agreement on what priorities the Boolean operators should have, and the designers of different programming languages make different choices. The choice made in Pascal is not the most common one, so persons familiar with other programming languages must be careful when using Boolean operators in Pascal.

The Boolean operators are most frequently used in expressions like

```
(I = J) OR (I < J + K)
```

Such expressions correspond to conditions stated in English using the words *not, and,* and *or.* For example, the expression just given corresponds to the following condition:

The value of I is equal to the value of J, or the value of I is less than the value of J + K

The parentheses in the expression are mandatory. This is because the Boolean operators have a higher priority than the relational operators. If the parentheses were not present, the computer would attempt to apply OR before applying the relational operators. That is, it would attempt to apply OR to the values of I and J, which not only doesn't make sense but results in an error. This is because the values of I and J are not Boolean and so the Boolean operators cannot be applied to them.

The parentheses assure that the relational operators will be applied before the Boolean operators. The parentheses also contribute to the readability of the expression, so in this respect Pascal may be ahead of some other languages that assign priorities to the Boolean operators in such a way as to allow the parentheses to be omitted.

Now let's look at a Boolean expression that involves all the rules we have discussed in this section. This expression is much more complicated than those usually encountered in practice:

```
(11 < 3 * 2 + 5) OR (6 * 2 = 4 * 3) AND NOT (2 + 2 = 4)
```

We begin by working out the arithmetic expressions inside the parentheses—multiplications first and then additions:

```
(11 < 6 + 5) OR (12 = 12) AND NOT (2 + 2 = 4)
(11 < 11) OR (12 = 12) AND NOT (4 = 4)
```

Continuing to work out the parts of the expression that are in parentheses, the relational operators are applied next:

```
FALSE OR TRUE AND NOT TRUE
```

Of the Boolean operators, NOT has the highest priority

```
FALSE OR TRUE AND FALSE
```

The Boolean operator with the next highest priority is AND, after which comes OR:

```
FALSE OR FALSE
        FALSE
```

The value of the original Boolean expression, then, is FALSE.

Exercises

1. Evaluate the following expressions:

(a) `3 * 2 + 4 * 5`   (b) `9 DIV 3 * 3`
(c) `7 * 3 - 5`   (d) `5.7 - 3.0 / 2.0`

2. Evaluate the following expressions:

(a) `3 * (4 + 5)`   (b) `(7 + 4) * (5 - 3)`
(c) `(9 + 7) DIV 3`   (d) `3 * (5 + 2 * (7 - 4)) + 5`

3. Evaluate the following expressions:

(a) `SQR(9)`   (b) `SQRT(9 + 7)`
(c) `3 * ROUND(6.7) + 5`   (d) `SQRT(SQR(5) + SQR(12))`

4. Write a single expression that will

(a) add the values of X and Y;
(b) add the values of U and V;
(c) multiply the sums obtained in (a) and (b); and
(d) take the square root of the product.

Show, step by step, how to evaluate your expression with 2.0 for the value of X, 6.0 for the value of Y, 7.0 for the value of U, and 11.0 for the value of V.

5. Evaluate the following expressions:

(a) `10 < 5`   (b) `'A' > 'A'`
(c) `9 <= 9`   (d) `(3 < 5) AND (2 = 4)`

6. The maximum size of a package that can be sent by first class mail is 100 inches in combined length and girth. That is, the length of the package plus its girth cannot exceed 100 inches. Write a program to input the length, width, and height of a package and print out its combined length and girth. The combined length and girth should be computed from the length, width, and height in a single statement.

7. Modify the program of Exercise 6 so that it will print the Boolean value TRUE if the package can be sent by first class mail and the Boolean value FALSE if it cannot. (This exercise cannot be done in UCSD Pascal, which will not print Boolean values.)

8. Write a program to compute the volume of a sphere, given its radius. The formula for the volume of a sphere is

$$V = \frac{4}{3}\pi r^3$$

where V is the volume of the sphere and r is its radius. The expression r^3, read "r cube," is equivalent to $r \times r \times r$. Pascal does not provide a standard function for computing the cube of a number. We can either write out the two multiplications.

```
RADIUS * RADIUS * RADIUS
```

or we can square the radius and then multiply the result by the radius:

```
SQR(RADIUS) * RADIUS
```

9. Your doctor has ordered you to go on a diet. For the next four weeks you will be eating less than you would need to stay at the same weight. For each 3500 calories less than you need, you will lose one pound. For the first week you will eat 1200 calories a day less than you need; for the second week, 1000 calories a day less; for the third week, 850 calories a day less; and for the fourth week, 600 calories a day less. Write a program to print all the above information in a sensible form and to calculate and print how much weight you will lose during your four-week diet.

10. You are given the same situation as in Exercise 9, but you have to approach it from the opposite point of view. That's because you're going to Bermuda in four weeks, and you want to wear a swimsuit you rashly bought on sale. To wear the swimsuit, you must weigh no more than 130 pounds. Write a program to input your present weight and tell you how many calories you must give up each day until you leave. As before, you reduce by the same number of calories each day for a week. During the first week you must lose one third of the total; during the second and third weeks, one quarter each week; and during the final week, the remaining one sixth.

Chapter 5

REPETITION

The programs we have written so far may have seemed trivial or useless. Who needs to write a computer program to work out the sales tax on a single purchase or to compute the volume of a single container? Instead of wasting time writing a program, it's easier to do the calculation directly, perhaps with the aid of a pocket calculator.

On the other hand, if we need to compute the sales tax on thousands of purchases or compute the volumes of hundreds of containers, using a computer makes more sense. By writing a program once and using it hundreds or thousands of times, we can indeed save ourselves much labor.

In short, for a computer program to be useful, some of its statements need to be executed more than once. This repeated use could come about simply because the entire program is executed repeatedly. But usually, some of the statements will be executed more than once during a single execution of the entire program. *Repetition* is the programming technique of having some statements in a program executed more than once.

Useful as repetition is, it must be carefully controlled, lest the program attempt to repeat some statements forever (a common programming error). Pascal provides three statements for controlling repetition: the FOR statement, the WHILE statement, and the REPEAT-UNTIL statement.

The FOR Statement

The FOR statement is best introduced with an example:

```
FOR I := 1 TO 5 DO
   WRITE('*')
```

When the FOR statement is executed, the WRITE statement is executed five times. The computer prints:

```
* * * * *
```

The WRITE statement is indented to show that it is part of the FOR statement.

On the first repetition the value of I is 1, on the second repetition the value of I is 2, and so on. We can see this by having the computer execute:

```
FOR I := 1 TO 5 DO
    WRITE(I:4)
```

The computer prints:

```
1    2    3    4    5
```

By using DOWNTO in place of TO, we can make the computer count backwards:

```
FOR I := 5 DOWNTO 1 DO
    WRITE(I:4)
```

The computer prints:

```
5    4    3    2    1
```

The limits between which the computer is to count can be given by expressions:

```
FOR I := 3 + 2 TO 4 * 3 - 1 DO
    WRITE(I:4)
```

The computer prints:

```
5    6    7    8    9   10   11
```

The FOR statement provides for only a single statement following the word DO. But that statement can be a *compound statement*—a sequence of statements bracketed by BEGIN and END. For example, the compound statement

```
BEGIN
    WRITE('AA');
    WRITE('BB.')
END
```

prints the pattern:

AABB.

The FOR statement

```
FOR I := 1 TO 5 DO
   BEGIN
     WRITE('AA');
     WRITE('BB.')
   END
```

prints the pattern:

AABB.AABB.AABB.AABB.AABB.

   The repeated statement is considered to be part of the FOR statement. This means that the semicolons separating the FOR statement
from the surrounding statements come before the FOR and after the repeated statement. For example:

```
X := 3.5;
FOR I := 1 TO 5 DO WRITE(I:4);
Y := 7.9
```

By writing the repeated statement on the same line as the rest of the
FOR statement, we emphasize that WRITE(I:4) is part of the FOR state-
ment. Therefore, we are not surprised that the semicolon separating the
FOR statement from the statement Y := 7.9 occurs after WRITE(I:4).
Even though we usually write the repeated statement on a line by itself,
the punctuation remains the same:

```
X := 3.5;
FOR I := 1 TO 5 DO
   WRITE(I:4);
Y := 7.9
```

   The same principle applies when the repeated statement is a compound statement:

```
X := 3.5;
FOR I := 1 TO 5 DO
   BEGIN
     WRITE('AA');
     WRITE('BB.')
   END;
Y := 7.9
```

In this case the FOR statement consists of everything from the word
FOR through the word END. Therefore, the semicolon separating the
FOR statement from the following statement comes after the word END.

Programs Using the FOR Statement

Personal Investment. Suppose you start with a certain amount in your savings account and deposit a certain amount each month. If interest is paid at a given rate and compounded monthly, how much will you have in your account after a given number of months?

Figure 5-1 shows a program for solving this problem. We use AMOUNT for the amount currently in the account, DEPOSIT for the monthly deposit, YEARLYRATE for the yearly interest rate, and MONTHS for the number of months in question. In an interactive dialog with the user, the program obtains the starting value of AMOUNT as well as the values DEPOSIT, YEARLYRATE, and MONTHS.

```
PROGRAM INVESTMENT;
(* COMPUTE AMOUNT RESULTING FROM MONTHLY DEPOSITS IN
   A SAVINGS ACCOUNT.  ASSUME INTEREST IS COMPOUNDED
   MONTHLY *)
VAR
   AMOUNT,                 (* AMOUNT IN ACCOUNT *)
   DEPOSIT,                (* MONTHLY DEPOSIT *)
   YEARLYRATE,             (* YEARLY INTEREST RATE AS PERCENT *)
   MONTHLYRATE,            (* MONTHLY INTEREST RATE AS DECIMAL *)
   INTEREST: REAL;         (* INTEREST FOR CURRENT MONTH *)

   MONTHS,                 (* NUMBER OF MONTHS DEPOSITS MADE *)
   I: INTEGER;             (* COUNTER *)
BEGIN
   WRITE('AMOUNT IN YOUR ACCOUNT NOW? ');
   READLN(AMOUNT);
   WRITE('MONTHLY DEPOSIT? ');
   READLN(DEPOSIT);
   WRITE('YEARLY INTEREST RATE AS PERCENT? ');
   READLN(YEARLYRATE);
   WRITE('NUMBER OF MONTHS? ');
   READLN(MONTHS);
   MONTHLYRATE := YEARLYRATE / 1200.0;
   FOR I := 1 TO MONTHS DO
      BEGIN
         AMOUNT := AMOUNT + DEPOSIT;
         INTEREST := AMOUNT * MONTHLYRATE;
         AMOUNT := AMOUNT + INTEREST
      END;
   WRITELN('AFTER ', MONTHS, ' MONTHS YOU WILL HAVE',
           AMOUNT:8:2, ' DOLLARS')
END.
```

FIGURE 5-1. This program computes the amount resulting from monthly deposits in a savings account. Note that the value calculated for AMOUNT on one repetition serves as data for the next repetition.

Interest is normally given as a yearly percentage rate. To solve the problem, we need a monthly interest rate expressed as a decimal. To convert the yearly rate to a monthly rate, we must divide by 12.0; to convert the percentage to a decimal, we must divide by 100.0. We could calculate the value of MONTHLYRATE, the monthly decimal rate, with

```
MONTHLYRATE := YEARLYRATE / 12.0 / 100.0
```

But since dividing by 12.0 and then by 100.0 is the same as dividing by 1200.0, we can use the simpler statement:

```
MONTHLYRATE := YEARLYRATE / 1200.00
```

The general approach that we use in this program can be applied to many other problems. Given the amount in the account at the beginning of the month, the monthly deposit, and the interest rate, it's easy to calculate the amount in the account at the end of the month. We simply repeat this calculation for the number of months desired. The amount in the account at the end of one month is the amount present at the beginning of the next month. The result calculated on one repetition (the amount at the end of the month) becomes part of the data (the amount at the beginning of the next month) for the calculation done on the next repetition.

The value of AMOUNT is the amount currently in the account. When the monthly deposit is made, its value is added to the amount in the account:

```
AMOUNT := AMOUNT + DEPOSIT
```

To compute the interest earned for a particular month, we multiply the amount in the account by the monthly interest rate:

```
INTEREST := AMOUNT * MONTHLYRATE
```

At the end of the month, the interest earned is added to the amount already in the account:

```
AMOUNT := AMOUNT + INTEREST
```

These three statements start with the value of AMOUNT at the beginning of a given month and compute the value of AMOUNT at the end of the month. To compute the amount in the account after a given number of months, we execute these statements for each month in question. The value computed for AMOUNT on one repetition provides part of the data used in the calculation done on the next repetition:

```
FOR I := 1 TO MONTHS DO
   BEGIN
      AMOUNT := AMOUNT + DEPOSIT;
      INTEREST := AMOUNT * MONTHLYRATE
      AMOUNT := AMOUNT + INTEREST
   END
```

Fibonacci's Problem.   The mathematician Leonardo Fibonacci posed the following problem: Suppose that a pair of rabbits has one pair of offspring each month, and each new pair becomes fertile at the age of one month. If we start with one fertile pair, and none of the rabbits die, how many pairs will we have after a year's time?

Figure 5-2 shows a program for solving a slightly generalized version of Fibonacci's problem. The approach is the same as for the investment program. We write statements that, given the number of pairs and the number of fertile pairs at the beginning of the month, compute the corresponding numbers for the beginning of the next month. These statements are repeated for the number of months in question.

We use PAIRS for the number of pairs alive at the beginning of the month and FERTILEPAIRS for the number of those pairs that are fertile. During the current month, each of the fertile pairs will have one pair of offspring. Thus, the number of pairs at the beginning of next month is calculated by

```
PAIRSNEXTMONTH := PAIRS + FERTILEPAIRS
```

```
PROGRAM FIBONACCI;
(* SOLVE FIBONACCI'S RABBIT PROBLEM *)
VAR
    PAIRS,                  (* PAIRS AT START OF MONTH *)
    FERTILEPAIRS,           (* FERTILE PAIRS AT START OF MONTH *)
    PAIRSNEXTMONTH,         (* PAIRS AT START OF NEXT MONTH *)
    MONTHS,                 (* NUMBER OF MONTHS CONSIDERED *)
    I: INTEGER;             (* COUNTER *)
BEGIN
    WRITE('STARTING NUMBER OF PAIRS? ');
    READLN(PAIRS);
    WRITE('STARTING NUMBER OF FERTILE PAIRS? ');
    READLN(FERTILEPAIRS);
    WRITE('NUMBER OF MONTHS? ');
    READLN(MONTHS);
    FOR I := 1 TO MONTHS DO
      BEGIN
        PAIRSNEXTMONTH := PAIRS + FERTILEPAIRS;
        FERTILEPAIRS := PAIRS;
        PAIRS := PAIRSNEXTMONTH
      END;
    WRITELN('AFTER ', MONTHS, ' MONTHS YOU WILL HAVE ',
            PAIRS, ' PAIRS')
END.
```

FIGURE 5-2. This program solves a slightly generalized version of Fibonacci's rabbit problem. Note that the values calculated for PAIRS and FERTILEPAIRS on one repetition serve as data for the next repetition.

We now have to calculate the values that PAIRS and FERTILEPAIRS will have at the beginning of next month, so that these values can be used for next month's calculation. A newly born pair becomes fertile after a month's time. All the pairs alive at the beginning of this month will be fertile at the beginning of next month, whereas the pairs born this month will not be. Thus, the number of fertile pairs at the beginning of next month equals the total number of pairs at the beginning of this month:

```
FERTILEPAIRS := PAIRS
```

We have already calculated the number of pairs at the beginning of next month; we assign this value to PAIRS:

```
PAIRS := PAIRSNEXTMONTH
```

(Why can't we just update the value of PAIRS with

```
PAIRS := PAIRS + FERTILEPAIRS
```

and avoid using the variable PAIRSNEXTMONTH?)

To solve Fibonacci's original problem, we start with one fertile pair and allow the rabbits to reproduce for 12 months:

```
STARTING NUMBER OF PAIRS? 1
STARTING NUMBER OF FERTILE PAIRS? 1
NUMBER OF MONTHS? 12
AFTER 12 MONTHS YOU WILL HAVE 377 PAIRS
```

The assumptions of Fibonacci's problem are clearly chosen for simplicity rather than because they reflect the actual behavior of rabbits. With more realistic assumptions, however, programs similar to Figure 5–2 can be applied to real-world ecological problems.

The Inventor's Request.   According to an old tale, the inventor of chess was called before the king and told to name her own reward. The inventor replied: "All I ask is one grain of wheat for the first square of my chessboard, two grains for the second square, four grains for the third square, and so on for all 64 squares, doubling the number of grains for each square." Should the king agree to this seemingly modest request?

Figure 5–3 shows the program to solve this problem. Our approach should by now be familiar. We will write statements to be repeated for all 64 squares of the chessboard. The results calculated on one repetition will be used as data on the next.

Let the value of GRAINS be the number of grains on the square being examined and the value of TOTAL be the number of grains on all the squares examined so far. We start with one grain on the first square, so the initial value of GRAINS is 1.0. And before any squares have been

```
PROGRAM WHEAT;
(* COMPUTE AMOUNT OF WHEAT REQUESTED BY INVENTOR *)
VAR
    GRAINS,              (* GRAINS ON CURRENT SQUARE *)
    TOTAL: REAL;         (* ACCUMULATOR FOR TOTAL NUMBER OF GRAINS *
    SQUARE: INTEGER;     (* NUMBER OF CURRENT SQUARE *)
BEGIN
    GRAINS := 1.0;       (* ONE GRAIN ON FIRST SQUARE *)
    TOTAL := 0.0;        (* CLEAR ACCUMULATOR *)
    FOR SQUARE := 1 TO 64 DO
        BEGIN
            TOTAL := TOTAL + GRAINS;
            GRAINS := 2.0 * GRAINS
        END;
    WRITELN('INVENTOR REQUESTED', GRAINS, ' GRAINS')
END.
```

FIGURE 5–3. **This program computes the amount of wheat requested by the inventor of chess. GRAINS and TOTAL are declared as real variables rather than integer variables because of the anticipated large value of the result.**

examined, the value of TOTAL is zero. Therefore, we assign GRAINS and TOTAL their initial values as follows:

```
GRAINS := 1.0;
TOTAL := 0.0
```

For each square, we first add the number of grains for that square to the running total:

```
TOTAL := TOTAL + GRAINS
```

Then, we compute the number of grains for the next square:

```
GRAINS := 2.0 * GRAINS
```

Repeating these two statements 64 times computes the total number of grains on all 64 squares of the chessboard:

```
FOR I := 1 TO 64 DO
    BEGIN
        TOTAL := TOTAL + GRAINS;
        GRAINS := 2.0 * GRAINS
    END
```

When the program is executed, it prints

```
INVENTOR REQUESTED  1.84467E19 GRAINS
```

The inventor requested over 18 billion billion grains of wheat, considerably more than the current yearly production for the entire world.

Nested FOR Statements

The program in Figure 5-4 prints the following pattern:

```
*
**
***
****
*****
```

Two FOR statements are needed to print this pattern—one to print the five lines and one to print the proper number of asterisks on each line. The second FOR statement is part of the first. When one statement occurs as part of another statement of the same kind, the statements are said to be *nested*. The program in Figure 5-4 uses nested FOR statements.

We will develop the program using *stepwise refinement*. In this widely used method of program construction, we begin by outlining the program in a mixture of Pascal and English. We then replace the English parts either by Pascal statements or by a combination of Pascal and English. The process continues until all the English parts have been replaced by Pascal statements.

We begin by noting that the pattern contains five rows of asterisks. The first row contains one asterisk, the second row contains two asterisks, and so on. Our first outline, then, looks like this:

```
FOR I := 1 TO 5 DO
    "Print I asterisks and advance to the
    next line in the printout"
```

```
PROGRAM PATTERN;
(* PRINT A TRIANGULAR PATTERN *)
VAR
    I, J: INTEGER;
BEGIN
    FOR I := 1 TO 5 DO
        BEGIN
            FOR J := 1 TO I DO
                WRITE('*');
            WRITELN
        END
END.
```

FIGURE 5-4. **This program, which prints a triangular pattern, illustrates nested FOR statements.**

The English parts are enclosed in double quotation marks to distinguish them from Pascal statements. (Don't confuse the English parts with Pascal strings, which are enclosed in *single* quotation marks.) The phrase "I asterisks" means the number of asterisks determined by the current value of I. If the value of I is 1, then one asterisk is to be printed; if the value of I is 2, then two asterisks are to be printed; and so on.

An obvious refinement is to separate the tasks of printing the asterisks and advancing to the next line. This gives us:

```
FOR I := 1 TO 5 DO
    BEGIN
        "Print I asterisks"
        "Advance to the next line in the printout"
    END
```

To print I asterisks, that is, the number of asterisks determined by the value of I, we use a FOR statement:

```
FOR J := 1 TO I DO
    WRITE('*')
```

Note that the value of I determines the number of asterisks printed. To go to the next line in the printout, we use the statement:

```
WRITELN
```

Replacing the English statements by the corresponding Pascal statements, we get

```
FOR I := 1 TO 5 DO
    BEGIN
        FOR J := 1 TO I DO
            WRITE('*');
        WRITELN
    END
```

The WHILE Statement

The FOR statement requires us to state in advance how many repetitions will be carried out. Sometimes, however, we may not know beforehand how many repetitions are to be done. We may only know when the time has come to stop the repetitions. Put another way, we may want the repetitions to be continued as long as a certain condition is true. When the condition becomes false, the repetitions are to terminate. The WHILE statement allows us to control repetition in this way.

The WHILE statement has the following general form:

```
WHILE Boolean expression DO
    statement
```

The computer evaluates the Boolean expression; if its value is TRUE, the statement is executed. This process is repeated as long as the Boolean expression has the value TRUE when it is evaluated. When the Boolean expression is evaluated and found to have the value FALSE, the repetition terminates and the computer goes on to the next statement in the program. As with FOR statements, the repeated statement can be either a simple or a compound statement.

For example, consider the following:

```
I := 0;
WHILE I <= 20 DO
   I := I + 5
```

This causes the statement I := I + 5 to be executed repeatedly. Since each execution increases the value of I by 5, I takes on the values 0, 5, 10, 15, 20, and 25. Before each repetition the value of I is checked to see if it is less than or equal to 20. When the value of I is 0, 5, 10, 15, or 20, this test is passed and the repeated statement is executed. But when the value of I is 25, the value of the Boolean expression I <= 20 is FALSE, the repetitions are terminated, and the computer goes on to the next statement in the program.

We can get the successive values of I printed out by using a compound statement:

```
I := 0;
WHILE I <= 20 DO
   BEGIN
      WRITE(I:4);
      I := I + 5
   END
```

When these statements are executed, the computer prints:

```
0   5  10  15  20
```

The final value of I, 25, isn't printed. Why?

If the value of the Boolean expression is FALSE the first time the expression is evaluated, the repeated statements will not be executed at all. For example, consider:

```
I := 21;
WHILE I <= 20 DO
   BEGIN
      WRITE(I:4);
      I := I + 5
   END
```

No values are printed. Since the value of I <= 20 is FALSE the first time the expression is evaluated, the repeated statement is not executed, no printing takes place, and the value of I remains 21.

The program in Figure 5–5 shows an application of the WHILE statement. Suppose an eccentric employer offers to pay you one cent for your first day on the job, two cents the next day, four cents the day after that, and so on. How many days must you work to earn a million dollars? This is obviously a variation on the inventor-of-chess problem, except that we are dealing with cents instead of grains of wheat and with days instead of squares on the chessboard.

On the other hand, there is one fundamental difference. In the inventor-of-chess problem, we knew in advance that our calculations were to be carried out for the 64 squares of the chessboard. In this version of the problem we don't know in advance how many days the calculations are to be carried out for. We only know that they are to be repeated until a million dollars has been earned. The number of days involved is the solution to the problem, not part of the given data. For this reason we will control the repetition with the WHILE statement instead of the FOR statement.

We use DAILYWAGES for the amount paid each day, DAYS-WORKED for the number of days worked so far, and TOTALWAGES for the amount earned so far. The first day's pay is one cent. Before the calculation begins, the number of days worked and the total amount

```
PROGRAM MILLIONAIRE;
(* COMPUTE HOW LONG IT WILL TAKE TO BECOME A
   MILLIONAIRE IF YOU GET PAID ONE CENT THE
   FIRST DAY, TWO CENTS THE SECOND DAY, FOUR
   CENTS THE THIRD DAY, AND SO ON *)
CONST
   MILLIONDOLLARS = 1E8;   (* $1,000,000 = 100,000,000 CENTS *)
VAR
   DAILYWAGES, TOTALWAGES: REAL;
   DAYSWORKED: INTEGER;
BEGIN
   DAILYWAGES := 1.0;
   DAYSWORKED := 0;
   TOTALWAGES := 0.0;
   WHILE TOTALWAGES < MILLIONDOLLARS DO
      BEGIN
         TOTALWAGES := TOTALWAGES + DAILYWAGES;
         DAYSWORKED := DAYSWORKED + 1;
         DAILYWAGES := 2.0 * DAILYWAGES
      END;
   WRITELN('AFTER ', DAYSWORKED, ' DAYS YOU WILL HAVE',
           TOTALWAGES / 100.0, ' DOLLARS')
END.
```

FIGURE 5–5. This program is similar to Figure 5–3, except the number of times the calculations are to be repeated is not given in advance, but rather is one of the results to be calculated.

earned are both zero. Thus we assign the variables their initial values as follows:

```
DAILYWAGES  := 1.0;
DAYSWORKED  := 0;
TOTALWAGES  := 0.0
```

The constant MILLIONDOLLARS is defined to be one million dollars, expressed in cents. Our calculations for each day will be repeated as long as the value of TOTALWAGES is less than the value of MILLIONDOLLARS:

```
WHILE TOTALWAGES < MILLIONDOLLARS DO
   "Add the value of DAILYWAGES to the value of
   TOTALWAGES, count another day, and double the
   value of DAILYWAGES"
```

Replacing the English description with the corresponding Pascal statements, we get:

```
WHILE TOTALWAGES < MILLIONDOLLARS DO
   BEGIN
      TOTALWAGES := TOTALWAGES + DAILYWAGES;
      DAYSWORKED := DAYSWORKED + 1;
      DAILYWAGES := 2.0 * DAILYWAGES
   END
```

When the program is executed, the computer prints

```
AFTER 27 DAYS YOU WILL HAVE  1.34218E6 DOLLARS
```

Reading Data

One of the most frequent applications of repetition is to read and process a series of data items, such as data on every employee, customer, or inventory item. A question arises as to the best way to let the program know when all the data has been processed. We will look at three solutions to this problem now, and we will see a fourth one later in the chapter.

Item Counts.   The simplest way to tell the program how much data it is to process is to let the first data value be the number of items to be processed. For example, if the program is to process a series of real numbers, the input data might be

```
5  3.78  9.63  5.42  8.76  9.14
```

The 5 indicates that there are five real numbers to be processed. If there were seven, the input data might be

```
7   3.78   9.63   5.42   8.76   9.14   2.81   9.12
```

The following statements will read and process this data:

```
READ(COUNT);
FOR I := 1 TO COUNT DO
   BEGIN
      READ(X);
      "Process the value of X"
   END
```

The first statement reads the number of items to be processed into the integer variable COUNT. In the FOR statement the value of COUNT determines how many real numbers will be read and processed. For simplicity, these statements are in noninteractive form, but they can be easily converted to a form suitable for an interactive program. For example, the program could prompt the user to enter the number of items to be processed, then prompt the user for each real number to be entered.

This method works well if the input data file was created by another computer program. If the input data was created manually, however, the user has to count the number of items to be processed, which can be inconvenient if there are hundreds or thousands of items. Counting data items is a job the computer should do, not the user.

Sentinels.   Another approach is to use a special value, called a *sentinel*, to designate the end of the data. The sentinel value must not be a permissible data value, since otherwise ordinary data values could be mistaken for the sentinel. For example, suppose the program must process a series of real numbers, all of which are less than 100.0. We can use any value greater than or equal to 100.0 as a sentinel. If we choose 999.0 as the sentinel value, the input data might look like this:

```
3.78   9.63   5.42   8.76   9.14   999.0
```

or like this:

```
3.78   9.63   5.42   8.76   9.14   2.81   9.12   999.0
```

The following statements will process this data:

```
READ(X);
WHILE X <> 999.0 DO
   BEGIN
      "Process the value of X"
      READ(X)
   END
```

The first READ statement reads the first data value. The WHILE statement checks to see if the value read was the sentinel. If it was not, the value is processed and a new value of X is read. The operation "process the current value of X and read a new value for X" will be repeated until the value of X is found equal to the sentinel value, at which time the repetitions will terminate.

Note that the READ statements are arranged so that a newly read data value is always tested before it is processed. If the newly read value is the sentinel, the repetition is terminated and the value is not processed. One is sometimes tempted to write:

```
X := 0.0;
WHILE X <> 999.0 DO
    BEGIN
        READ(X);
        "Process the value of X"
    END
```

This version has the advantage of using only one READ statement, but it has the fatal disadvantage that the sentinel value is processed as if it were a legitimate data value. There is no provision for stopping the repetitions after the sentinel has been read but before it is processed.

Sentinels can be used for both interactive and noninteractive processing. Since Pascal provides a better method (the EOF predicate) for noninteractive processing, sentinels are used most frequently in interactive programs.

The EOF Predicate. A *predicate* is a function that returns a Boolean value. The end-of-file predicate, EOF, takes a file as its actual parameter. If the end of the file has been reached, EOF returns the value TRUE. If the file still contains data to be processed, EOF returns the value FALSE. Thus the value of EOF(INPUT) is TRUE or FALSE depending on whether or not the end of the standard input file has been reached. The actual parameter for EOF can be omitted, in which case the standard input file is assumed. Thus the expressions EOF and EOF(INPUT) are equivalent.

For example, if the standard input file contains a series of real numbers, we can process them as follows:

```
WHILE NOT EOF(INPUT) DO
    BEGIN
        READ(X);
        "Process the value of X"
    END
```

Suppose the standard input file contains the following values:

```
3.78  9.63  5.42  8.76  9.14
```

The value of EOF(INPUT) is initially FALSE and remains FALSE as long as the file still contains data to be read. After the value of 9.14 has been read, however, the value of EOF(INPUT) becomes TRUE and remains

TRUE thereafter. Thus after 9.14 has been processed, the value of NOT EOF(INPUT) is found to be FALSE and the repetitions terminate.

EOF is normally used for noninteractive programming. To be sure, some versions of Pascal will set the value of EOF to TRUE when a special combination of keys is pressed, thus allowing an interactive user to signal the end of the input data. But special combinations of keys are apt to be confusing to many users, so sentinels seem best for interactive programs. Later in this chapter we will look at the alternative of specifically asking the user whether the program should continue or terminate.

Two Examples.   Figures 5–6 and 5–7 both show programs for computing workers' wages, given the number of hours each person worked and that person's hourly pay rate. The program in Figure 5–6 is interactive and uses a sentinel to detect the end of the input data. The program in Figure 5–7 is noninteractive and uses EOF to detect the end of the input data.

The program in Figure 5–6 prompts the user to enter the number of hours worked by the first employee. If the sentinel value 999.0 is entered, the repeated statements are not executed and execution of the program terminates. Otherwise, the user is prompted to enter the person's hourly rate, and the worker's wages are calculated and printed. A WRITELN statement creates a blank line on the screen to separate the data for different workers. The user is then prompted to enter the hours worked by the next employee.

```
PROGRAM PAY;
(* COMPUTE EMPLOYEES' WAGES *)
VAR
    HOURS,                  (* HOURS WORKED *)
    RATE,                   (* AMOUNT PAID PER HOUR *)
    WAGES: REAL;            (* WAGES EARNED *)
BEGIN
    WRITE('HOURS WORKED? ');
    READLN(HOURS);
    WHILE HOURS <> 999.0 DO
        BEGIN
            WRITE('HOURLY RATE? ');
            READLN(RATE);
            WAGES := HOURS * RATE;
            WRITELN('WAGES ARE', WAGES:8:2);
            WRITELN;
            WRITE('HOURS WORKED? ');
            READLN(HOURS)
        END
END.
```

FIGURE 5–6. An interactive program for computing employees' wages. A sentinel is used to terminate the repetition when all the data has been processed.

Whenever a new value is read for HOURS, the value is checked to see if it is equal to the sentinel value, 999.0. If so, the repetitions terminate, as does the execution of the program. If the value of HOURS is not 999.0, then the program requests a value for RATE, then calculates and prints the value of WAGES.

The dialog with the program goes like this:

```
HOURS WORKED? 38.5
HOURLY RATE? 9.45
WAGES ARE 363.83


HOURS WORKED?
```

At this point, if the user enters the sentinel value 999.0, the program terminates. Otherwise, it requests the hourly rate and computes the workers wages.

The program in Figure 5-7 assumes that the data will be read from a previously prepared file, such as a deck of punched cards or a disk file. The input is arranged in lines, each of which contains a worker's ID number, the number of hours worked, and the amount the worker earns per hour. The printout produced by the program is a table with the column headings ID NUMBER, HOURS, RATE, and WAGES.

The program begins by printing the column headings and skipping a line to separate the column headings from the data. As long as

```
PROGRAM PAYROLL;
(* COMPUTE EMPLOYEES' WAGES *)
VAR
    IDNUMBER: INTEGER;      (* EMPLOYEE IDENTIFICATION NUMBER *)
    HOURS,                  (* HOURS WORKED *)
    RATE,                   (* AMOUNT PAID PER HOUR *)
    WAGES: REAL;            (* WAGES EARNED *)
BEGIN
    WRITELN('ID NUMBER':14, 'HOURS':14, 'RATE':14,
            'WAGES':14);
    WRITELN;
    WHILE NOT EOF(INPUT) DO
        BEGIN
            READLN(IDNUMBER, HOURS, RATE);
            WAGES := HOURS * RATE;
            WRITELN(IDNUMBER:14, HOURS:14:1, RATE:14:2,
                    WAGES:14:2)
        END
END.
```

FIGURE 5-7. A noninteractive program for computing employees' wages. The predicate EOF is used to terminate the repetition when all the data has been processed.

EOF(INPUT) remains FALSE, the program reads the data for a worker, computes the worker's wages, and prints both the data read and the calculated wages.

Note that the same field width is used for the column headings and the data values, assuring that the column heads will line up with the columns. We could have used different field widths for different columns, as long as the same field width was used for each column head and the data in that column. If the input data is:

```
1734   38.5   9.45
2897   45.7  15.28
3702   25.1  18.75
4921   41.3  10.30
```

the output looks like this:

ID NUMBER	HOURS	RATE	WAGES
1734	38.5	9.45	363.83
2897	45.7	15.28	698.30
3702	25.1	18.75	470.63
4921	41.3	10.30	425.39

For much of our later work, Figure 5–6 can be used as a model for interactive programs, and Figure 5–7 can be used as a model for noninteractive programs.

The REPEAT Statement

Pascal provides still another statement for controlling repetition, the REPEAT statement, which has the following form:

```
REPEAT
    statements
UNTIL Boolean expression
```

Any number of statements, separated by semicolons, can be placed between REPEAT and UNTIL. Since the words REPEAT and UNTIL form a natural pair of brackets, no BEGIN and END are needed.

The statements between REPEAT and UNTIL are executed, after which the Boolean expression is evaluated. If the value of the Boolean expression is TRUE, no more executions of the repeated statements take place, and the computer goes on to the next statement in the program. If the value of the Boolean expression is FALSE, the repeated statements are executed again (after which, the Boolean expression is checked again, and so on).

For example, the statements:

```
I := 0;
REPEAT
    WRITE(I:4);
    I := I + 5
UNTIL I > 20
```

cause the computer to print:

```
0    5   10   15   20
```

After the value 20 is printed, the statement:

```
I := I + 5
```

changes the value of I to 25. Now the value of I > 20 is TRUE and no more repetitions take place.

The most important distinction of the REPEAT statement is that the value of the Boolean expression is checked *after* the repeated statements have been executed, not before. This means that the repeated statements are always executed at least once. We can make this distinction clear by comparing two similar sets of statements, one using WHILE and the other using REPEAT:

```
I := 21;                       I := 21;
WHILE I <= 20 DO               REPEAT
    BEGIN                          WRITE(I:4);
        WRITE(I:4);                I := I + 5
        I := I + 5             UNTIL I > 20
    END
```

The statements on the left produce no printout. The statements on the right cause the computer to print the value 21. When the statements on the left have finished executing, the value of I is 21; when the statements on the right have finished executing, the value of I is 26.

The difference between the two examples is, of course, that in the example on the left the repeated statements are not executed, whereas in the example on the right they are executed once. This is because the WHILE statement checks the Boolean expression before each execution of the repeated statements, whereas REPEAT checks it afterward.

The REPEAT statement is useful when the condition controlling the repetition cannot be checked until after the repeated statements have been executed. Perhaps the repeated statements read the data that is to be checked, or perhaps they compute values that are to be compared.

The REPEAT statement provides us with still another way of repeating a calculation until there is no more data to be processed. After processing one set of data, the program can ask the user to enter Y if another set of data is to be processed, and N otherwise. If the user enters Y, the program will go on to obtain and process another set of data. If the user enters N, the program terminates.

Letting CONTINUE be a character variable, we can outline such a program as follows:

```
REPEAT
    "Obtain and process a set of data"
    WRITELN('PROCESS ANOTHER SET OF DATA (Y/N)? ');
    READLN(CONTINUE)
UNTIL CONTINUE <> 'Y'
```

```
PROGRAM INVESTMENTS;
(* INVESTMENT PROGRAM WITH REPEAT-UNTIL STATEMENT *)
VAR
    AMOUNT,                 (* AMOUNT IN ACCOUNT *)
    DEPOSIT,                (* MONTHLY DEPOSIT *)
    YEARLYRATE,             (* YEARLY INTEREST RATE AS PERCENT *)
    MONTHLYRATE,            (* MONTHLY INTEREST RATE AS DECIMAL *)
    INTEREST: REAL;         (* INTEREST FOR CURRENT MONTH *)

    MONTHS,                 (* NUMBER OF MONTHS DEPOSITS MADE *)
    I: INTEGER;             (* COUNTER *)

    CONTINUE: CHAR;         (* PROCESS ANOTHER SET OF DATA? *)
BEGIN
    REPEAT
        WRITE('AMOUNT IN YOUR ACCOUNT NOW? ');
        READLN(AMOUNT);
        WRITE('MONTHLY DEPOSIT? ');
        READLN(DEPOSIT);
        WRITE('YEARLY INTEREST RATE AS PERCENT? ');
        READLN(YEARLYRATE);
        WRITE('NUMBER OF MONTHS? ');
        READLN(MONTHS);
        MONTHLYRATE := YEARLYRATE / 1200.0;
        FOR I = 1 TO MONTHS DO
            BEGIN
                AMOUNT := AMOUNT + DEPOSIT;
                INTEREST := AMOUNT * MONTHLYRATE;
                AMOUNT := AMOUNT + INTEREST
            END;
        WRITELN('AFTER ', MONTHS, ' MONTHS YOU WILL HAVE',
                AMOUNT:8:2, ' DOLLARS');
        WRITELN;
        WRITE('PROCESS ANOTHER SET OF DATA (Y/N)? ');
        READLN(CONTINUE)
    UNTIL CONTINUE <> 'Y'
END.
```

FIGURE 5–8. The program of Figure 5–1, modified to process more than one set of data. After each set of data has been processed, the program inquires whether the user wishes to process another set.

If the user enters Y for CONTINUE, the program obtains and processes another set of data. If any other character is entered, the repetition terminates.

In Figure 5-8, this technique is used to modify the investment program so that it will process data for any number of investments.

Exercises

1. Write a program to compute the sum of the integers from 1 through 100.

2. The sequence of numbers

0, 1, 1, 2, 3, 5, 8, 13, 21, . . .

is known as *Fibonacci's sequence* and has applications in mathematics and computer science. The first two numbers of the sequence are 0 and 1; each remaining number is the sum of the two preceding ones. Write a program to print any specified number of terms of the Fibonacci sequence. For example, if the user requests six terms, the program will print:

0, 1, 1, 2, 3, 5

Make sure the program works if the user requests one or two terms. *Hint:* How is the Fibonacci sequence related to Fibonacci's rabbit problem?

3. Modify the program for Fibonacci's rabbit problem so that it inputs the initial number of pairs, the initial number of fertile pairs, and the number of pairs you wish to end up with. The program will tell you how many months must elapse before the number of pairs equals or exceeds the desired number.

4. The king has just been told how many grains of wheat were requested by the inventor of chess. Resisting the temptation to have the inventor executed on the spot, the king decides to see how far the country's grain surplus will go in satisfying the inventor's request. Write a program to input the available number of grains of wheat and calculate the number of squares of the chessboard that the available wheat would take care of if used to satisfy part of the inventor's request.

5. Modify either version of the program for computing workers' wages so that, after all the data has been processed, the program prints the number of workers processed and the total wages earned by all the workers.

6. Modify the program of Figure 5-8 so that it will only accept Y or N as responses to the question

PROCESS ANOTHER SET OF DATA (Y/N)?

If the user enters some character other than Y or N, the program will repeat the question. The question will continue to be repeated until the
user's response is either Y or N.

7. Write a program to print the pattern:

```
* * * * *
* * * *
* * *
* *
*
```

8. Write a program to print the pattern:

```
     *
    * * *
   * * * * *
  * * * * * *
 * * * * * * * *
```

9. Write a program to print the pattern:

```
     *
    * * *
   * * * * *
  * * * * * *
 * * * * * * * *
  * * * * * * *
   * * * * *
    * * *
     *
```

10. Write a program to print a bar graph, as follows. The input consists
of a series of real numbers, each of which is to be represented by a
horizontal line of asterisks. The number of asterisks in each line equals
the value of the corresponding real number, rounded to the nearest integer. Thus 12.4 is represented by 12 asterisks, while 12.5 and 12.6 are
each represented by 13 asterisks. If the input data is:

```
15.8 21.3 24.9 28.5 36.0 26.6 19.3 10.1 3.5
```

the output looks like this:

```
* * * * * * * * * * * * * * * *
* * * * * * * * * * * * * * * * * * * * *
* * * * * * * * * * * * * * * * * * * * * * * * *
* * * * * * * * * * * * * * * * * * * * * * * * * * * *
* * * * * * * * * * * * * * * * * * * * * * * * * * * * * * * * * * * *
* * * * * * * * * * * * * * * * * * * * * * * * * * *
* * * * * * * * * * * * * * * * * * *
* * * * * * * * * *
* * * *
```

11. Modify the program of Exercise 10 so that the bars are numbered on the left and the value being plotted is printed immediately to the right of each bar:

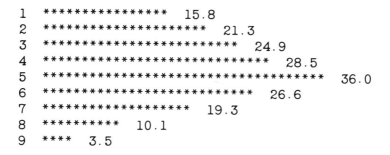

```
1   ***************    15.8
2   ********************    21.3
3   ************************    24.9
4   ****************************    28.5
5   ***********************************    36.0
6   *************************    26.6
7   *****************    19.3
8   **********    10.1
9   ****    3.5
```

12. On a trip a stamp collector visits three other collectors. The collector both buys stamps from and sells stamps to each host. Write a program to keep track of the collector's money. The input to the program is

• the amount of money with which the collector starts;

• a series of positive and negative amounts of money, continuing up to the first zero amount, representing transactions with the first host;

• a second series of positive and negative amounts, starting just after the first zero amount and continuing up to the next zero, representing transactions with the second host;

• a third series of positive and negative amounts, terminated by the end of file, representing transactions with the third host.

Positive amounts represent sales of stamps, for which money is received; negative amounts represent purchases, for which money must be paid. Your program should print the amounts in three columns, one column for the transactions with the first host, one for the transactions with the second host, and one for the transactions with the third. At the foot of each column print the total of all the transactions in that column. Also print the amount of money that the collector brings home from the trip.

Chapter 6

SELECTION

In *selection* the computer selects one of several alternative sets of instructions for execution. Which alternative the computer selects depends on the conditions that hold when the program is executed. When we write the program, we provide instructions for each of the different situations that can arise when the program is executed. We also instruct the computer how to determine which situation prevails and which instructions to execute in that situation.

Selection is essential for letting the computer respond flexibly to its input. A program that always does the same thing regardless of its input isn't going to hold our attention very long. To give just one example, a game-playing program that always makes the same moves regardless of what moves the player makes won't be much fun to play with.

One-Way Selection

In one-way selection the computer checks the value of a Boolean expression before executing a certain statement. If the value of the expression is TRUE, the statement is executed. If the value is FALSE, the statement is not executed.

In Pascal one-way selection is specified using the IF statement, which has the following form:

IF *Boolean expression* THEN
    statement

When the computer comes to the IF statement, it evaluates the Boolean expression. If the value of the expression is TRUE, the statement is executed. Otherwise, the statement is skipped, and the computer goes on to the next statement in the program. The statement can be either simple or compound.

For example, let's modify our program for computing workers' wages to take overtime into account. All time in excess of 40 hours is overtime, and workers are paid "time and a half for overtime." That is, every hour in excess of 40 is counted as if it were actually an hour and a half.

For every hour worked in excess of 40 hours, then, an extra half hour is to be added to the hours actually worked. If the value of HOURS is the number of hours actually worked, the number of extra hours is given by:

```
0.5 * (HOURS - 40.0)
```

and the value of HOURS is modified as follows:

```
HOURS := HOURS + 0.5 * (HOURS - 40.0)
```

This modification is to be used only for persons who worked more than 40 hours. If we applied it to someone who worked less than 40 hours, we would penalize that person a half hour for every hour less than 40 that was worked—definitely not what we intend. We use one-way selection to apply the modification only if the person in question worked more than 40 hours:

```
IF HOURS > 40.0 THEN
    HOURS := HOURS + 0.5 * (HOURS - 40.0)
```

Figure 6–1 shows the complete program for computing employees' wages including overtime.

Two-Way Selection

In one-way selection a statement is either executed or not executed, depending on the value of a Boolean expression. In two-way selection one statement is executed if the value of a Boolean expression is TRUE, and another statement is executed if the value is FALSE. No matter what the value of the Boolean expression, one of the two statements will be executed.

Two-way selection uses a slightly different form of the IF statement:

```
IF Boolean expression THEN
    statement-1
ELSE
    statement-2
```

For example, let's look at another method for handling overtime wages. If a person worked 40 hours or less, that person's hours are all paid for at the regular rate. The wages are calculated by

```
WAGES := HOURS * RATE
```

```
PROGRAM PAY1;
(* COMPUTE EMPLOYEES' WAGES INCLUDING OVERTIME *)
VAR
    HOURS,               (* HOURS WORKED *)
    RATE,                (* AMOUNT PAID PER HOUR *)
    WAGES: REAL;         (* WAGES EARNED *)
BEGIN
    WRITE('HOURS WORKED? ');
    READLN(HOURS);
    WHILE HOURS <> 999.0 DO
        BEGIN
            WRITE('HOURLY RATE? ');
            READLN(RATE);
            IF HOURS > 40.0 THEN
                HOURS := HOURS + 0.5 * (HOURS - 40.0);
            WAGES := HOURS * RATE;
            WRITELN('WAGES ARE', WAGES:8:2);
            WRITELN;
            WRITE('HOURS WORKED? ');
            READLN(HOURS)
        END
END.
```

FIGURE 6-1. **The program for computing employees' wages, modified to pay time-and-a-half for overtime.**

Now consider someone who worked more than 40 hours. The first 40 hours are paid for at the regular rate:

```
40.0 * RATE
```

The remaining hours are paid for at one and a half times the regular rate:

```
1.5 * RATE * (HOURS - 40.0)
```

The wages are calculated by:

```
WAGES := 40.0 * RATE + 1.5 * RATE * (HOURS - 40.0)
```

To see that the correct calculation is done depending on how many hours each person worked, we use a two-way selection:

```
IF HOURS <= 40.0 THEN
    WAGES := HOURS * RATE
ELSE
    WAGES := 40.0 * RATE + 1.5 * RATE * (HOURS - 40.0)
```

The Blackjack Dealer's Algorithm. In the game of blackjack a player is initially dealt two cards and has the option of taking additional cards on later rounds. The object of the game is for the total value of the hand —the sum of the values of all the cards—to be as high as possible. The total value must not go over 21, however. If it does, the player "busts" and loses.

On each round after the cards have been dealt, the player has the option of "hitting"—taking another card—or "staying"—electing not to take any more cards. A player hits in an attempt to raise the value of his hand. The player stays if he fears an additional card would make the value of his hand exceed 21.

The blackjack dealer plays a hand just as the players do. But the dealer has no options: if the value of the hand is 16 or less, the dealer must take another card. If the value of the hand is greater than 16, but not greater than 21, the dealer must stay. If the value of the hand is greater than 21, the dealer busts.

A further complication arises in connection with the values of the cards. The cards 2 through 10 are counted at their face values (regardless of suit). The face cards (jack, queen, and king) are counted as 10. But the ace can be counted as either 1 or 11. It is counted as 11 if it does not put the value of the hand over 21. If counting an ace as 11 *would* put the value of the hand over 21, the ace is counted as 1.

The value of a hand is called the *count*. A count that is obtained by counting an ace as 11 is said to be *soft*. In a given hand no more than one ace will ever be counted as 11, since to do so would always put the count over 21. Therefore, a hand can only be soft by virtue of one ace being counted as 11.

We want to write a program to simulate a blackjack dealer. The program will request the user to enter the values of the cards drawn. Aces are entered as 1s (it's up to the program to decide when an ace should be counted as 11). Cards 2 through 10 are represented by their values, and face cards are represented by 10s. After a sufficient number of cards have been drawn, the program indicates whether the dealer stays or busts, and prints the dealer's final count:

```
CARD DRAWN? 5
CARD DRAWN? 10
CARD DRAWN? 4
THE DEALER STAYS
THE DEALER'S COUNT IS 19
```

In this example, an ace is counted as 11:

```
CARD DRAWN? 1
CARD DRAWN? 7
THE DEALER STAYS
THE DEALER'S COUNT IS 18
```

In this example, the dealer busts:

```
CARD DRAWN? 8
CARD DRAWN? 4
```

```
CARD DRAWN? 10
THE DEALER BUSTS
THE DEALER'S COUNT IS 22
```

Using the integer variable COUNT for the dealer's count, we outline the program as follows:

```
"Initialize variables"
REPEAT
   "Obtain value of card drawn and update
   COUNT.  Make sure that an ace is counted
   properly as either 1 or 11"
UNTIL COUNT > 16
IF COUNT <= 21 THEN
   WRITELN('THE DEALER STAYS')
ELSE
   WRITELN('THE DEALER BUSTS');
WRITELN('THE DEALER''S COUNT IS ', COUNT)
```

Before any cards are drawn, the dealer's count is zero; therefore COUNT is initialized to zero. We use the Boolean variable SOFTCNT to record whether or not the count is currently soft. SOFTCNT has the value TRUE if the count is soft and the value FALSE otherwise. Since the count cannot be soft until an ace has been drawn, SOFTCNT receives the initial value FALSE:

```
COUNT := 0;
SOFTCNT := FALSE
```

The program reads the value of each card into the integer variable CARD and uses the value of CARD to update the value of COUNT:

```
WRITE('CARD DRAWN? ');
READLN(CARD);
COUNT := COUNT + CARD
```

An ace is entered and counted as 1. If the count is not already soft, however, we should count the ace as 11. We can do this by adding 10 to the count (the ace has already been counted as 1, remember). We also set SOFTCNT to TRUE to record that the count is now soft:

```
IF (CARD = 1) AND NOT SOFTCNT THEN
   BEGIN
      COUNT := COUNT + 10;
      SOFTCNT : = TRUE
   END
```

We aren't through yet. An ace can only be counted as 11 if doing so does not take the count over 21. If the count goes over 21, and an ace is being counted as 11, then the ace must be counted as 1. We make this change by subtracting 10 from the value of COUNT and setting SOFTCNT to FALSE:

```
IF (COUNT > 21) AND SOFTCNT THEN
    BEGIN
        COUNT := COUNT - 10;
        SOFTCNT := FALSE
    END
```

Figure 6–2 shows the complete program for simulating a blackjack dealer.

```
PROGRAM DEALER;
(* SIMULATE BLACKJACK DEALER *)
VAR
    COUNT,                      (* CURRENT COUNT OF DEALER'S HAND *)
    CARD: INTEGER;              (* CARD JUST DRAWN *)
    SOFTCNT: BOOLEAN;           (* ACE BEING COUNTED AS 11? *)
BEGIN
    COUNT := 0;
    SOFTCNT := FALSE;
    REPEAT
        WRITE('CARD DRAWN? ');
        READLN(CARD);
        COUNT := COUNT + CARD;
        (* COUNT ACE AS 11 ... *)
        IF (CARD = 1) AND NOT SOFTCNT THEN
            BEGIN
                COUNT := COUNT + 10;
                SOFTCNT := TRUE
            END;
        (* ... BUT NOT IF IT TAKES COUNT OVER 21 *)
        IF (COUNT > 21) AND SOFTCNT THEN
            BEGIN
                COUNT := COUNT - 10;
                SOFTCNT := FALSE
            END
    UNTIL COUNT > 16;
    IF COUNT <= 21 THEN
        WRITELN('THE DEALER STAYS')
    ELSE
        WRITELN('THE DEALER BUSTS');
    WRITELN('THE DEALER''S COUNT IS ', COUNT)
END.
```

FIGURE 6–2. This program simulates a blackjack dealer.

Multiway Selection

We have looked at one-way selection and two-way selection. But why stop there? Why not go on and select one statement for execution out of an arbitrary number of possible ones?

Selecting from more than two alternatives is known as *multiway selection*. In Pascal we can accomplish multiway selection either with the IF statement we have already studied or with the CASE statement, which is especially designed for multiway selection.

Nested IF Statements. Since we are going to be talking about a number of Boolean expressions and statements in this section, let's adopt some abbreviations to make our work easier. We will use $b1$, $b2$, $b3$, and $b4$ to represent arbitrary Boolean expressions and $s1$, $s2$, $s3$, and $s4$, to represent arbitrary statements.

Using these abbreviations, the two forms of the IF statement can be written as follows:

```
IF b1 THEN              IF b1 THEN
    s1                      s1
                       ELSE
                           s2
```

The two forms are identical except that the one on the right has an "ELSE part."

Since the statements $s1$ and $s2$ can be any Pascal statements, they can also be IF statements, in which case we will have nested IF statements. For example, if we let $s1$ be an IF statement, we get the following:

```
IF b1 THEN
    IF b2 THEN
        s3
    ELSE
        s4
ELSE
    s2
```

When the computer executes this statement, it starts by evaluating the Boolean expression $b1$. If the value is FALSE, statement $s2$ is executed. If the value is TRUE, however, the computer executes the indented IF statement. If the value of $b2$ is TRUE, statement $s3$ is executed; if the value of $b2$ is FALSE, statement $s4$ is executed. We can make a table showing which statement will be executed for each possible combination of the values of $b1$ and $b2$.

b1	b2	statement executed
FALSE	FALSE	s2
FALSE	TRUE	s2
TRUE	FALSE	s4
TRUE	TRUE	s3

Going back to our original format for the IF statement, we can let s2 rather than s1 be another IF statement:

```
IF b1 THEN
    s1
ELSE
    IF b2 THEN
        s3
    ELSE
        s4
```

If the value of b1 is TRUE, s1 is executed. If the value of b1 is FALSE, the value of b2 detemines whether s3 or s4 is executed. Again, we can use a table to show which statements are executed for which values of the Boolean expressions:

b1	b2	statement executed
FALSE	FALSE	s4
FALSE	TRUE	s3
TRUE	FALSE	s1
TRUE	TRUE	s1

So far all the IF statements in our examples have had ELSE parts. But of course some IF statements may not have ELSE parts, since the ELSE part is optional. When we use nested IF statements, some of which do not have ELSE parts, an additional complication arises.

Consider the following statement, which is shown indented in two ways, only one of which is correct:

```
IF b1 THEN                      IF b1 THEN
    IF b2 THEN                      IF b2 THEN
        s3                              s3
    ELSE                       ELSE
        s4                         s4
```

The question is, with which IF does the ELSE part go? The left-hand version shows the ELSE matched with the second IF; the right-hand version shows it matched with the first IF. Which is correct?

The computer (specifically, the Pascal language processor) pays no attention to indentation. It cannot, for indentation is optional—we could just as well have written the statement as

IF *b1* THEN IF *b2* THEN *s3* ELSE *s4*

So the computer is going to execute both versions exactly the same way. One version is correct in the sense that it reflects what the computer is going to do, and the other is incorrect in that it is misleading and does not reflect the way the computer is going to execute the statements.

In Pascal, the rule for ELSE parts is this: An ELSE part always goes with the nearest preceding IF that does not already have an ELSE part. Therefore, the indentation on the left is correct, and the one on the right is highly misleading.

Multiway Selection Using IF Statements. We have seen several ways in which IF statements can be nested, and there are other possibilities we have not looked at. For each different nesting scheme, the conditions under which each statement will be executed are different. And some of the schemes have tricky features, such as the problem of matching IFs and ELSEs.

Matters would be simplifed if we settled on one particular nesting scheme, memorized its properties, and used it for all our needs. This nesting scheme would constitute a multiway selection version of the IF statement.

A nesting scheme that can be used to meet many of our multiway selection needs is the following:

```
IF b1 THEN
    s1
ELSE
    IF b2 THEN
        s2
    ELSE
        IF b3 THEN
            s3
        ELSE
            s4
```

Each IF statement is nested into the ELSE part of the preceding one. The construction can be extended to any number of IFs. That is, *s4* in the example could be still another IF statement.

Under what conditions will each of the statements be executed? If the value of *b1* is TRUE, *s1* is executed. If the value of *b1* is FALSE but the value of *b2* is TRUE, then *s2* is executed. If the values of both *b1* and *b2* are FALSE, but the value of *b3* is TRUE, then *s3* is executed. Finally, if the values of all three Boolean expressions are FALSE, *s4* is executed. As before, we can use a table to summarize the conditions under which each statement is executed:

b1	b2	b3	statement executed
TRUE	TRUE	TRUE	s1
TRUE	TRUE	FALSE	s1
TRUE	FALSE	TRUE	s1
TRUE	FALSE	FALSE	s1
FALSE	TRUE	TRUE	s2
FALSE	TRUE	FALSE	s2
FALSE	FALSE	TRUE	s3
FALSE	FALSE	FALSE	s4

We can think of this kind of IF statement as representing a list of Boolean expressions and another list of statements to be executed, like this:

```
b1      s1
b2      s2
b3      s3
        s4
```

To find out which statement will be executed, go down the list of Boolean expressions until you find the first expression whose value is TRUE. The corresponding statement will be executed. If none of the Boolean expressions are TRUE, the last statement is executed—the one that does not correspond to any Boolean expression.

Previously, we wrote this kind of IF statement in such a way as to emphasize the nesting of one IF statement inside another. We can also write it so as to emphasize the list of Boolean expressions and the corresponding list of statements:

```
IF b1 THEN
    s1
ELSE IF b2 THEN
    s2
ELSE IF b3 THEN
    s3
ELSE
    s4
```

It is this easily understood form of the IF statement that we will use for multiway selection. It can, of course, contain as many ELSE IF parts as needed, so it can handle as many Boolean expressions and corresponding statements as we want. Also, the final ELSE part can be omitted. If the ELSE part is omitted and none of the Boolean expressions are TRUE, then none of the statements are executed, and the computer goes on to the next statement in the program.

The program of Figure 6–3 uses multiway selection to classify triangles as equilateral, isosceles, or scalene. A triangle is equilateral if all three sides have the same length, isosceles if any two sides have the same length, and scalene if no two sides have the same length.

The program uses the integer variables A, B, and C for the lengths of the three sides of a triangle. The following statement classifies a triangle:

```
IF (A = B) AND (B = C) THEN
    WRITELN('EQUILATERAL')
ELSE IF (A = B) OR (A = C) OR (B = C) THEN
    WRITELN('ISOSCELES')
ELSE
    WRITELN('SCALENE')
```

If the value of

```
(A = B) AND (B = C)
```

```
PROGRAM TRIANGLES;
(* CLASSIFY TRIANGLES AS EQUILATERAL, ISOSCELES,
   OR SCALENE *)
VAR
   A, B, C: INTEGER;       (* SIDES OF TRIANGLE *)
BEGIN
   WRITE('ENTER SIDES OF TRIANGLE (0 TO TERMINATE): ');
   READ(A);
   WHILE A <> 0 DO
      BEGIN
         READLN(B, C);
         IF (A = B) AND (B = C) THEN
            WRITELN('EQUILATERAL')
         ELSE IF (A = B) OR (A = C) OR (B = C) THEN
            WRITELN('ISOSCELES')
         ELSE
            WRITELN('SCALENE');
         WRITELN;
         WRITE('ENTER SIDES OF TRIANGLE (0 TO TERMINATE): ');
         READ(A)
      END
END.
```

FIGURE 6–3. This program classifies triangles as equilateral, isosceles, or scalene. Note that the more restrictive requirements for an equilateral triangle are checked before the less restrictive ones for an isosceles triangle.

is TRUE, then all three sides of the triangle are equal, and the triangle is equilateral. (Note that if the values of A and B are equal, and if the values of B and C are equal, then the values of A and C must also be equal, since both are equal to the value of B.) If the value of

```
(A = B) OR (A = C) OR (B = C)
```

is TRUE, then two sides are equal, and the triangle is isosceles. If neither of these two expressions has the value TRUE, then no two sides of the triangle are equal, and the triangle is scalene.

Note that we perform the most restrictive test first. Every equilateral triangle is also an isosceles triangle, but the reverse is not true. If we tested for isosceles triangles before testing for equilateral ones, we would never find any equilateral triangles, since they would all have been classified as isosceles. As it is, triangles that fail the more restrictive test for equilateral triangles can be given the less restrictive test for isosceles triangles. Triangles that fail both tests must be scalene.

Before looking at the program in Figure 6–3, we might expect the values of A, B, and C to be read with a single READLN statement, such as:

```
READLN(A, B, C)
```

Instead, we find that A is read with a READ statement, whereas B and C are read with a READLN statement. Why aren't all three values read with the same statement?

The CASE Statement. Sometimes we can find an expression whose value determines which statements are to be executed. When this is possible, the CASE statement is easier to use than the multiway selection form of the IF statement. What's more, the computer can execute the CASE statement faster.

We can illustrate the CASE statement with a simple example:

```
CASE I OF
    1: s1;
    2: s2;
    3: s3;
    4: s4
END
```

The value of I determines which statement will be executed. If the value of I is 1, s1 will be executed; if the value of I is 2, s2 will be executed; and so on. If the value of I is outside the range 1 through 4, some versions of Pascal will report an error, while others will just go on to the next statement in the program without executing any of the statements controlled by the CASE statement.

It's possible to label a statement with more than one value. For example

```
CASE J — 3 OF
    1, 2, 3: s1;
    4, 5: s2;
    6, 7, 8: s3
END
```

If the value of J − 3 is 1, 2 or 3, then s1 is executed. If the value of J − 3 is 4 or 5, then s2 is executed. And if the value of J − 3 is 6, 7, or 8, then s3 is executed. If the value of J − 3 is outside the range 1 through 8, none of the statements will be executed, and some versions of Pascal will report an error.

The expression whose value determines which statement is to be executed is called the *selector*. The value of the selector is not restricted to being an integer; it can be any data type we have studied except REAL. For example, if GRADE is a variable of type CHAR, we can use the following CASE statement to convert a letter grade to an integer score:

```
CASE GRADE OF
    'A': SCORE := 4;
    'B': SCORE := 3;
    'C': SCORE := 2;
    'D': SCORE := 1;
    'F': SCORE := 0
END
```

Figure 6–4 shows a program to calculate the commissions earned by salespeople. Each salesperson is classified as *temporary*, *regular*, or *senior*; the rules for calculating a salesperson's commission depend on the class to which the salesperson belongs.

After obtaining the amount a person sold, the program prompts the user to enter the person's classification:

```
T(EMPORARY, R(EGULAR, OR S(ENIOR?
```

This form of prompt, which is familiar to users of UCSD Pascal, indicates that the user is to enter T for temporary, R for regular, or S for senior. The character entered by the user is read into the character variable CLASS. A WHILE statement checks to see that the user entered T, R, or S; if some other character was entered, the user is prompted (repeatedly, if need be) to enter a valid character.

The value of CLASS determines how the salesperson's commission will be calculated:

```
CASE CLASS OF
    'T': "Calculate commission for temporary salesperson"

    'R': "Calculate commission for regular salesperson"

    'S': "Calculate commission for senior salesperson"
END
```

```
PROGRAM SALESCOMMISSION;
(* COMPUTE COMMISSIONS FOR THREE CLASSES OF SALESPEOPLE *)
VAR
    SALES, COMMISSION: REAL;
    CLASS: CHAR;
BEGIN
    WRITE('SALES? ');
    READLN(SALES);
    WHILE SALES > 0.0 DO
        BEGIN
            WRITE('T(EMPORARY, R(EGULAR, OR S(ENIOR? ');
            READLN(CLASS);
            WHILE      (CLASS <> 'T') AND (CLASS <> 'R')
                  AND (CLASS <> 'S') DO
                BEGIN
                    WRITE('ENTER T, R, OR S: ');
                    READLN(CLASS)
                END;
            CASE CLASS OF
                'T': COMMISSION := 0.1 * SALES;

                'R': IF SALES <= 10000.0 THEN
                        COMMISSION := 0.15 * SALES
                     ELSE
                        COMMISSION :=   0.15 * SALES
                                      + 0.05 * (SALES - 10000.0);

                'S': IF SALES <= 5000.0 THEN
                        COMMISSION := 0.2 * SALES
                     ELSE
                        COMMISSION :=   0.2 * SALES
                                      + 0.05 * (SALES - 5000.0)
            END; (* CASE *)
            WRITELN('COMMISSION IS ', COMMISSION:8:2);
            WRITELN;
            WRITE('SALES? ');
            READLN(SALES)
        END
END.
```

FIGURE 6-4. **This program computes the commissions of salespeople. A different computation is used depending on whether a salesperson is temporary, regular, or senior.**

A temporary salesperson earns commission at a flat 10% rate:

```
COMMISSION := 0.1 * SALES
```

A regular salesperson earns 15% commission on the first $10,000 of sales and 20% (an extra 5%) on the amount by which the sales exceed $10,000:

```
IF SALES <= 10000.0 THEN
    COMMISSION := 0.15 * SALES
ELSE
    COMMISSION :=   0.15 * SALES
              + 0.05 * (SALES - 10000.0)
```

A senior salesperson earns 20% commission on the first $5000 of sales and 25% (an extra 5%) on the amount by which the sales exceed $5000:

```
IF SALES <= 5000.0 THEN
    COMMISSION := 0.2 * SALES
ELSE
    COMMISSION :=   0.2 * SALES
              + 0.05 * (SALES - 5000.0)
```

Exercises

1. A package cannot be sent by first class mail if it weighs more than 70 pounds or if the sum of its length and girth exceeds 100 inches. Write a program to input the length, width, height, and weight of a package, and print whether the package can be sent by first class mail. If it cannot, the program should state whether the package is too large, too heavy, or both.

2. Modify the program in Exercise 1 so that the dimensions of the package can be entered in any order. The program will take the longest dimension to be the length and the other two dimensions to be the width and height.

3. Write a program to input the temperatures that were recorded each hour on a particular day and output the high and low temperatures for the day. (*Hint:* Let the values of HIGH and LOW be the highest and lowest temperatures that have been inputted so far. Start off by setting the values of both HIGH and LOW to the first temperature read. If the temperature just read is greater than the value of HIGH, it becomes the new value of HIGH; if it is less than the value of LOW, it becomes the new value of LOW.)

4. Suppose that in the data for Exercise 3, each temperature is followed by the time at which it was recorded. Modify the program so that it prints not only the high and low temperatures but the times at which the high and low were recorded. If the high or low was recorded more than once, the earliest time should be printed.

5. The salespeople for a certain company work in three territories, numbered 1, 2, and 3. At the end of each month, each salesperson turns in the following data—ID number, territory number, and the amount sold. Thus

1134   2   375.24

means that the salesperson with ID number 1134 sold $375.24 worth in territory 2. Write a program to process this data as follows: The printout will consist of four columns. The first column contains the salespersons' ID numbers. The remaining three columns correspond to territories 1, 2, and 3. For each person, the amount sold will be printed in the proper column depending on whether it was sold in territory 1, 2, or 3. At the foot of each territory column, print the total sales for that territory.

6. A business supply firm prices a certain kind of typewriter ribbon as follows:

Quantity Ordered	Price per Dozen Ribbons
1 dozen	$27
2–4 dozen	$26
5–9 dozen	$24
10 dozen or more	$21

Write a program to input how many dozens of ribbons were ordered and print the total cost of the order.

7. Write a program to input three characters and output them in alphabetical order. Thus, if the user enters XQA, the program prints AQX.

8. Suppose we are given a sequence of numbers such as:

1   3   8   9   4   12   25   24   17   19   19   35   28   40

Those segments of the sequence that are in nondecreasing order are called *runs*. For the sequence given, the runs are

```
 1   3   8   9
 4   12   25
24
17   19   19   35
28   40
```

Note that the end of each run (except the last one) is signalled by a *step-down*—a larger value followed by a smaller value. Write a program to read a sequence of numbers and print each run on a separate line.

9. The owner of a paint store, knowing that all colors can be obtained by mixing white (coded as W), cyan (C), magenta (M), and yellow (Y), decides to stock only those four colors. He plans to use a desktop computer to tell him how to mix any requested color from the four in stock. You are to write the program for the owner's computer. Your program should be able to mix the following colors:

Color	Code	Mixture	
Red	R	M + Y	(magenta and yellow)
Blue	B	C + M	
Green	G	C + Y	
Purple	P	B + R	
Orange	O	R + Y	
Turquoise	T	B + G + W	
Brown	N	R + G	
Black	K	C + Y + M	
Gray	A	K + W	

What's more, each color can be light (its code is preceded by L), dark (code preceded by D), very light or very dark (code preceded by VL or VD), or faded (code preceded by F). Light is achieved by adding white (very light by adding W + W), dark by adding black (very dark by adding K + K), and faded by adding gray (A).

The user enters the code for the desired color; the program responds with the proportions in which the stock colors should be mixed:

```
COLOR REQUESTED? LP
WHITE: 1   CYAN: 1    MAGENTA: 2    YELLOW: 1
```

Thus to get light purple, we mix together one part white, one part cyan, two parts magenta, and one part yellow. Note that Pascal terminates each input line with a blank space; your program can use this space to determine when the entire color code has been read.

You can improve the program by having it input the number of gallons of paint ordered and print how many gallons of each stock color should go into the mixture.

10. Write a program to simulate a simple pocket calculator. The allowed sequences of input are an integer, followed by one of the operators +, −, *, or / (implement / with DIV), followed by another integer, and so on. Or the operator may be =, which means print out the current value in the accumulator; following =, another operator is expected. The operator may also be C, to clear the accumulator, or S, to stop the program. All blanks should be ignored.

Chapter 7

FUNCTIONS
AND PROCEDURES

Functions and procedures are building blocks for constructing programs. We can assemble a program from functions and procedures, rather than directly from Pascal statements, just as an automobile is assembled from parts such as tires, sparkplugs, and headlights, rather than directly from rubber, glass, and metal.

Using such building blocks offers three advantages: (1) When we are working on one building block we can focus our attention on that part of the program alone, allowing us to break our work down into manageable parts. (2) In a large programming project, different people can work on different building blocks at the same time. (3) If a building block is needed more than one place in the program, we can write it once and use it as many times as needed.

Functions

We have already seen how to use standard, predefined functions such as SQR, SQRT, TRUNC, and ROUND. Now we will see how to define our own functions for jobs that were not anticipated by the designers of Pascal.

We define a function with a *function declaration*. For example, let's define a function FRAC that returns the fractional part of a real number —the part to the right of the decimal point. The following are some examples of FRAC:

Expression	Value
FRAC(3.14)	0.14
FRAC(245.75)	0.75
FRAC(5.0)	0.0

The following is the function declaration for FRAC:

```
FUNCTION FRAC(X: REAL): REAL;
(* RETURN FRACTIONAL PART OF REAL NUMBER *)
BEGIN
    FRAC := X - TRUNC(X)
END;
```

A function declaration has the same structure as a program, with two exceptions. (1) The function begins with a *function header* instead of a program header. (2) The statement part is followed by a semicolon instead of a period.

The function header for FRAC is

```
FUNCTION FRAC(X: REAL): REAL;
```

The reserved word FUNCTION introduces the function header. Next comes the name of the function, FRAC. Following the name of the function, the *formal parameters* are declared. (The formal parameter declarations are enclosed in parentheses.) The formal parameters correspond to the actual parameters that will be supplied when the function is used. The formal parameter declaration

```
X: REAL
```

tells us that the function will take one parameter, which must be a real number. The value of the actual parameter will be assigned to X. Finally, the ": REAL" at the end of the function header specifies that this function will return a real value. The function header is terminated by a semicolon.

A function declaration can have a constant definition part and a variable declaration part, just like a program. Because of the simplicity of FRAC, it does not define any constants or declare any variables.

In the statement part of the function declaration, we have only one statement:

```
FRAC := X - TRUNC(X)
```

which computes the value to be returned and assigns it to the name of the function. We indicate the value a function is to return by assigning that value to the function name. No matter how many statements there are in the statement part, at least one of them must assign a value-to-be-returned to the function name. Otherwise, the value of the function will be undefined.

Now let's see how a user-defined function works. Suppose that the following statement appears in a program in which FRAC has been declared:

```
Z := FRAC(3.14)
```

When the computer encounters the function name FRAC, it sets up a private memory area for the function to use. This private memory area has two memory locations, X and FRAC. FRAC serves as the name not only of the entire function but also of one of the private memory locations, the one that holds the value the function is to return.

Next, the value of the actual parameter is assigned to the formal parameter, X:

```
X := 3.14
```

Now, the statements in the statement part are executed:

```
FRAC := X - TRUNC(X)
```

and the value 0.14 is stored in the location named FRAC. When the statement part has been executed, the contents of the location FRAC are substituted for the function designator in the program that called the function. In effect, the assignment

```
Z := FRAC
```

takes place. Thus, we can think of

```
Z := FRAC(3.14)
```

as equivalent to:

```
X := 3.14;
FRAC := X - TRUNC(X);
Z := FRAC
```

When the function name appears on the left-hand side of an assignment operator, it acts just like any other variable. When the function name appears in an expression, however, it has a different meaning, one we will go into later. For now, inside a function declaration the function name will only appear on the left-hand side of the assignment operator.

The ideas we have been discussing also hold when the actual parameter is an expression and the function designator is itself used in an expression. For example, the statements:

```
Y := 3.14;
Z := 2.5 + FRAC(2.0 * Y + 0.5)
```

are equivalent to

```
Y := 3.14;
X := 2.0 * Y + 0.5;
FRAC := X - TRUNC(X);
Z := 2.5 + FRAC
```

The value 6.78 is assigned to X, and the value 0.78 is assigned to FRAC. The value assigned to Z is 3.28.

In a program function and procedure declarations come after variable declarations. Figure 7-1 demonstrates how FRAC can be declared and used in a program. Execution begins with the statement part of the main program. The statement part of the function declaration is executed only when the function is used, or *called*, in the main program. Function and procedure declarations are on much the same footing with constant definitions and variable declarations—they provide the computer with information it will need to execute the statement part of the main program.

A user-defined function can have more than one formal parameter. For example, consider a function that computes the volume of a box, given its length, width, and height. The function header could be written

```
FUNCTION VOLUME(LENGTH: REAL; WIDTH: REAL;  HEIGHT: REAL): REAL;
```

The formal parameter declarations use the same punctuation as ordinary variable declarations, except that no semicolon is used before the closing parenthesis. As in ordinary variable declarations, we don't have to repeat the identifier REAL:

```
PROGRAM FRACDEMO;
(* ILLUSTRATE FUNCTION DECLARATION AND INVOCATION *)
VAR
   V: REAL;

FUNCTION FRAC(X: REAL): REAL;
(* RETURN FRACTIONAL PART OF REAL NUMBER *)
BEGIN
   FRAC := X - TRUNC(X)
END; (* FRAC *)

BEGIN (* MAIN PROGRAM *)
   WRITE('INPUT REAL NUMBER (0 TO TERMINATE): ');
   READLN(V);
   WHILE V <> 0.0 DO
     BEGIN
        WRITELN('FRACTIONAL PART IS ', FRAC(V):8:6);
        WRITELN;
        WRITE('INPUT REAL NUMBER (0 TO TERMINATE): ');
        READLN(V)
     END
END.
```

FIGURE 7-1. This program "exercises" the function FRAC. Note that the statement part of FRAC is executed only when FRAC is called in the main program.

```
FUNCTION VOLUME(LENGTH, WIDTH, HEIGHT: REAL): REAL;
```

The complete function declaration follows:

```
FUNCTION VOLUME(LENGTH, WIDTH, HEIGHT: REAL): REAL;
(* COMPUTE VOLUME OF BOX *)
BEGIN
   VOLUME := LENGTH * WIDTH * HEIGHT
END;
```

When this function is called, memory locations are reserved for VOLUME, LENGTH, WIDTH, and HEIGHT in the function's private memory area. The value assigned to VOLUME is returned as the value of the function. For example,

```
WRITELN(VOLUME(9.0, 5.0, 3.0):8:2)
```

is equivalent to

```
LENGTH := 9.0;
WIDTH := 5.0;
HEIGHT := 3.0;
VOLUME := LENGTH * WIDTH * HEIGHT;
WRITELN(VOLUME:8:2)
```

The computer prints the value 135.00.

Now let's look at a slightly more complicated function. The "factorial" of an integer greater than 0 is defined as the product of all the integers from 1 through the integer in question. For example, the factorial of 3 is 1 * 2 * 3 or 6. Let's define a function FACTORIAL whose value is the factorial of its actual parameter:

Expression	Value
FACTORIAL(3)	6
FACTORIAL(4)	24
FACTORIAL(5)	120
FACTORIAL(6)	720

Figure 7–2 shows the program PRINTFACTORIALS, which contains the declaration for the FACTORIAL function. To compute the factorial of the value of N, we set the variable FACT to 1 and multiply it by each of the integers in the range 1 through the value of N:

```
FACT := 1;
FOR I := 1 TO N DO
   FACT := FACT * I;
FACTORIAL := FACT
```

```
PROGRAM PRINTFACTORIALS;
(* EXERCISE FACTORIAL FUNCTION *)
VAR
   M: INTEGER;

FUNCTION FACTORIAL(N: INTEGER): INTEGER;
(* COMPUTE THE FACTORIAL OF N *)
VAR
   FACT, I: INTEGER;
BEGIN
   FACT := 1;
   FOR I := 1 TO N DO
      FACT := FACT * I;
   FACTORIAL := FACT
END; (* FACTORIAL *)

BEGIN (* MAIN PROGRAM *)
   WRITELN('NUMBER':14, 'FACTORIAL':14);
   WRITELN;
   FOR M := 1 TO 7 DO
      WRITELN(M:14, FACTORIAL(M):14)
END.
```

FIGURE 7-2. This program exercises the FACTORIAL function.

Note that FACT and I are declared in the variable declaration part of the function FACTORIAL. Variables declared by a function or procedure are said to be *local* to that function or procedure. When the function or procedure is called, memory locations for the local variables are reserved in the function's or procedure's private memory area.

Suppose that FACTORIAL is called with the following statement:

```
J := FACTORIAL(5)
```

When this statement is executed, the computer sets up a private memory area containing locations named N, I, FACT, and FACTORIAL. In effect, the following statements are executed:

```
N := 5;
FACT := 1;
FOR I := 1 TO N DO
   FACT := FACT * I;
FACTORIAL := FACT;
J := FACTORIAL
```

Here's a mistake you might be tempted to make. You might think you can eliminate the variable FACT by writing the statement part of the function as

```
FACTORIAL := 1;
FOR I := 1 TO N DO
   FACTORIAL := FACTORIAL * I
```

Unfortunately, the function name can be used as a variable only on the left-hand side of the assignment operator. Thus the statement

```
FACTORIAL := FACTORIAL * I
```

is incorrect. We must use the variable FACT for calculating the factorial, then assign the value of FACT to FACTORIAL after the calculation is complete.

Procedures

A function is limited in that it can return only a single value to the calling program. Often we want a "building block" to return several values. Or we might not want to return any value at all, but take some other action, such as printing a message to the user. A *procedure* frees us from always having to return exactly one value.

For example let's write a procedure that calculates the volume of a box but prints the volume instead of returning it to the calling program:

```
PROCEDURE PRINTVOL(LENGTH, WIDTH, HEIGHT: REAL);
VAR
   V: REAL;
BEGIN
   V := LENGTH * WIDTH * HEIGHT;
   WRITELN('VOLUME: ', V:8:2)
END;
```

The structure of a procedure is the same as that of a function or a program except that a *procedure header* is used in place of a program header or a function header. A procedure header differs from a function header in only two respects: (1) the reserved word PROCEDURE is used instead of FUNCTION, and (2) no data type is given for a value to be returned, since a procedure does not use the procedure name to return a value.

A procedure is called using a *procedure statement*, which consists of the procedure name followed by the list of actual parameters. The parameter list is enclosed in parentheses. For example, the procedure statement

```
PRINTVOL(9.0, 5.0, 3.0)
```

causes the computer to print:

```
VOLUME:   135.00
```

In effect, the procedure statement is equivalent to

```
LENGTH := 9.0;
WIDTH := 5.0;
HEIGHT := 3.0;
V := LENGTH * WIDTH * HEIGHT;
WRITELN('VOLUME: ', V:8:2)
```

What we have done, in effect, is to define a new command for the computer to carry out, the PRINTVOL command. All we have to do is issue the command PRINTVOL and provide the necessary actual parameters in order to have the computer carry out the calculations and print the result. Once the procedure has been written, we can issue this command whenever we need a volume calculated and printed. We can use the command without having to worry about the details of how the computer carries it out.

Incidentally, READ, READLN, WRITE, and WRITELN are all predefined procedures. Although we sometimes, for convenience, speak of a READ statement or a WRITELN statement, the input and output statements are all special cases of the procedure statement. The input and output procedures do, however, have some special features not available for user-defined procedures, such as the field-width parameters in WRITE and WRITELN.

Value and Variable Parameters. Suppose we want to return the results of a procedure's calculations to the calling program instead of printing them out. How can we do this? An obvious way is to use the formal parameters. The formal parameters are used to communicate data from the calling program to the procedure. Why not use them to communicate in the opposite direction as well?

Unfortunately, the kinds of parameters we have used so far are not suitable for this purpose. These parameters are the names of locations in procedure's private memory area. Assigning values to these parameters changes the procedure's private memory area but has no effect whatever on the calling program. Such parameters are known as *value parameters*, since they can be used only to pass values from the calling program to a function or procedure.

To get around this difficulty, Pascal also provides *variable parameters*. The actual parameter corresponding to a variable parameter must be a variable; constants and expressions are not allowed. The actual parameter is, in effect, substituted for the formal parameter throughout the procedure. If a new value is assigned to the formal parameter, the same value is also assigned to the actual parameter.

For example, the program in Figure 7–3 uses a procedure BOX, which computes the volume and length-plus-girth of a box from its length, width, and height. We pass the length, width, and height to the procedure with the value parameters L, W, and H. The procedure returns its results via the variable parameters V (volume) and LPG (length-plus-girth). The procedure header looks like this:

```
PROCEDURE BOX(L, W, H: REAL; VAR V, LPG: REAL);
```

```
PROGRAM BOXES;
(* EXERCISE THE PROCEDURE BOX *)
VAR
   LENGTH, WIDTH, HEIGHT,
   VOLUME, LENGTHPLUSGIRTH: REAL;

PROCEDURE BOX(L, W, H: REAL; VAR V, LPG: REAL);
(* COMPUTE VOLUME AND LENGTH-PLUS-GIRTH OF BOX *)
BEGIN
   V := L * W * H;
   LPG := L + 2.0*(W + H)
END; (* BOX *)

BEGIN (* MAIN PROGRAM *)
   WRITE('ENTER LENGTH, WIDTH, AND HEIGHT: ');
   READ(LENGTH);
   WHILE LENGTH > 0.0 DO
      BEGIN
         READLN(WIDTH, HEIGHT);
         BOX(LENGTH, WIDTH, HEIGHT, VOLUME, LENGTHPLUSGIRTH);
         WRITELN('VOLUME IS ', VOLUME:8:3);
         WRITELN('LENGTH-PLUS-GIRTH-IS ', LENGTHPLUSGIRTH:8:3);
         WRITELN;
         WRITE('ENTER LENGTH, WIDTH, AND HEIGHT: ');
         READ(LENGTH)
      END
END.
```

FIGURE 7-3. This program illustrates variable parameters. When the procedure BOX is called, VOLUME is, in effect, substituted for V in the statement part of BOX, and LENGTHPLUSGIRTH is substituted for LPG.

The reserved word VAR indicates that V and LPG are variable parameters. Declarations of variable parameters must always begin with VAR; if VAR is omitted, the parameters are considered to be value parameters.

In the main program BOX is called with the following procedure statement:

```
BOX(LENGTH, WIDTH, HEIGHT, VOLUME, LENGTHPLUSGIRTH)
```

When this statement is executed, the *values* of LENGTH, WIDTH, and HEIGHT are assigned to the value parameters L, W, and H. On the other hand, the *variables* VOLUME and LENGTHPLUSGIRTH are, in effect, substituted for the variable parameters V and LPG. When, in the statement part of the procedure, an assignment is made to V:

```
V := L * W * H
```

the effect is the same as if the assignment had been made to VOLUME:

```
VOLUME := L * W * H
```

In the same way an assignment to LPG

```
LPG := L + 2.0 * (W + H)
```

is equivalent to an assignment to LENGTHPLUSGIRTH:

```
LENGTHPLUSGIRTH := L + 2.0 * (W + H)
```

We are already familiar with one application of variable parameters. The parameters of the input procedures READ and READLN are variable parameters. Therefore, when statements such as

```
READLN(I, J, K)
```

are executed, the values read are assigned to the actual parameters, the variables I, J, and K.

The Scopes of Identifiers

The definitions, declarations, and statements that follow a function or procedure header are known as a *block*. Thus, a program consists of a program header followed by a block, and a function or procedure declaration consists of a function or procedure header followed by a block. For the function FACTORIAL, for example, the function header is

```
FUNCTION FACTORIAL(N: INTEGER): INTEGER;
```

and the block is

```
VAR
   FACT, I: INTEGER;
BEGIN
   FACT := 1;
   FOR I := 1 TO N DO
      FACT := FACT * I;
   FACTORIAL := FACT
END
```

A variable declaration applies only to the block containing the declaration. We can only refer to the variable inside this block. Outside the block containing the declaration the variable is not declared, and a reference to it is meaningless.

The part of the program in which it is meaningful to refer to an identifier is called the *scope* of the identifier. The scope of a variable, then, is the block in which it is declared. In the function FACTORIAL the scope of I and FACT is the block containing their declarations.

The program PRINTFACTORIALS, Figure 7–2, has two blocks. One block begins immediately after the program header and extends all the way to the end of the program. The other block begins immediately after the function header and extends to the end of the function declaration, that is, to the end of the statement part of the factorial function.

It's convenient to designate a block with the program, function, or procedure name that appears in the immediately preceding program, function, or procedure header. Therefore, we will refer to the block that begins immediately after the program header as PRINTFACTORIALS and the block that begins immediately after the function header as FACTORIAL.

One variable, M, is declared in the block PRINTFACTORIALS. Therefore, M may be referred to anywhere within this block. Since the function declaration is a part of this block, the variable M could be referred to from within the function declaration (although, in fact, it isn't). That is, M is accessible from both PRINTFACTORIALS and FACTORIAL.

The variables I and FACT are declared in the block FACTORIAL and can be accessed from anywhere inside this block. However, I and FACT cannot be accessed from any part of the program outside the block FACTORIAL. In particular, they cannot be accessed from the statement part of the main program.

Using complete programs to illustrate these points can be clumsy. It's more convenient to use diagrams instead. In the diagram for PRINT-FACTORIALS, which is shown in Figure 7–4, each block is represented by a box. M can be accessed from anywhere inside the outer block or the inner block. I and FACT can be accessed only from inside the inner block. It's helpful to think of the boxes representing the blocks as made

FIGURE 7–4. This diagram illustrates the blocks and declarations in the program PRINTFACTORIALS.

of one-way glass. From inside the FACTORIAL block, it's possible to look out and see the variable M. But from outside the FACTORIAL block, it isn't possible to look in and see the variables I and FACT.

The body of a function or procedure is a block and so can contain other function or procedure declarations. These declarations can, in turn, contain still other function and procedure declarations, and so on. Such declarations are said to be *nested*; Figure 7-5 illustrates nested function and procedure declarations. The main program in Figure 7-5 is named P. In P two functions or procedures (it doesn't matter which) named Q1 and Q2 are declared. Finally, inside Q1 another function or procedure named R is declared.

The variables A and B are declared in the outermost block, the main program P. They can therefore be accessed from everywhere inside that block. Specifically, A and B can be accessed from P, Q1, Q2,

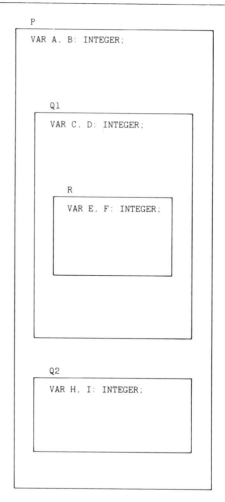

FIGURE 7-5. This diagram illustrates a program P containing declarations for functions or procedures Q1 and Q2. Q1, in turn, declares a function or procedure R.

and R. The variables C and D can be accessed from Q1 and R; they cannot be accessed from P or Q2. The variables H and I can be accessed only from Q2.

Again, if you think of the boxes in the diagram as made of one-way glass that allows you to look out of a block but not into one, you should have no difficulty determining which declarations can be "seen" from any part of the program.

Figure 7–6 illustrates still another aspect of the accessibility of variables. What's different about this example is that the same identifier has been declared in more than one block. Thus, there is an A in P and an A in Q1, a B in P and a B in Q2, and an F in Q1 and an F in Q2.

The first thing to note is that variables declared in different blocks have nothing to do with one another, even though they happen to have the same name. Thus, the A declared in P refers to a different memory location than the A declared in Q1; the B declared in P refers to a different memory location than the P declared in Q2; and the F declared in Q1 refers to a different memory location than the F declared in Q2.

Because of this, a statement can have different meanings depending on where it occurs in the program. For example, if

F := 25

occurs in the statement part of Q1, it assigns 25 to the variable F declared in Q1. If the same statement occurs in the statement part of Q2, it assigns 25 to an entirely different variable, the F declared in Q2.

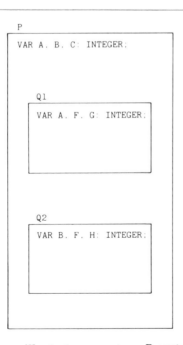

FIGURE 7–6. This diagram illustrates a program P containing declarations for functions or procedures Q1 and Q2. Variables named A are declared in P and Q1; variables named B are declared in P and Q2; and variables named F are declared in Q1 and Q2.

Now consider the statement

```
A := 100
```

If this statement is located in P or Q2, it assigns 100 to the variable A declared in P. But what if the statement is located in Q1? From what we have said so far, there are two variables named A that might be accessible from Q1: the A declared in P and the A declared in Q1. To which A does the statement apply?

The rule is this: When the declarations of several variables with the same name are valid at a particular point in the program, then the name refers to the variable with the smallest scope. Thus in Q1 the statement

```
A := 100
```

refers to the A declared in Q1, since this variable has a smaller scope than the A declared in P. We can think of the declaration of A in Q1 as "hiding" the declaration of A in P, so that only the former declaration can be seen from inside Q1. A little thought will show that this rule is the only reasonable one; any other would make it impossible to refer to the A declared in Q1 at all.

In the same way, the statement

```
B := B + 1
```

refers to the B declared in P if the statement is located in P or Q1. If the statement is located in Q2, however, it refers to the B declared in Q2.

The scope rules for constant identifiers, and for the type identifiers we will begin to work with in the following chapter, are the same as for variables. We need to look a bit more closely, however, at how the scope rules apply to the names and formal parameters of functions and procedures.

The name of a function or procedure is considered to be declared in the block containing the function or procedure declaration. The formal parameters, on the other hand, are considered to be declared in the block that follows the function or procedure heading. For example, consider the function outlined as follows:

```
FUNCTION F(I, J, K: INTEGER): INTEGER;
VAR
    M, N, P: INTEGER;
BEGIN
    . . .
END;
```

F is declared in the block containing the function declaration, whereas I, J, K, M, N, and P are all declared in the block F, the block following the function header. Figure 7–7 illustrates the scopes of these identifiers.

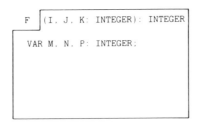

FIGURE 7-7. In a function or procedure declaration the formal parameters and local variables are considered declared in the block that follows the function or procedure header. The function or procedure name, however, is considered declared in the block containing the function or procedure declaration.

As we have seen Pascal allows us to give distinct variables, constants, functions, and so on, the same name, provided they are declared in different blocks. But this doesn't mean we should rush out and start writing programs in which many different entities all have the same name. Identifiers are not in short supply, and using different ones to refer to different entities will contribute immeasurably to the readability of your programs. The use of the same name for different things occurs mainly when different people write different functions and procedures. In this case the different people may happen to use the same name in different ways. The Pascal scope rules keep these different uses of the same name from interfering with one another.

Global Variables

As mentioned earlier variables declared in a function or procedure are said to be *local* to a function or procedure. Variables not declared in a function or procedure, but accessible from it, are said to be *global* to the function or procedure. In most cases global variables are declared in the main program. When we refer to global variables without further qualification we will mean variables declared in the main program.

The statements in a function or procedure can refer to a global variable provided there is no local variable having the same name. They can use the values of the global variables and assign new values to them. Thus, global variables provide another way of passing data to and from a procedure or function. Values to be passed to a function or procedure can be assigned to global variables before the function or procedure is called. The function or procedure can assign values to global variables, and these values can be accessed by the main program after the function or procedure returns.

There is, however, a disadvantage to passing data in this way. When data is passed using parameters, we can look at the function designator or procedure statement and see at a glance the values passed to a function or procedure and the variables in the calling program to which a procedure is given access. But with global variables we have to examine every statement in the function or procedure to see if it refers to a global variable before we can be sure what data the function or procedure uses and what values it returns. If we think of the function or procedure header, containing the formal parameter declarations, as the "front door" of the function or procedure, then global variables let data sneak in and out the "back door".

Because of this disadvantage, formal parameters are usually preferred to global variables. Nevertheless, there are two situations in which global variables are often used:

1. We want to preserve some values from one call of the function or procedure to the next. This cannot be done with local variables. Every time a function or procedure is called, a new private memory area is set up for the local variables. Any values assigned to these variables are lost when the function or procedure returns. The next time the function or procedure is called, the private memory area will be set up anew.

2. Sometimes, many of the functions and procedures in a program manipulate some common data structure, say a large table. In this case the table can be assigned to a global variable, and all the functions and procedures can refer to this global variable to carry out their manipulations. We will see examples of this situation later in the book.

A good example of the first situation is a *pseudorandom number generator*. Pseudorandom numbers are numbers that appear to have been chosen at random but which were actually computed by a function or procedure. Pseudorandom numbers provide the unpredictability for game-playing programs. They are also important in other areas such as simulation and cryptography.

Typically, a pseudorandom number generator works with a value called the *seed*, which is the current value of the pseudorandom number. The function or procedure carries out a calculation on the seed to get a new seed—a new pesudorandom number. Each new pseudorandom number is obtained by carrying out a calculation on the previous one.

Let's use the global real variable SEED to hold the current value of the pseudorandom number. The value SEED has to be preserved from one call on the pseudorandom number function to the next, since the new value of SEED is always calculated from the old value.

There are many schemes for calculating pesudorandom numbers, some of which are adapted to the characteristics of particular computers. We will use a quick-and-dirty method that works on all computers and is suitable for noncritical applications, such as computer games. It would probably not be suitable for more demanding applications where the pseudorandom numbers must have specific statistical properties. The new value of the SEED is calculated from the old value as follows:

```
SEED := SQR(SEED + 3.1415927);
SEED := SEED - TRUNC(SEED)
```

That is, a constant is added to the value of SEED (the mathematical constant *pi* was chosen here), and the sum is squared. The integer part of the result is subtracted off, leaving only the fractional part. It is largely the effect of dropping the integer part of the result that makes the resulting numbers appear to be random.

Since our calculation retains only the fractional part of the result, our random numbers will be fractions—that is, their values will range from 0.0 up to, but not including, 1.0.

What we usually need is not a random fractional value but rather a random integer in a particular range. For a guessing game we might need a random integer in the range of 1 through 100; to simulate the rolling of ordinary dice, we need random integers in the range of 1 through 6; with random integers in other ranges, such as 1 through 10, we can simulate the special dice used in some role-playing games. How can we convert the value of SEED into an integer ranging from 1 through the value of N?

To be specific, suppose we need random integers in the range of 1 through 100. If real numbers are stored with six significant digits, the value of SEED ranges from 0.0 through 0.999999. Consequently, the value of 100 * SEED ranges from 0.0 through 99.9999. The value of

```
TRUNC(100 * SEED)
```

ranges from 0 through 99, and the value of

```
TRUNC(100 * SEED) + 1
```

ranges from 1 through 100. Generalizing, we see that the value of

```
TRUNC(N * SEED) + 1
```

ranges from 1 through the value of N.

The following function yields a pseudorandom integer in the range 1 through the value of the actual parameter:

```
FUNCTION RANDOM(N: INTEGER): INTEGER;
(* RETURNS PSEUDORANDOM INTEGER IN RANGE 1-N
   REFERS TO AND MODIFIES GLOBAL VARIABLE SEED *)
BEGIN
   SEED := SQR(SEED + 3.1415927);
   SEED := SEED - TRUNC(SEED);
   RANDOM := TRUNC(N * SEED) + 1
END;
```

Thus, RANDOM(6) yields a random integer in the range of 1 through 6; RANDOM(100) yields a random integer in the range of 1 through 100; and so on. Figure 7-8 shows a guessing game program using the function RANDOM.

```
PROGRAM GAME;
(* PLAY GUESSING GAME WITH USER *)
VAR
    SEED: REAL;
    ANSWER: CHAR;
    NUMBER, GUESS: INTEGER;

FUNCTION RANDOM(N: INTEGER): INTEGER;
(* RETURNS PSEUDORANDOM INTEGER IN RANGE 1-N
    REFERS TO AND MODIFIES GLOBAL VARIABLE SEED *)
BEGIN
    SEED := SQR(SEED + 3.1415927);
    SEED := SEED - TRUNC(SEED);
    RANDOM := TRUNC(N * SEED) + 1
END; (* RANDOM *)

BEGIN (* MAIN PROGRAM *)
    WRITE('ENTER A NUMBER BETWEEN 0 AND 1: ');
    READLN(SEED);
    WRITELN;
    WRITELN('I AM THINKING OF A NUMBER FROM 1 THROUGH 100.');
    WRITELN('YOU ARE TO TRY TO GUESS THE NUMBER.');
    WRITELN('I WILL TELL YOU WHETHER YOUR GUESS IS RIGHT');
    WRITELN('OR WHETHER IT IS TOO LARGE OR TOO SMALL.');
    REPEAT
        NUMBER := RANDOM(100);
        WRITELN;
        WRITE('I HAVE MY NUMBER.  WHAT IS YOUR GUESS? ');
        REPEAT
            READLN(GUESS);
            IF GUESS > NUMBER THEN
                WRITE('TOO LARGE.  TRY AGAIN: ')
            ELSE IF GUESS < NUMBER THEN
                WRITE('TOO SMALL.  TRY AGAIN: ')
        UNTIL GUESS = NUMBER;
        WRITELN('YOU ARE RIGHT.  CONGRATULATIONS!');
        WRITELN('WOULD YOU LIKE TO PLAY AGAIN?');
        WRITE('ANSWER Y (YES) OR N (NO): ');
        READLN(ANSWER);
    UNTIL ANSWER <> 'Y';
    WRITELN('I HAVE ENJOYED PLAYING WITH YOU.')
END.
```

FIGURE 7-8. In this guessing-game program the function RANDOM uses and modifies the value of the global variable SEED.

Recursion

A function or procedure can call other functions or procedures. For example, the function RANDOM calls the standard functions SQR and TRUNC. A function or procedure can even call *itself*, a situation known as *recursion*. It sometimes happens that, after making some progress towards solving a problem, we arrive at a simplified version of the same problem. When a function or procedure for solving the problem arrives at this point, it can call itself to solve the simplified version of the original problem. Such a call is said to be recursive.

Like repetition, recursion can fail to terminate. The recursive function or procedure can call itself again and again without making any progress toward solving the original problem. For recursion to terminate, two conditions must hold: (1) The function or procedure must always call itself to solve a *simplified* version of the original problem. (2) Repeated simplification must lead to a trivial version of the problem that can be solved without any further recursive calls.

The Factorial Function. We recall that the factorial of the value of N is the product of all the integers from 1 through the value of N. It's easy to see that the following statements are true:

```
FACTORIAL(1) = 1
FACTORIAL(2) = 2 * 1                 = 2 * FACTORIAL(1)
FACTORIAL(3) = 3 * 2 * 1             = 3 * FACTORIAL(2)
FACTORIAL(4) = 4 * 3 * 2 * 1         = 4 * FACTORIAL(3)
```

Thus, to compute the value of FACTORIAL(2), we can compute the value of FACTORIAL(1) and multiply the result by 2. To compute the value of FACTORIAL(3), we can compute the value of FACTORIAL(2) and multiply the result by 3. To compute the value of FACTORIAL(4), we can compute the value of FACTORIAL(3) and multiply by the result by 4. In general, to compute the value of FACTORIAL(N), we can compute the value of FACTORIAL(N – 1) and multiply the result by the value of N. A Pascal FACTORIAL function can call itself to compute the value of FACTORIAL(N – 1).

A recursive function or procedure must always be able to handle two cases—the trival case that can be solved without any further recursive calls and the nontrivial case that is solved by calling the procedure or function recursively. For the FACTORIAL function the trivial case occurs when the value of the actual parameter, N, is 1. We can write a recursive version of the factorial function as follows:

```
FUNCTION FACTORIAL(N: INTEGER): INTEGER;
BEGIN
  IF N = 1 THEN
     FACTORIAL := 1
  ELSE
     FACTORIAL := N * FACTORIAL(N – 1)
END;
```

Note that the identifier FACTORIAL is used in two different ways. When FACTORIAL appears on the left-hand side of the assignment operator it refers to the memory location used to store the result returned by the function. When FACTORIAL appears on the right-hand side of the assignment operator it refers to the FACTORIAL function and causes a recursive call to that function.

If FACTORIAL is called with the actual parameter 4, it calls itself with the actual parameter 3. When FACTORIAL is called with the actual parameter 3, it calls itself with the actual parameter 2, and so on. Thus, the following sequence of calls to FACTORIAL take place:

```
FACTORIAL(4)
FACTORIAL(3)
FACTORIAL(2)
FACTORIAL(1)
```

When FACTORIAL is called with the actual parameter 1 it returns the value 1 without making any further recursive calls. When the call FACTORIAL(1) returns the value 1 the value of FACTORIAL(2) can be calculated as:

```
2 * FACTORIAL(1) = 2 * 1 = 2
```

When the call FACTORIAL(2) returns the value 2 the value of FACTORIAL(3) can be calculated as:

```
3 * FACTORIAL(2) = 3 * 2 = 6
```

When the call FACTORIAL(3) returns the value 6 the value of FACTORIAL(4) can be calculated as:

```
4 * FACTORIAL(3) = 4 * 6 = 24
```

The Towers of Hanoi. Figure 7–9 illustrates an otherwise tricky puzzle that's easy to solve with the aid of recursion. We have three pegs labeled A, B, and C. Peg A contains three disks numbered, in order of increasing size, 1, 2, and 3. The problem is to move the three disks from peg A to peg C using peg B as needed during the process. The disks must

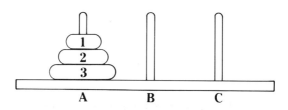

FIGURE 7–9. The Towers of Hanoi problem. The three disks are to be moved from peg A to peg C, via peg B if necessary. The disks must be moved one at a time, and a larger disk may never be placed on top of a smaller one. The problem can be generalized to any number of disks.

be moved one at a time, and we can never place a larger disk on top of a smaller one. The problem easily generalizes to any number of disks. The number of pegs remains three, however.

After some thought, the following plan emerges:

1. Move disks 1 and 2 from peg A to peg B

2. Move disk 3 from peg A to peg C

3. Move disks 1 and 2 from peg B to peg C

Figure 7–10 illustrates this solution. Step 2 can be accomplished in a single move. Steps 1 and 3, however, require more than one move. Two disks must be moved, and we can only move one disk at a time.

Starting Configuration:

After Step 1:

After Step 2:

After Step 3:

FIGURE 7–10. A plan for solving the Towers of Hanoi problem. Step 1 moves disks 1 and 2 to peg B. Step 2 moves disk 3 to peg C. Step 3 moves disks 1 and 2 to peg C. Step 2 can be done in one move; steps 1 and 3 each involve several moves. A procedure for solving the problem can call itself recursively to carry out steps 1 and 3.

It's easy to generalize this plan to an arbitrary number of disks. Letting N represent the number of disks, we have

1. Move N – 1 disks from peg A to peg B

2. Move disk N from peg A to peg C

3. Move N – 1 disks from peg B to peg C

"Disk N" is the disk whose number is equal N.

We want to write a recursive procedure MOVE to print out step-by-step instructions for moving the disks. For step 2 of the plan the procedure will just print instructions for moving the disk in question. For steps 1 and 3 the procedure will call itself recursively to solve the simpler problem of moving N – 1 disks. The trivial case—the one than can be solved without further recursive calls—is the problem of moving zero disks, which can be solved without taking any action.

The formal parameters for MOVE are declared as follows:

```
MOVE(NUMBER: INTEGER; SOURCE, DEST, AUX: CHAR)
```

NUMBER represents the number of disks to be moved—three in Figure 7–9. SOURCE represents the peg from which the disks are to be moved—peg A in Figure 7–9. DEST represents the peg to which the disks are to be moved—peg C in Figure 7–9. AUX represents the auxiliary peg on which disks will be placed temporarily—peg B in Figure 7–9.

The statement part of MOVE implements our plan for moving an arbitrary number of disks:

```
IF NUMBER > 0 THEN
   BEGIN
      MOVE(NUMBER - 1, SOURCE, AUX, DEST);
      WRITELN('MOVE DISK ', NUMBER, ' FROM PEG ', SOURCE,
             ' TO PEG ', DEST);
      MOVE(NUMBER - 1, AUX, DEST, SOURCE)
   END
```

If the value of NUMBER is 0, then we have the trivial problem of moving zero disks, and no action needs to be taken. Otherwise, MOVE is called recursively to move NUMBER – 1 disks from the original source peg to the original auxiliary peg. The original destination peg serves as the auxiliary peg for this move. Next, instructions are printed to move one disk, whose number equals the value of NUMBER, from the source peg to the destination peg. Finally, MOVE is again called recursively to move NUMBER – 1 disks from the original auxiliary peg to the original destination peg. The original source peg serves as the auxiliary peg for this move.

Figure 7–11 shows a complete program for solving the Towers-of-Hanoi problem. MOVE is called with the procedure statement

```
MOVE(COUNT, 'A', 'C', 'B')
```

COUNT, whose value is obtained from the user, specifies the number of disks to be moved. A is the source peg, C is the destination peg, and B is the auxiliary peg. For the three-disk problem, the program prints:

```
MOVE DISK 1 FROM PEG A TO PEG C
MOVE DISK 2 FROM PEG A TO PEG B
MOVE DISK 1 FROM PEG C TO PEG B
MOVE DISK 3 FROM PEG A TO PEG C
MOVE DISK 1 FROM PEG B TO PEG A
MOVE DISK 2 FROM PEG B TO PEG C
MOVE DISK 1 FROM PEG A TO PEG C
```

```
PROGRAM HANOI;
(* SOLVE TOWERS-OF-HANOI PROBLEM *)
VAR
    COUNT: INTEGER;

PROCEDURE MOVE(NUMBER: INTEGER: SOURCE, DEST, AUX: CHAR);
(* MOVE SPECIFIED NUMBER OF DISKS FROM THE SOURCE PEG TO
   THE DESTINATION PEG WITH THE AID OF THE AUXILIARY PEG *)
BEGIN
    IF NUMBER > 0 THEN
        BEGIN
            MOVE(NUMBER - 1, SOURCE, AUX, DEST);
            WRITELN('MOVE DISK ', NUMBER, ' FROM PEG ', SOURCE,
                    ' TO PEG ', DEST);
            MOVE(NUMBER - 1, AUX, DEST, SOURCE)
        END
END;   (* MOVE *)

BEGIN (* MAIN PROGRAM *)
    WRITE('HOW MANY DISKS? ');
    READLN(COUNT);
    WRITELN;
    MOVE(COUNT, 'A', 'C', 'B')
END.
```

FIGURE 7-11. A program for solving the Towers of Hanoi problem. In the recursive procedure MOVE, the trivial case—the one that can be solved without any recursive calls—consists of moving zero disks and requires no action.

Exercises

When you are requested to write a function or procedure, you should also write a program to "exercise" the function or procedure by providing it with data and printing the results that it produces.

1. Write a function

```
WAGES(HOURS, RATE)
```

whose actual parameters are the hours a person worked and the amount paid per hour. The value of the function is the WAGES the person earned, with time-and-half for hours in excess of 40.

2. Write a function

```
MAXIMUM(M, N)
```

that returns the value of the largest of its two actual parameters.

3. Write function

```
RANDOM1(M, N)
```

that return a pseudorandom integer ranging from the value of M through the value of N.

4. The value of

```
POWER(M, N)
```

is computed by starting with 1 and multiplying repeatedly by the value of M. The value of N determines the number of times we multiply by the value of M:

```
POWER(3, 0) = 1
POWER(3, 1) = 1 * 3 = 3
POWER(3, 2) = 1 * 3 * 3 = 9
POWER(3, 3) = 1 * 3 * 3 * 3 = 27
```

Write the function POWER.

5. Write a recursive version of the function POWER based on the following two statements:

```
POWER(M, 0) = 1
POWER(M, N) = M * POWER(M, N - 1)
```

6. For the Towers of Hanoi problem rewrite the procedure MOVE so that the "trivial case" consists of moving one disk instead of moving zero disks. Your version of MOVE will be more efficient, since it won't waste time calling procedures that do nothing. On the other hand, your version will be slightly more complicated than the one in the book.

7. You have five neighbors and want to make a note of which ones are home on a particular Sunday morning (so you know who is available to help you mow the village green). You can represent which neighbors are home by a five-digit code number. The first (leftmost) digit of the code is 1 if neighbor 1 is home and 0 otherwise; the second digit of the code is 1 if neighbor 2 is home and 0 otherwise; and so on. The code 10010 indicates that neighbors 1 and 4 are home, 01100 indicates that neighbors 2 and 3 are home, and so on. If we represent neighbor 1 by the code 10000, neighbor 2 by 01000, and so on, the code representing who is home is the sum of the individual codes for the neighbors who are at home. For example, if neighbors 1, 3, and 5 are home, the code for who is home is $10000 + 00100 + 00001 = 10101$.

Write a function

```
HOME(CODE)
```

whose actual parameter is a five-digit code and whose value is the number of neighbors who are at home. (*Hint:* you will need DIV and MOD.)

8. Mathematicians often write 1000 as 10^3, since three 10s multiplied together give 1000. In the same way 100 can be written 10^2 and 10 itself as 10^1. By convention, 10^0 equals 1. The same notation can be applied to numbers other than 10. Thus, 2^3 equals 8, 2^2 equals 4, 2^1 equals 2, and 2^0 equals 1.

In Exercise 7 neighbor 1 was represented by 10^4; neighbor 2, by 10^3; neighbor 3, by 10^2; neighbor 4, by 10^1; and neighbor 5, by 10^0. You can reorganize this code for use with other objects in two ways. First, it's convenient to let 10^0 represent object 0, 10^1 represent object 1, 10^2 represent object 2, and so on. Second, if you use 2^0, 2^1, 2^2, and so on, instead of 10^0, 10^1, 10^2, and so on, you can code many more objects without exceeding the value of MAXINT. For example, if objects 3, 5, and 8 are present, then the corresponding code is $2^3 + 2^5 + 2^8 = 8 + 32 + 256 = 296$. Rewrite the function HOME (from Exercise 7) to return the total number of objects as before, using a code based on 2^0, 2^1, 2^2, and so on. Do not assume any maximum number of coded objects. Use repetition rather than recursion.

9. Write a recursive version of the function HOME from Exercise 8.

10. This is a simple exercise in computer simulation—using a computer program to show what would happen in a real-world situation under certain hypothetical circumstances.

Acid rain has killed off all the fish in your local lake, and you are in charge of restocking it for the summer. You want a computer program to work out how many bass and perch will be left by Labor Day in September if you stock the lake with a certain number of each in May.

Suppose your program uses the variables B and P for the populations of bass and perch. As the populations change, so will the values of B and P. In principle the values of B and P should change continuously. In practice, since programs must work step by step, some changes will be made daily, some weekly, and some every four weeks. The calculations for the four-week changes are based on the average populations over the previous four weeks. The calculations for the one-week changes are based on the average populations over the previous week. The calculations for the daily changes are based on the current populations, that is, the current values of B and P. Your simulation should run sixteen weeks and print a report showing the populations at the end of each week.

The changes are specified by giving the numerical factors that govern them, such as the percentage of the populations killed in a certain period of time for a certain reason. Pascal variable names are suggested for each numerical factor. The changes that take place every four weeks are governed by the following factors:

(1) The percentage of the average populations killed every four weeks by the acidity of the water (A)

(2) The percentage of the average populations killed every four weeks by accidents and mysterious causes (M)

The weekly changes are governed by the following factors:

(3) The percentage of bass (FB) and of perch (FP) taken by fishermen every week

(4) The number of perch the cats will catch each week (PC). The cats will be able to catch perch only if the average perch population that week is not below a certain minimum level (MP)

The daily changes are governed by the following factors:

(5) The maximum proportion of bass to perch that will allow the perch to find enough food each day (BP). If the proportion of bass to perch exceeds the value of BP, then every increase of 0.1 over the value of BP means the death of 0.1% of the perch population.

(6) The net increase or decrease in the numbers of bass (IB) and perch (IP) each day due to fish swimming into or out of the lake

Your program should call a separate procedure to make each of the changes 1 through 6. The main program must input the initial bass and perch populations as well as the various numerical factors governing the simulation, compute the one-week and four-week averages required by some of the procedures, call the necessary procedures to make changes—daily, weekly, and every four-weeks— and print the report showing the populations at the end of each week.

Write your program using the method of *top-down design*—write the main program first, then write the procedures it calls. While working on the main proram, you don't have to worry about the detailed rules for each kind of change. You need consider the details of a particular change only when you write the corresponding procedure.

Chapter 8

THE SIMPLE DATA TYPES

There are two aspects to computer programming: (1) organizing the data to be processed, and (2) specifying the processing to be carried out. So far, we have concentrated on the statements that do the processing. With this chapter we shift our attention to methods of organizing the data to be processed.

In Pascal data is organized with the help of a system of *data types*. These data types are classified into *simple*, *structured*, and *pointer* types. The simple types are those whose values cannot be broken down into simpler components. The structured types are those whose values *can* be broken down into simpler components. The pointer types are those whose values are used to locate data items in the computer's memory.

The simple types, the ones we will consider in this chapter, are further divided into the *ordinal* data types and the type REAL. The ordinal data types can be used for such purposes as counting, designating statements to be executed, or designating entries in tables. For example, the ordinal data types can be used for the control variable in a FOR statement and the selector in a CASE statement. The type REAL, on the other hand, can be used only for real-number arithmetic. For this reason we will concentrate on the ordinal types and have little more to say about the type REAL.

Ordinal Data Types

Standard Data Types. We are already familiar with the four standard data types: INTEGER, REAL, BOOLEAN, and CHAR. Of these, IN-TEGER, BOOLEAN, and CHAR are ordinal data types. As just mentioned, REAL is the one simple data type that is not an ordinal data type.

Data Type Definitions.   Pascal allows programmers to define new data types beyond the standard ones whose definitions are built into the language. To illustrate type definitions, let's give new names to the standard data types:

```
TYPE
    FIXED = INTEGER;
    FLOAT = REAL;
    BIT = BOOLEAN;
    CHARACTER = CHAR;
```

We can now declare:

```
VAR
    I, J, K: FIXED;
    X, Y, Z: FLOAT;
    P, Q: BIT;
    C: CHARACTER;
```

When these declarations are processed the type definitions will be consulted to determine what values each variable can have. Thus, I, J, and K can have integer values; X, Y, and Z can have real values; P and Q can have Boolean values; and C can have character values.

Data type definitions follow constant definitions and precede variable declarations. Thus, the various definitions and declarations at the beginning of a block must occur in the following order:

• constant definitions

• type definitions

• variable declarations

• function and procedure declarations

Any definition or declaration parts not needed for a particular program can be omitted, of course. But those present must be in the order shown.

Enumerated Types.   Pascal allows programmers to define new ordinal types by listing, or enumerating, the values of each new type. The values of enumerated types are represented by identifiers. The following are some definitions of enumerated types:

```
TYPE
    DAY = (SUN, MON, TUE, WED, THURS, FRI, SAT);
    COLOR = (RED, ORANGE, YELLOW, GREEN, BLUE, INDIGO, VIOLET);
    CHESSMAN = (PAWN, KNIGHT, BISHOP, ROOK, QUEEN, KING);
    MONTH = (JAN, FEB, MAR, APR, MAY, JUN, JULY, AUG,
            SEPT, OCT, NOV, DEC);
    GRADE = (F, D, C, B, A);
```

Type DAY, for example, consists of seven values denoted by the identifiers SUN, MON, TUE, WED, THURS, FRI, and SAT. The order in which the identifiers are listed is important, since it allows us to define the relations "precedes" and "follows" for the type. Thus for type DAY, SUN precedes MON and TUE precedes FRI. Similarly, SAT follows FRI and FRI follows MON.

If we declare the variable D by

```
VAR
    D: DAY;
```

then the possible values of D are SUN, MON, TUE, and so on. Assignments such as

```
D := MON
```

and

```
D := SAT
```

are valid.

Note that the standard type BOOLEAN could be defined by

```
BOOLEAN = (FALSE, TRUE);
```

however, this definition is built into Pascal and must not be supplied by the programmer.

The same identifier cannot be used for values of more than one enumerated type. If we define

```
RANK = (PRIVATE, CORPORAL, SERGEANT, LIEUTENANT,
        CAPTAIN, MAJOR, COLONEL, GENERAL);
```

then we cannot also define

```
OFFICER = (LIEUTENANT, CAPTAIN, MAJOR, COLONEL, GENERAL);
```

since doing so would make LIEUTENANT, CAPTAIN, MAJOR, COLONEL, and GENERAL values of more than one enumerated type. Later in the chapter we will see how OFFICER can be defined as a *subrange type*.

When declaring variables, we can describe the type directly without bothering to define a type identifier:

```
VAR
    S: (WINTER, SPRING, SUMMER, FALL);
```

The possible values of S are WINTER, SPRING, SUMMER, and FALL.

There is no type identifier, however, that refers to the type described by (WINTER, SPRING, SUMMER, FALL).

When declaring formal parameters and the values returned by functions, however, we must use type identifiers; type descriptions are not allowed. Suppose, for example, we want to declare a function NEXT whose value is the season following the one supplied as its actual parameter. We must define a type identifier.

```
TYPE
    SEASON = (WINTER, SPRING, SUMMER, FALL);
```

and use this identifier to declare the formal parameter for NEXT and the value that it returns:

```
FUNCTION NEXT(S: SEASON): SEASON;
```

Subrange Types. For every ordinal type we can define a new type whose values are some subrange of the previously defined type. For example,

```
DIGIT = 0..9;
```

defines a subrange of type INTEGER whose values are 0 through 9;

```
WORKDAY = MON..FRI;
```

defines a subrange of type DAY whose values are MON through FRI; and

```
OFFICER = LIEUTENANT..GENERAL;
```

defines a subrange of type RANK whose values are LIEUTENANT through GENERAL.

The type whose values are used to define a subrange type is called the *host* type. All operations that can be performed on values of the host type can also be performed on values of the subrange type. The only difference between the subrange type and the host type is that the values of the subrange type are required to lie in the specified subrange.

For example, suppose I and N are declared as follows:

```
VAR
    I: INTEGER;
    N: DIGIT;
```

The assignment

```
I := N
```

is always valid, since a value of type DIGIT is also a value of type INTEGER. On the other hand, the assignment

```
N := I
```

is valid only if the value of I lies in the range of 0 through 9. A value of type INTEGER is also a value of type DIGIT only if it lies in the range of 0 through 9.

All the operations that can be carried out on integers can be carried out on digits as well. For example, the statements

```
N := 5;
N := N - 3;
N := 2 * N
```

are valid (when executed in the order shown), since in every case the value assigned to N lies in the range of 0 through 9. On the other hand, consider

```
N := 7;
N := N + 3
```

After 7 is assigned to N, the value of N + 3 is 10. When an attempt is made to assign 10 to N, the computer reports an error.

Operations on Ordinal Data Types

An *order* is defined for the values of any ordinal type. For integers this order is the usual numerical order. For Boolean values FALSE precedes TRUE. For characters the order is given by the collating sequence for a particular computer system. For enumerated types the order of the values is the order in which they are listed in the type definition. The order for a subrange type is the same as for the host type.

As a consequence of this ordering, the relational operators

```
=   <   >   <=   >=   <>
```

can be applied to the values of any ordinal type. The following illustrates relational operators applied to values of enumerated types:

Expression	Value
SUN < THURS	TRUE
RED >= BLUE	FALSE
MAR > APR	FALSE
F = A	FALSE
QUEEN > ROOK	TRUE

The functions PRED and SUCC apply to values of all ordinal types. PRED returns the value (if any) immediately preceding the value of the actual parameter. SUCC returns the value (if any) immediately following the value of the actual parameter. The following illustrates PRED and SUCC applied to integer values:

Expression	Value
PRED(5)	4
PRED(4)	3
SUCC(5)	6
SUCC(4)	5

For integers, PRED(I) has the same value as I – 1 and SUCC(I) has the same value as I + 1. We don't actually need PRED and SUCC for integers, since I – 1 and I + 1 can be used instead. But no arithmetic operations are defined for BOOLEAN, CHAR, and enumerated types, so for these PRED and SUCC are needed. The following illustrates PRED and SUCC applied to values of various ordinal types:

Expression	Value
SUCC(SUN)	MON
PRED(MON)	SUN
PRED(TRUE)	FALSE
SUCC(FALSE)	TRUE
PRED('Y')	'X'
SUCC('Y')	'Z'
SUCC(ROOK)	QUEEN
PRED(QUEEN)	ROOK

The predecessor of the first value of a particular type and the successor of the last value are undefined. Therefore, the following expressions are not defined:

PRED(FALSE)	SUCC(TRUE)
PRED(SUN)	SUCC(SAT)
PRED(PAWN)	SUCC(KING)
PRED(JAN)	SUCC(DEC)
PRED(F)	SUCC(A)

The values of enumerated types are numbered, starting with 0 for the first value. For example, the values of type DAY are numbered as follows:

```
DAY = (SUN, MON, TUE, WED, THURS, FRI, SAT);
        0    1    2    3     4     5    6
```

The numbers are called the *ordinal numbers* of the corresponding values. Pascal has a standard function, ORD, which returns the ordinal number of its actual parameter:

Expression	Value
ORD(SUN)	0
ORD(MON)	1
ORD(TUE)	2
. . .	. . .
ORD(SAT)	6

The ORD function can be applied to values of other ordinal types as well. For integer values ORD simply returns the value of its actual parameter. For Boolean values ORD(FALSE) equals 0 and ORD(TRUE) equals 1. For character values the ordinal numbers of the characters depend on the collating sequence. The following examples assume the ASCII character set:

Expression	Value
ORD('A')	65
ORD('B')	66
ORD('C')	67
ORD('Z')	90
ORD('0')	48
ORD('9')	57

For type CHAR only there is a function, CHR, which converts ordinal numbers back into the corresponding characters:

Expression	Value
CHR(65)	'A'
CHR(90)	'Z'
CHR(48)	'0'
CHR(57)	'9'

Again, the values shown assume the ASCII character set.

One use of CHR is to obtain the nonprinting characters used for control purposes. For example, the ASCII character CHR(7) is the *bell character*, which causes the computer terminal to ring a bell or sound a beep. The following procedure can be executed to bring some matter of importance to the user's attention:

```
PROCEDURE ALARM;
CONST
   BELL = 7;   (* ASCII code to ring bell *)
VAR
   I: INTEGER;
BEGIN
   FOR I := 1 TO 10 DO
      WRITE(CHR(BELL))
END;
```

Another important use of ORD and CHR is to convert between the numerals '0' through '9' and the corresponding integers. If the value of C is a numeral,

```
ORD(C) - ORD('0')
```

converts the numeral to the corresponding integer:

Expression	Value
ORD('0') – ORD('0')	0
ORD('1') – ORD('0')	1
ORD('2') – ORD('0')	2
. . .	. . .
ORD('9') – ORD('0')	9

To convert an integer in the range of 0 through 9 to the corresponding numeral, we use

```
CHR(I + ORD('0'))
```

which yields the values

Expression	Value
CHR(0 + ORD('0'))	'0'
CHR(1 + ORD('0'))	'1'
CHR(2 + ORD('0'))	'2'
. . .	. . .
CHR(9 + ORD('0'))	'9'

CHAR is the only data type for which a function is provided to convert ordinal numbers into their corresponding values. We can, however, easily write such functions for other data types. For example, suppose type CRANGE is defined by

```
CRANGE = 0..6;
```

The following function will convert a value of type CRANGE into the corresponding color:

```
FUNCTION CLR(N: CRANGE): COLOR;
BEGIN
    CASE N OF
        0: CLR := RED;
        1: CLR := ORANGE;
        2: CLR := YELLOW;
        3: CLR := GREEN;
        4: CLR := BLUE;
        5: CLR := INDIGO;
        6: CLR := VIOLET
    END
END;
```

The types CRANGE and COLOR are assumed defined in the main program. In fact, global identifiers are used much more frequently for data types than for variables. It's common to define all data types in the main program. Since the type identifiers are then global, all procedures and functions can make use of the defined types.

Any ordinal type can be used for the control variable in a FOR statement and the selector expression in a CASE statement. For example, if D is a variable of type DAY, then

```
FOR D := MON TO FRI DO
    s1
```

causes statement s1 to be executed five times. The first time the value of D equals MON, the second time the value of D equals TUE, and so on.

The following statement will print a table of the uppercase letters and their ordinal numbers:

```
FOR C := 'A' TO 'Z' DO
    WRITELN(C, ORD(C):5)
```

By executing statements of this form, you can explore the character set your computer uses.

If M is a variable of type CHESSMAN, the following is valid:

```
CASE M OF
    PAWN: s1;
    KNIGHT: s2;
    BISHOP: s3;
    ROOK: s4;
    QUEEN: s5;
    KING: s6
END
```

If the value of M is PAWN, s1 is executed; if the value of M is BISHOP, s2 is executed; and so on.

Exercises

1. Write a program to print the alphabet. The program should print both the uppercase and the lowercase letters.

2. Write two functions, VALUE and NUMERAL, to convert between the numerals '0' through '9' and the corresponding integers. The actual parameter for VALUE is a character in the range of '0' through '9'; the value returned is the corresponding integer. The actual parameter for NUMERAL is an integer in the range of 0 through 9; the value returned is the corresponding numeral. Use subrange types for the actual parameters and values returned. Write a program to exercise VALUE and NUMERAL.

3. The procedures READ and READLN will not read values of enumerated types from cards or computer terminals. We must write functions and procedures to do this job. Suppose values of type DAY are entered as follows (a small b represents a blank space):

Mb   Tb   Wb   TH   Fb   Sb   SU

Write a function to read two characters and return the corresponding value of type DAY.

4. Write a program to simulate a very simple version of a well-known board game in which pieces circle a board, collecting money each time around and landing on various places along the way. The places around this board are Start, Lamprey, Townhall, Willey, Bank, Mill, Library, Nicholls, Zionhill, and Church. From Church you must go back to Start to complete the circuit around the board. Define the places as values of an enumerated type and declare a procedure that will print out the name of any given place.

Start a piece off at Start with $250 and collect $50 every time the piece passes Start again. If the piece lands on Start, collect $100. Every other place on the board costs $20 to land on, except Church, which is free, and Bank, which pays you $10 interest. The number of positions you advance is determined by rolling a die, which is simulated by the function RANDOM from Chapter 7. For each roll, print the value on the die, the placed landed on, the money paid out or received, and the new balance. Stop when you run out of money or reach $2000.

5. You are driving from Portland in Maine to Miami along interstate route 95 testing an emergency, "low-tech" signaling system, which uses carrier pigeons at various towns along the way. You are to write a program to compute how many pigeons will be needed to carry the messages. Define an enumerated type for the towns, which are Portland, Boston, New Haven, New York, Philadelphia, Washington, D.C., Richmond, Raleigh, Florence, Savannah, Jacksonville, and Miami.

As you reach each town, you have to send a message to some other town on the route. The input to your program will contain the destination town, in the form of the first two letters of its name (except use NY for New York and NH for New Haven). So the first line of input will be the town to which a message should be sent from Portland; the second line, the destination of the message from Boston; and so on, for 12 lines in all.

Each distance between two adjacent towns is called a *stage*, and each group of three stages is called a *stretch*. A pigeon can fly a maximum distance of one stretch, so a message going from Jacksonville to New Haven would need at least three pigeons. Unfortunately, each message dispatched towards a destination farther than one stretch away requires an extra pigeon for each extra stretch—to insure against difficulties in transferring the message at the relay points. So, to take a message from Jacksonville to New Haven, six pigeons would be needed —three to fly from Jacksonville to Raleigh, two to fly from Raleigh to Philadelphia, and one to fly from Philadelphia to New Haven.

Chapter 9

STRUCTURED TYPES: ARRAYS

A structured type, you recall, is one whose values are made up of simpler components. Different methods of organizing the component values give rise to different structured data types.

One way of organizing values is to arrange them in lists or tables. Structured data types using this method of organization are known as *array types*; the lists and tables themselves are called *arrays*.

One-Dimensional Arrays

We can think of a one-dimensional array as a *list* of values, such as the following:

```
1.   25
2.    4
3.   39
4.   17
5.    2
```

The values on the list—25, 4, 39, 17, and 2—are referred to as *components*. The integers 1 through 5, known as *index values*, label the components for easy reference. Thus, we can refer to component 3 (whose value is 39), component 1 (whose value is 25), component 4 (whose value is 17), and so on.

Let LIST be the data type whose values are lists of five integers. LIST is defined in Pascal as follows:

```
TYPE
   LIST = ARRAY[1..5] OF INTEGER;
```

This definition mentions two data types. The type mentioned in brackets is the *index type*, whose values will be used to label components. The index type must be an ordinal type; frequently it is a subrange of type INTEGER. In the definition of LIST the index type is the subrange 1..5. The other type mentioned in the definition, the one following the word OF, is the *component type*, the type of the components making up a value of the type being defined. There is no restriction on the component type. Thus, each value of type LIST is a five-component list. The components are integers and are labeled with the values 1 through 5.

Suppose we declare variables A and B to be of type LIST:

```
VAR
    A, B: LIST;
```

A and B are known as *array variables*, since their values are arrays. Specifically, the possible values of A and B are lists of five integers. Suppose, for example, the value of A is the list we have been discussing. We can indicate this as follows:

Variable	Value	
A	1.	25
	2.	4
	3.	39
	4.	17
	5.	2

Only the components are stored in memory. The index values do not have to be stored because, given any index value, the computer can calculate the address of the memory location containing the corresponding component.

To refer to a particular component of an array, we write the index of the desired component after the array variable. The index is enclosed in brackets. Thus A[1] refers to component 1 of the value of A; A[2] refers to component 2 of the value of A, and so on. The variables A[1], A[2], A[3], A[4], and A[5] are called *indexed variables*; their values are as follows:

Variable	Value
A[1]	25
A[2]	4
A[3]	39
A[4]	17
A[5]	2

Indexed variables can be used in any of the ways permissible for nonindexed variables. We can write their values, use their values in expressions, read new values for them, and assign new values to them. For example, the statements

```
A[1] := 95;
A[3] := 71;
A[5] := 11
```

change the first, third, and fifth components of A as follows:

Variable	Value
A[1]	95
A[2]	4
A[3]	71
A[4]	17
A[5]	11

Note that the second and fourth components of A remain unchanged, since no new values were assigned to the corresponding indexed variables.

We can also use indexed variables in expressions. For example, if the components of A have the values just given, then the statements

```
I := A[1] - A[2];
J := 2 * A[3];
K := A[4] * A[5]
```

assign I, J, and K the following values:

Variable	Value
I	91
J	142
K	187

We can read values into indexed variables with READ and READLN statements, and we can write the values of indexed variables with WRITE and WRITELN statements:

```
READLN(A[1], A[2], A[3], A[4], A[5]);
WRITELN(A[5]:4, A[4]:4, A[3]:4, A[2]:4, A[1]:4)
```

If the input data for the READLN statement is

```
10   15   20   25   30
```

the WRITELN statement prints

```
30   25   20   15   10
```

Ordinal types such as BOOLEAN, CHAR, and enumerated types can also be used as index types. For example, recall the types DAY and CHESSMAN defined in Chapter 8:

```
TYPE
    DAY = (SUN, MON, TUE, WED, THURS, FRI, SAT);
    CHESSMAN = (PAWN, KNIGHT, BISHOP, ROOK, QUEEN, KING);
```

The following array variables use these types as index types:

```
VAR
    HOURS: ARRAY[DAY] OF REAL;
    VALUE: ARRAY[CHESSMAN] OF INTEGER;
```

The indexed variables for the array HOURS are:

```
HOURS[SUN]     HOURS[MON]    HOURS[TUE]    HOURS[WED]
HOURS[THURS]   HOURS[FRI]    HOURS[SAT]
```

We could use these variables to record the number of hours an employee worked each day of the week. For example,

```
HOURS[MON] := 7.4
```

records the fact that the employee worked 7.4 hours on Monday.

We could use the array VALUE to record the relative values of the different kinds of chessmen:

```
VALUE[PAWN]  := 1;        VALUE[KNIGHT] := 3;
VALUE[BISHOP] := 3;       VALUE[ROOK]  := 5;
VALUE[QUEEN]  := 9;       VALUE[KING]  := 1000
```

(Theoretically, the king is priceless, but the needs of chess-playing programs are often best served by assigning the king a large but finite value.)

In a chess-playing program each side is usually given a material score, which equals the sum of the values of all that side's chessmen. Suppose the value of MATERIAL is the material score for a particular side. If that side loses its queen, the material score would be updated as follows

```
MATERIAL := MATERIAL - VALUE[QUEEN]
```

As with ordinary variables, we sometimes use a simplified, shorthand terminology when talking about arrays. Strictly speaking, a variable such as A (which was defined earlier in this section) is an *array variable* and its value—the list of five numbers—is the *array*. For simplicity, however, we often use the term *array* for both the variable and its value, letting the context show which is meant in each case. We will sometimes use the name of the array variable to refer to its value. Thus, we might speak of "the third component of A" instead of "the third component of the value of A." Likewise, we will sometimes use the indexed variables A[1], A[2], A[3]. and so on as names of the components of A. Thus, we might say "A[1] is 95" or "A[2] is less than A[3]."

Using One-Dimensional Arrays

Arrays and FOR Statements. Arrays and FOR statements work very well together. The FOR statement steps the value of a variable through a series of index values, which are used to refer to the corresponding components of the array. Thus we can step through all or part of an array, carrying out the same operation on each component.

For example, let's add up the values of the components of array A using the integer variable SUM to accumulate the total:

```
SUM := 0;
FOR I := 1 TO 5 DO
   SUM := SUM + A[I]
```

These statements are equivalent to the following:

```
SUM := 0;
SUM := SUM + A[1];
SUM := SUM + A[2];
SUM := SUM + A[3];
SUM := SUM + A[4];
SUM := SUM + A[5]
```

This example illustrates an important property of arrays. The index does not have to be a constant; it can be any expression that yields a value of the index type. Therefore, we do not have to specify the index value for an array variable when we write the program; the value can be computed by the program. For example, the value of the index might depend on the data that the program inputs. Or, as in the case of

```
SUM := SUM + A[I]
```

we can write a statement once but have it executed many times, each time with a different value for the index.

The program in Figure 9–1 reads 24 temperatures, one for each hour of the day, and then computes the high, low, and average temperatures for the day. The 24 temperatures are stored in the array TEMP declared by:

```
VAR
   TEMP: ARRAY[1..24] OF REAL;
```

We use a FOR statement to read each of the 24 components of this array:

```
FOR I := 1 TO 24 DO
   READ(TEMP[I]);
```

To compute the average temperature, we add up all 24 temperatures and divide by 24.0. The sum of all the temperatures is accumulated in the real variable TOTAL:

```
PROGRAM TEMPERATURES;
(* ILLUSTRATE PRINCIPLES OF ARRAY PROCESSING *)
VAR
    TEMP: ARRAY[1..24] OF REAL;
    TOTAL, AVERAGE, HIGH, LOW: REAL;
    I: INTEGER;
BEGIN
    (* READ DATA *)
    WRITE('ENTER 24 TEMPERATURES: ');
    FOR I := 1 TO 24 DO
        READ(TEMP[I]);
    WRITELN;

    (* COMPUTE AVERAGE TEMPERATURE *)
    TOTAL := 0.0;
    FOR I := 1 TO 24 DO
        TOTAL := TOTAL + TEMP[I];
    AVERAGE := TOTAL / 24.0;
    WRITELN('AVERAGE TEMPERATURE: ', AVERAGE:6:1);

    (* COMPUTE HIGH AND LOW TEMPERATURES *)
    LOW := TEMP[1];
    HIGH := TEMP[1];
    FOR I := 2 TO 24 DO
        IF TEMP[I] < LOW THEN
            LOW := TEMP[I]
        ELSE IF TEMP[I] > HIGH THEN
            HIGH := TEMP[I];
    WRITELN('LOW TEMPERATURE: ', LOW:6:1);
    WRITELN('HIGH TEMPERATURE: ', HIGH:6:1)
END.
```

FIGURE 9-1. **This program reads 24 temperatures, one for each hour of the day, and computes the high, low, and average temperatures.**

```
TOTAL := 0.0;
FOR I := 1 TO 24 DO
    TOTAL := TOTAL + TEMP[I];
AVERAGE := TOTAL / 24.0
```

To compute the high and low for the day, we begin by setting both LOW and HIGH to the first component of the array. As we step through the array, we compare each component with the values of LOW and HIGH. If a component is less than the value of LOW, that component becomes the new value of LOW. If a component is greater than the value of HIGH, that component becomes the new value of HIGH. After we have stepped through the entire array, the values of LOW and HIGH are equal to the largest and smallest components of the array:

```
LOW  := TEMP[1];
HIGH := TEMP[1];
FOR I := 2 TO 24 DO
    IF TEMP[I] < LOW THEN
        LOW := TEMP[I]
    ELSE IF TEMP[I] > HIGH THEN
        HIGH := TEMP[I]
```

Assignment, Input, and Output. Most operations in Pascal are carried out on individual components of an array—the values of the indexed variables—rather than on the array as a whole. However, if A and B are two array variables of the same type, the assignment operator will assign the value of one array variable (the entire array) to the other array variable. For example, if A and B are declared by

```
VAR
    A, B: ARRAY[1..5] OF INTEGER;
```

then

```
A := B
```

has the same effect as:

```
FOR I := 1 TO 5 DO
    A[I] := B[I]
```

The value of B[1] is assigned to A[1], the value of B[2] is assigned to A[2], the value of A[3] is assigned to B[3], and so on.

As we saw in the temperatures program, the components of an array must be read in one by one; Pascal does not provide for reading an entire array in a single operation. Thus, to read the five components of the array A, we must use

```
FOR I := 1 TO 5 DO
    READ(A[I])
```

If the input data is

```
17   29   14   38   75
```

then 17 is assigned to A[1], 29 is assigned to A[2], 14 is assigned to A[3], and so on.

In the same way we can use a FOR statement to print out an array component by component. If we do the actual printing with a WRITE statement, the values of the components will all be printed on the same line. For example, if A has the values read in the last paragraph, then

```
FOR I := 1 TO 5 DO
    WRITE(A[I]:4)
```

causes the computer to print:

```
17   29   14   38   75
```

On the other hand, if we do the printing with a WRITELN statement

```
FOR I := 1 TO 5 DO
   WRITELN(A[I])
```

each component is printed on a separate line:

```
17
29
14
38
75
```

Translation Tables.   We often find it convenient to represent the same information in different ways—that is, using values of different data types. When this is done we usually need to translate values from one type to another. Arrays come in handy for this purpose.

For example, recall the type COLOR defined in Chapter 8:

```
TYPE
   COLOR = (RED, ORANGE, YELLOW, GREEN, BLUE, INDIGO, VIOLET);
```

Values of enumeration types cannot be written out directly. Suppose we want to print R for red, O for orange, Y for yellow, and so on. We can use an array to translate values of type COLOR into the characters that are to be printed. Let T be declared by

```
VAR
   T: ARRAY[COLOR] OF CHAR;
```

and assign values to the components of T as follows:

```
T[RED]    :=    'R';     T[ORANGE] := 'O';
T[YELLOW] := 'Y';        T[GREEN]  :=  'G';
T[BLUE]   :=    'B';     T[INDIGO] := 'I';
T[VIOLET] := 'V'
```

If CL is a variable of type COLOR, the value of T[CL] is the character corresponding to the value of C, which can be printed with:

```
WRITE(T[CL])
```

For example,

```
FOR CL := RED TO VIOLET DO
   WRITE(T[CL])
```

causes the computer to print:

ROYGBIV

Arrays such as T are sometimes called *translation tables*, since they serve to translate values from one data type to another.

Packed Arrays

The description of an array type can be prefixed with the reserved word PACKED, as in

PACKED ARRAY[1..5] OF BOOLEAN

The prefix PACKED instructs the language processor to store the values of a structured type as compactly as possible, even if this means packing more than one value into each memory location. The advantage of a packed type is, of course, that its values take up less memory than might otherwise be the case. The disadvantage is that the computer usually takes longer to access a component of a packed value, since not only must it access the memory location containing the component, it must also separate the desired component from the others sharing the same memory location.

The types of arrays most commonly packed are arrays of CHAR and BOOLEAN. A character or Boolean value might take up only a small part of a memory location, so storing more than one value per location can save considerable space. Also, arrays of subrange types can be packed effectively, since the computer requires less memory to store values of type 0..7, say, than to store values of type INTEGER.

Whether or not values of a particular type should be packed depends on how those values are represented inside the computer. Thus, the amount of memory saved in packing a particular kind of array, and the time lost in accessing its components, will vary from one version of Pascal to another.

The components of packed arrays can be referred to just like those of any other array. For example, if PC is declared by

VAR
    PC: PACKED ARRAY[1..5] OF CHAR;

then the references

C := PC[3];
PC[5] := 'A'

are valid.

If may be much faster to pack or unpack an entire array in a single operation than it would be to refer repeatedly to packed values. For this reason Pascal provides two procedures, PACK and UNPACK, for efficiently transferring data between packed and unpacked arrays. To see how these procedures work, let's declare arrays A and Z as follows:

```
VAR
    A: ARRAY[1..10] OF CHAR;
    Z: PACKED ARRAY[1..7] OF CHAR;
```

The statement

```
PACK(A, 3, Z)
```

causes the values of A[3] through A[9] to be packed into Z. The actual parameter 3 designates the value of A[3] as the first value to be packed; the size of Z determines how many values will be packed. The PACK statement accomplishes the same result as:

```
FOR I := 1 TO 7 DO
    Z[I] := A[I + 2]
```

Going in the opposite direction, the statement

```
UNPACK(Z, A, 3)
```

causes the value of Z to be unpacked and its components stored in A[3] through A[9]. The size of Z determines how many values will be unpacked; the actual parameter 3 specifies that the first value unpacked will be stored in A[3]. The UNPACK statement accomplishes the same result as:

```
FOR I := 1 TO 7 DO
    A[I + 2] := Z[I]
```

Note that the entire array Z is always either packed or unpacked. On the other hand, as was the case in the examples, we can use only part of A to hold the values to be packed or the values that are unpacked.

UCSD Pascal does not provide the procedures PACK and UNPACK.

There is one limitation on access to packed arrays. Indexed variables (such as Z[3]) that refer to components of packed arrays cannot be substituted for variable parameters in procedures calls. Worse yet, READ and READLN are procedures with variable parameters. Thus statements such as

```
READ(Z[3])
```

are not permitted. Instead, we must write something like:

```
READ(C);
Z[3] := C
```

Strings

We are already familiar with string constants such as 'COMPUTER' and 'PROGRAMMER'. We now want to see how to declare variables that take strings as values. To do this, we need *string types*—data types whose values are strings. In standard Pascal we can use packed arrays of characters to define *fixed-length-string types*, so called because each string of a given type has the same length.

Fixed-length-string types require that we know in advance the lengths of the strings our programs will process. In many cases this information is not available. For example, a program might have to process a line typed by the user. The length of the line cannot be known when the program is written, since it will depend on the specific information that the user wishes to communicate to the program.

Because of the limited usefulness of fixed-length-string types, many versions of Pascal intended for real-world programming also provide variable-length-string types. Strings belonging to a variable-length-string type range in length from zero characters (the *null string*) up to some maximum length specified by the programmer. Unfortunately, since variable-length-string types are nonstandard, the details of their use vary from one version of Pascal to another. We will look at variable-length-string types as they are implemented in UCSD Pascal.

Fixed-Length-String Types.   A fixed-length-string type is a packed-array-of-characters type of the form

```
PACKED ARRAY[1..n] OF CHAR
```

where n is a positive integer constant. For example, let's define the type STR10 by:

```
TYPE
    STR10 = PACKED ARRAY[1..10] OF CHAR;
```

The values of type STR10 are all possible ten-character strings. Since every value of type STR10 must have exactly ten characters, the term fixed-length-string type is clearly appropriate. If we declare the variable M by

```
VAR
    M: STR10;
```

then the possible values of M are the strings of ten characters.

String constants are assumed to be of the types determined by their lengths. For example, in the assignment

```
M := 'PROGRAMMER'
```

'PROGRAMMER' is assumed to be of type:

```
PACKED ARRAY[1..10] OF CHAR
```

Since M and 'PROGRAMMER' are of the same type, the assignment is valid. On the other hand, the assignments

```
M := 'COMPUTER'
```

and

```
M := 'PROGRAMMING'
```

are both invalid, since the type of the constant on the right side of the assignment operator is not the same as the type of the variable on the left side. (The type of 'COMPUTER' is PACKED ARRAY[1..8] OF CHAR; the type of 'PROGRAMMING' is PACKED ARRAY[1..11] OF CHAR.)

We already know that the values of string constants can be printed with WRITE and WRITELN statements. Thus,

```
WRITELN('HELLO')
```

causes the computer to print:

```
HELLO
```

We can also use WRITE and WRITELN statements to print the values of string variables. Thus, the statements

```
M := 'SCIENTIFIC';
WRITELN(M)
```

cause the computer to print:

```
SCIENTIFIC
```

We can use field-width parameters if we wish. If the WRITELN statement in the preceding example were

```
WRITELN(M:15)
```

the computer would print:

```
bbbbbSCIENTIFIC
```

where the b's stand for the blank spaces that would actually be printed.

On the other hand, a fixed-length string must be read component by component, just as for any other array. For example, to read a ten-character value for M, we must use

```
FOR I := 1 TO 10 DO
   BEGIN
      READ(C);
      M[I] := C
   END
```

where C is a character variable. Note we cannot eliminate the need for C by writing

```
READ (M[I])
```

since M[I]—a component of a packed array—cannot be used as a variable parameter.

Fixed-length strings of the same type can be compared with the relational operators =, <, >, <=, >=, and <>. One string precedes a second string if the first string comes before the second in alphabetical order. Alphabetical order is, as usual, defined by the collating sequence for the character code being used. For example, the value of each of the following Boolean expressions is TRUE:

```
'JACK' < 'JOHN'
'BUD' > 'BOB'
'SUE' <> 'SAL'
'MARY' = 'MARY'
```

Let's look at an example of a program using fixed-length strings. Figure 9–2 shows a change-making program that uses arrays to hold the names and values of the bills and coins. Using arrays allows us to write the change-calculating statements just once for the entire program instead of having to write them once for each denomination that the program handles.

For the names of the bills and coins, we define the fixed-length-string type DENOMINATION, whose values are eight-character strings:

```
TYPE
   DENOMINATION = PACKED ARRAY[1..8] OF CHAR;
```

To hold the names and values of the bills and coins, we use two nine-component arrays, NAMES and VALUES:

```
VAR
   NAMES: ARRAY[1..9] OF DENOMINATION;
   VALUES: ARRAY[1..9] OF INTEGER;
```

For each value of I in the subrange 1..9 the value of NAMES[I] is the name of a bill or coin, and the value of VALUES[I] is the value of the bill or coin in cents. Arrays such as NAMES and VALUES are often called *parallel arrays*, since we can think of them as parallel columns in

```
PROGRAM CHANGE1;
(* CHANGE-MAKING PROGRAM USING ARRAYS *)
TYPE
   DENOMINATION = PACKED ARRAY[1..8] OF CHAR;
VAR
   NAMES: ARRAY[1..9] OF DENOMINATION;
   VALUES: ARRAY[1..9] OF INTEGER;
   AMOUNT: REAL;
   CHANGE, I: INTEGER;
BEGIN
   NAMES[1] := 'TWENTIES';  VALUES[1] := 2000;
   NAMES[2] := 'TENS    ';  VALUES[2] := 1000;
   NAMES[3] := 'FIVES   ';  VALUES[3] :=  500;
   NAMES[4] := 'ONES    ';  VALUES[4] :=  100;
   NAMES[5] := 'HALVES  ';  VALUES[5] :=   50;
   NAMES[6] := 'QUARTERS';  VALUES[6] :=   25;
   NAMES[7] := 'DIMES   ';  VALUES[7] :=   10;
   NAMES[8] := 'NICKELS ';  VALUES[8] :=    5;
   NAMES[9] := 'PENNIES ';  VALUES[9] :=    1;
   WRITE('AMOUNT TO BE RETURNED? ');
   READLN(AMOUNT);
   WHILE AMOUNT > 0.0 DO
      BEGIN
         WRITELN;
         CHANGE := ROUND(100.0 * AMOUNT);
         FOR I := 1 TO 9 DO
            BEGIN
               WRITELN(NAMES[I], (CHANGE DIV VALUES[I]):4);
               CHANGE := CHANGE MOD VALUES[I]
            END;
         WRITELN;
         WRITE('AMOUNT TO BE RETURNED? ');
         READLN(AMOUNT)
      END
END.
```

FIGURE 9–2. This version of the change-making program uses fixed-length strings to represent the names of the bills and coins. Note that each such name must be followed by enough blank spaces to make up an eight-character string.

a table. Each entry in the NAMES column gives the name of a denomination, and the corresponding entry in the VALUES column gives the value of the denomination.

The program begins by assigning values to the components of NAMES and VALUES. Note that each name is followed by enough blank spaces to make up an eight-character string (we say the names are *padded* with blanks). Note also an inconvenience of Pascal: When assigning constant values to the components of an array, we must write a separate assignment statement for each component. Some programming languages offer a shorthand notation that allows us to write the name of the array variable once and then simply list the values that are to be assigned to the components.

The program reads the amount to be returned, converts it to cents, and assigns the result to CHANGE. For each denomination, the statements

```
WRITELN(NAMES[I], (CHANGE DIV VALUES[I]):4);
CHANGE := CHANGE MOD VALUES[I]
```

are executed. The expression

```
CHANGE DIV VALUES[I]
```

computes the number of bills or coins of denomination NAMES[I] that are to be handed back. The WRITELN statement prints the denomination and the number. The expression

```
CHANGE MOD VALUES[I]
```

computes the amount of change still remaining to be handed back.

Variable-Length-String Types. Programs must frequently deal with strings whose lengths are not known in advance, such as strings entered by the user. For example, the user might enter a string listing the names of the files that the program is to process. The program must extract the files' names (whose lengths are also not known in advance) from the string.

For these kinds of jobs many versions of Pascal provide variable-length-string types. UCSD Pascal, for example, provides the built-in type STRING, whose values are strings ranging in length from 0 through 80 characters. If we declare the variable S by

```
VAR
    S: STRING;
```

then we can assign S any string whose length is 80 characters or less.

UCSD Pascal uses the same character-string constants for both fixed-length and variable-length strings. The context in which a constant appears determines which kind of string it represents. Thus 'COMPUTER' could be of type PACKED ARRAY[1..8] OF CHAR or of type STRING, depending on how it is used in a program. The following assignments to S are all valid:

```
S := 'COMPUTER';
S := 'PROGRAMMER';
S := 'ANTIDISESTABLISHMENTARIANISM';
S := ''
```

In the final assignment the two quotation marks with nothing in between represent the *null string*, the string with zero characters. Note

that there is no fixed-length null string, since we are not allowed to declare a packed array of characters having no components. Thus, in standard Pascal the string constant

' '

is invalid.

A variable-length-string variable can be indexed just like any other
array variable. For example, if the value of S is a 'COMPUTER', then
the value of S[1] is 'C', the value of S[2] is 'O', the value of S[3] is 'M',
and so on. However, we cannot refer to characters beyond the end of
the string currently assigned to the variable. Thus, if the value of S is
'COMPUTER', we cannot refer to S[9], S[10], and so on. On the other
hand, if the value of S is 'PROGRAMMER', the value of S[9] is 'E' and
the value of S[10] is 'R'.

If the maximum length of 80 characters for a variable-length string
is not satisfactory, we can specify the desired maximum length in
brackets following the type identifer STRING. Thus, the type
STRING[10] consists of all strings with lengths from 0 through 10 characters. Type STRING[80] is equivalent to type STRING. By specifying a
maximum length smaller than 80 characters, we can save space in memory. By using a larger maximum length, we give ourselves the capability
of handling longer strings. The largest maximum length allowed is 255
characters.

Note that all values of STRING[10] also belong to STRING[11],
STRING[12], and so on. For example, if S is a variable of type STRING
and T a variable of type STRING[10], the assignment

```
S := T
```

is always valid, since every value of type STRING[10] is also a value of
type STRING. On the other hand, the assignment

```
T := S
```

is valid only if the current value of S is no longer than ten characters.
Thus, the sequence

```
S := 'PROGRAMMER';
T := S
```

is valid, whereas

```
S := 'PROGRAMMING';
T := S
```

is not.

Values of variable-length-string variables can be read with READ
and READLN and written with WRITE and WRITELN:

```
WRITE('WHAT''S YOUR NAME? ');
READLN(S);
WRITELN('HELLO, ', S)
```

When these statements are executed, an exchange such as the following takes place:

```
WHAT'S YOUR NAME? JANE
HELLO, JANE
```

Variable-length strings can be compared for alphabetical order with the relational operators, and the strings being compared need not have the same length. When one string is equal to the initial part of another, the shorter string precedes the longer. Thus, the value of each of the following Boolean expressions is TRUE:

```
'JACK' < 'JACKSON'
'NEW' < 'NEW YORK'
'PRO' < 'PROGRAMMER'
```

UCSD Pascal provides a set of functions and procedures for manipulating variable-length strings. The CONCAT function *concatenates*, or joins together, any number of strings. Thus the value of

```
CONCAT('AL', 'TO', 'GET', 'HER')
```

is

```
'ALTOGETHER'
```

A *substring* is a part of a string: 'AL', 'TO', 'GET', and 'HER' are substrings of 'ALTOGETHER'. The function COPY returns a designated substring of a given string. A call to copy has the form

```
COPY(SOURCE, INDEX, SIZE)
```

where SOURCE is the string from which the substring is to be extracted, INDEX is the index of the first character of the substring, and SIZE is the length of the string. Thus, the value of

```
COPY('CONCATENATE', 4, 3)
```

is

```
'CAT'
```

The function

```
POS(PATTERN, SOURCE)
```

searches the string SOURCE for the first occurrence of a substring that matches the string PATTERN. If a matching substring is found, POS returns its position. Thus, the value of

```
POS('ATE', 'CONCATENATE')
```

is 5. Note that the position of the first (rather than the second) occurrence of 'ATE' is returned. If no matching substring is found, POS returns 0. Thus, the value of

```
POS('EAT', 'CONCATENATE')
```

is 0.

The function LENGTH returns the length of a string. Thus the value of

```
LENGTH('PROGRAMMING')
```

is 11. Note that the value of

```
LENGTH('')
```

is 0.

The procedure

```
INSERT(SOURCE, DESTINATION, INDEX)
```

inserts the value of SOURCE into the value of DESTINATION at the position given by the value of INDEX. The procedure

```
DELETE(DESTINATION, INDEX, SIZE)
```

deletes characters from the value of DESTINATION. The value of INDEX specifies where the characters will be deleted and the value of SIZE specifies how many. In each procedure DESTINATION is a variable parameter; only a variable may be substituted for it. The other parameters are value parameters.

For example, after executing the statements

```
S := 'ABCDEF';
INSERT('XY', S, 4)
```

the value of S is:

```
'ABCXYDEF'
```

If we now execute

```
DELETE(S, 5, 3)
```

the value of S is:

'ABCXF'

Figure 9-3 illustrates the use of variable-length strings in the change-making program. This version of the program prints out in words how many bills or coins of each denomination are to be returned. Thus, if the amount to be returned is $0.39, the program prints:

```
ONE QUARTER
ONE DIME
FOUR PENNIES
```

We use three parallel arrays, NS, NP, and VALUES, to store data about the denominations the program can handle. NS holds the names of the denominations in singular form, NP holds the names in plural form, and VALUES holds the values in cents. Note that we can use the index values of these three arrays to number the denominations: denomination 1 is the twenty-dollar bill, denomination 2 is the ten-dollar bill, and so on.

The array DIGITS holds the names of the numbers one through nine: ONE, TWO, THREE, and so on.

The statements that do the change calculations are

```
FOR I := 1 TO 9 DO
   BEGIN
      COUNT := CHANGE DIV VALUES[I];
      CHANGE := CHANGE MOD VALUES[I];
      IF COUNT > 0 THEN
         PRINTLINE(I, COUNT)
   END
```

The value of I is the denomination number. When the value of I is 1, the program is calculating the number of twenties to hand back; when the value of I is 2, the program is calculating the number of tens to hand back; and so on. The number of bills or coins to be handed back for denomination I is assigned to COUNT, and the change still remaining to be handed back is assigned to CHANGE. If the value of COUNT is 0, nothing is printed for denomination I. Otherwise, the procedure PRINTLINE is called to print the number of bills or coins of denomination I to be handed back. The parameters for PRINTLINE are the denomination number, I, and the bill or coin count, COUNT.

PRINTLINE uses COIN for the denomination number and COUNT for the number of bills or coins to be handed back. If the value of COUNT is 1, the singular form of the name of the bill or coin (which is stored in NS) must be used. The line to be printed, LINEOUT, is constructed as follows:

```
LINEOUT := CONCAT(DIGITS[COUNT], ' ' , NS[COIN])
```

```
PROGRAM CHANGE2;
(* CHANGE-MAKING PROGRAM USING ARRAYS AND STRINGS *)
VAR
   NS, NP, DIGITS: ARRAY[1..9] OF STRING;
   VALUES: ARRAYS[1..9] OF INTEGER;
   AMOUNT: REAL;
   CHANGE, COUNT, I: INTEGER;

PROCEDURE PRINTLINE(COIN, COUNT: INTEGER);
(* PRINT LINE GIVING NUMBER OF A SPECIFIC COIN
   OR BILL TO BE RETURNED.  NS, NP, AND DIGITS
   ARE GLOBAL VARIABLES *)
VAR
   LINEOUT: STRING;
BEGIN
   IF COUNT = 1 THEN
      LINEOUT := CONCAT(DIGITS[COUNT], ' ', NS[COIN])
   ELSE
      LINEOUT := CONCAT(DIGITS[COUNT], ' ', NP[COIN]);
   WRITELN(LINEOUT)
END; (* PRINTLINE *)

BEGIN (* MAIN PROGRAM *)
   NS[1] := 'TWENTY';  NP[1] := 'TWENTIES';  VALUES[1] := 2000;
   NS[2] := 'TEN';     NP[2] := 'TENS';      VALUES[2] := 1000;
   NS[3] := 'FIVE';    NP[3] := 'FIVES';     VALUES[3] :=  500;
   NS[4] := 'ONE';     NP[4] := 'ONES';      VALUES[4] :=  100;
   NS[5] := 'HALF';    NP[5] := 'HALVES';    VALUES[5] :=   50;
   NS[6] := 'QUARTER'; NP[6] := 'QUARTERS';  VALUES[6] :=   25;
   NS[7] := 'DIME';    NP[7] := 'DIMES';     VALUES[7] :=   10;
   NS[8] := 'NICKEL';  NP[8] := 'NICKELS';   VALUES[8] :=    5;
   NS[9] := 'PENNY';   NP[9] := 'PENNIES';   VALUES[9] :=    1;

   DIGITS[1] := 'ONE';    DIGITS[2] := 'TWO';
   DIGITS[3] := 'THREE';  DIGITS[4] := 'FOUR';
   DIGITS[5] := 'FIVE';   DIGITS[6] := 'SIX';
   DIGITS[7] := 'SEVEN';  DIGITS[8] := 'EIGHT';
   DIGITS[9] := 'NINE';

   WRITE('AMOUNT TO BE RETURNED? ');
   READLN(AMOUNT);
   WHILE AMOUNT > 0.0 DO
      BEGIN
         WRITELN;
         CHANGE := ROUND(100.0 * AMOUNT);
```

FIGURE 9–3. This version of the change-making program, which prints words
for both the number and name of each bill or coin, uses variable-length strings.
Note that none of the names have to be padded with blank spaces.

(FIGURE 9-3 continued)

```
FOR I := 1 TO 9 DO
   BEGIN
      COUNT := CHANGE DIV VALUES[I];
      CHANGE := CHANGE MOD VALUES[I];
      IF COUNT > 0 THEN
         PRINTLINE(I, COUNT)
   END;
   WRITELN;
   WRITE('AMOUNT TO BE RETURNED? ');
   READLN(AMOUNT)
END
END.
```

The value of COUNT selects the proper component of DIGITS, and the value of COIN selects the proper component of NS. Note that the blank space between the number and denomination must be provided explicitly as a parameter of CONCAT. CONCAT never automatically inserts blank spaces.

If the value of COUNT is greater than 1, then the plural forms of the names (stored in NP) must be used:

```
LINEOUT := CONCAT(DIGITS[COUNT], ' ', NP[COIN])
```

How could we change the declarations of NS, NP, DIGITS, and LINEOUT so as to save space in memory?

Multidimensional Arrays

The arrays we have discussed so far are called *one-dimensional* arrays since they extend in only one dimension—up and down the page. Sometimes we need tables in which the values extend in two dimensions—across the page as well as up and down. These tables are called two-dimensional arrays.

We can declare a two-dimensional array in Pascal as follows:

```
VAR
   T: ARRAY[1..4, 1..3] OF INTEGER;
```

The array T is a table of integers with four rows and three columns. The rows are labeled with index values 1 through 4; the columns are labeled with index values 1 through 3. For example, let's assume that the value of T is as follows:

T

	1	2	3
1	17	30	25
2	14	18	65
3	19	50	24
4	75	96	80

The integers on the left are the row indices and those at the top are the column indices. We can specify any position in the table by giving a row index and a column index. Thus, the value 65 is at the intersection of row 2 and column 3; the value 19 is at the intersection of row 3 and column 1; and so on. As was the case with one-dimensional arrays, the index values are not actually stored in the computer's memory.

Also as was the case with one-dimensional arrays, we can use indexed variables to refer to the components of a two-dimensional array. Two indices are required; The row index is given first, followed by the column index. Thus, T[3, 2] refers to the component in the third row and second column of T; the value of T[3, 2] is 50. Likewise, the value of T[I, J] refers to the component in the row determined by the value of I and the column determined by the value of J. (We sometimes express this by saying that the value of T[I, J] lies at the intersection of the Ith row and the Jth column of the value of T.)

The *dimension* of an array refers to the number of indices required to designate a particular component. Thus, a one-dimensional array requires one index; a two-dimensional array requires two indices; a three-dimensional array requires three; and so on. Pascal places no limit on the dimensions of arrays, so arrays of three and higher dimensions are allowed.

For example, consider the three-dimensional array B declared as follows:

```
VAR
    B: ARRAY[1..30, 1..5, 1..4] OF INTEGER;
```

One way to think of B is as a *book of tables*. The first index designates a particular page in the book, the second designates a particular row in the table on the selected page, and the third designates a column in the same table. Thus B[12, 3, 2] refers to the value found in the table on page 12 at the intersection of row 3 and column 2. Likewise, B[25, 4, 3] refers to the value found in the table on page 25 at the intersection of row 4 and column 3.

Using Two-Dimensional Arrays.   Let's look at a typical application of two-dimensional arrays. Suppose we are processing data from a political poll. There are three candidates running—Johnson, Roberts, and Saxon. The voters we are questioning are of three political persuasions

—Democrat, Republican, and Independent. We are interested in find-ing how many people of each political persuasion are interested in each candidate.

Suppose each voter questioned is asked for his or her political par-ty and candidate preference. The results of the poll can be summarized as follows:

	Johnson	Roberts	Saxon
Democrat	253	40	98
Republican	75	370	150
Independent	24	107	228

That is, of all the Democrats questioned, 253 were for Johnson, 40 were for Roberts, and 98 were for Saxon. Of all the Republicans questioned, 75 were for Johnson, 370 were for Roberts, and so on.

We can use a three-by-three array, COUNT, to store this data. The array variable COUNT is declared as follows:

```
VAR
    COUNT: ARRAY[1..3, 1..3] OF INTEGER;
```

The value of COUNT[1, 3] is the number of Democrats for Saxon, the value of COUNT[3, 2] is the number of Independents for Roberts, and so on.

We will use the index values to represent the parties and can-didates. Thus, in our data, we will code the three parties and the three candidates as follows:

Party	Code	Candidate	Code
Democrat	1	Johnson	1
Republican	2	Roberts	2
Independent	3	Saxon	3

Suppose the raw data obtained when the poll was taken is coded as follows. Two integers are recorded for each person questioned. The first integer is the code for the person's party, and the second integer is the code for the candidate the person prefers. Thus the data

```
2  1
```

represents a Republican who prefers Johnson, and

```
1  3
```

represents a Democrat who prefers Saxon.

Now let's write a procedure to input this kind of data and record in COUNT the number of people with each particular party affiliation and candidate preference.

Before the procedure starts to input data all the components of COUNT must be set to 0. The statement

```
COUNT[I, J] := 0
```

sets to 0 the component of COUNT determined by the values of I and J. If this statement is repeated with J taking on the values 1, 2, and 3.

```
FOR J := 1 TO 3 DO
   COUNT[I, J] := 0
```

then the Ith row of COUNT—the row designated by the value of I—is set to 0. If the last statement is repeated with I taking on the values 1, 2, and 3

```
FOR I := 1 TO 3 DO
   FOR J := 1 TO 3 DO
      COUNT[I, J] := 0
```

then all the components in the array are set to 0. Note that we have here an example of nested FOR statements—one FOR statement contained within another. Nested FOR statements are frequently used in processing multidimensional arrays.

The data for each person questioned is processed as follows:

```
READLN(P, C);
COUNT[P, C] := COUNT[P, C] + 1
```

where P and C are variables of type 1..3, a subrange of INTEGER. The computer reads the party affiliation (the value of P) and the candidate preference (the value of C) for a particular person and adds 1 to the value of COUNT[P, C]. The procedure GETDATA reads the data and counts the number of people with each party affiliation and candidate preference:

```
PROCEDURE GETDATA;
VAR
   P, C: 1..3;
BEGIN
   FOR P := 1 TO 3 DO
      FOR C := 1 TO 3 DO
         COUNT[P, C] := 0;
   WHILE NOT EOF(INPUT) DO
      BEGIN
         READLN(P, C);
         COUNT[P, C] := COUNT[P,C] + 1
      END
END;
```

We assume here that COUNT is a global variable. Remember that one use of global variables is to hold data that will be manipulated by a number of procedures. COUNT is a good example of this.

Having obtained the entries in COUNT, one thing we are interested in doing is printing those values out. To see what statements we need, we can reason much as we did with the statements that set the entries in COUNT to 0. The statement

```
WRITE(COUNT[P, C]:15)
```

prints the component of COUNT determined by the values of P and C. By repeating this statement with C taking on the values 1, 2, and 3, we can print a row of COUNT:

```
FOR C := 1 TO 3 DO
   WRITE(COUNT[P, C]:15)
```

After we have finished printing one row, we want the computer to go to a new line of printout so that the different rows of COUNT will be printed on different lines. This can be done by putting a WRITELN statement after the statement that prints a row:

```
FOR C := 1 TO 3 DO
   WRITE(COUNT[P, C]:15);
WRITELN
```

To get all three rows of COUNT printed, we repeat the preceding statements for P equal to 1, 2, and 3:

```
FOR P := 1 TO 3 DO
   BEGIN
      FOR C := 1 TO 3 DO
         WRITE(COUNT[P, C]:15);
      WRITELN
   END
```

For the sample data given previously, these statements produce the following printout:

```
253              40              98
 75             370             150
 24             107             228
```

Let's look at some of the other things we might want to do with the data in COUNT. For example, we might want to add up all the entries to get the total number of people questioned. Of course, we could have gotten this by counting the number of data entries when the data was read. But we want to see how to add up the components of a two-dimensional array, so we will do the calculation this way.

Let TOTAL be an integer variable. We start out by setting the value of TOTAL to 0. Then we add the value of each component of COUNT to the value of TOTAL. The statements that do this have a form that will be familiar by now:

```
TOTAL := 0;
FOR P := 1 TO 3 DO
   FOR C := 1 TO 3 DO
      TOTAL := TOTAL + COUNT[P, C]
```

One thing that obviously interests us is the total number of people who support each candidate. Let's declare an array variable CTOTAL to hold these totals:

```
VAR
   CTOTAL: ARRAY[1..3] OF INTEGER;
```

Thus, the value of CTOTAL[1] is the total number of people who favor Johnson; the value of CTOTAL[2] is the total number of people who favor Roberts; and so on. To compute the total for the Cth column—the column designated by the value of C—we use.

```
CTOTAL[C] := 0;
FOR P := 1 TO 3 DO
   CTOTAL[C] := CTOTAL[C] + COUNT[P, C]
```

To get the totals for all three candidates, we need to execute these statements for C equal to 1, 2, and 3:

```
FOR C := 1 TO 3 DO
   BEGIN
      CTOTAL[C] := 0;
      FOR P := 1 TO 3 DO
         CTOTAL[C] := CTOTAL[C] + COUNT[P, C]
   END
```

Likewise, we might want to know how many of the people questioned belong to each party. For instance, the totals for the candidates might not be very meaningful if the proportions of the people belonging to each party in the group questioned are not the same as for the population at large.

Let's use an array PTOTAL for the party totals:

```
VAR
   PTOTAL: ARRAY[1..3] OF INTEGER;
```

The value of PTOTAL[1] is the number of Democrats questioned; the value of PTOTAL[2], the number of Republicans; and so on.

To compute the total for the row corresponding to the value of P, we use:

```
PTOTAL[P] := 0;
FOR C := 1 TO 3 DO
    PTOTAL[P] := PTOTAL[P] + COUNT[P, C]
```

To get the totals for all three parties, we repeat the statements just given for P equal to 1, 2, and 3:

```
FOR P := 1 TO 3 DO
   BEGIN
      PTOTAL[P] := 0;
      FOR C := 1 TO 3 DO
          PTOTAL[P] := PTOTAL[P] + COUNT[P, C]
   END
```

Exercises

1. Write a program to input a list of real numbers and calculate their average. The program should then print the numbers on the list, with each number accompanied by the word ABOVE, AVERAGE, or BELOW, depending on whether the number in question is greater than, equal to, or less than the average.

2. In the program TEMPERATURES suppose the value of TEMP[1] is the temperature recorded at 1 A.M.; the value of TEMP[2], the temperature recorded at 2 A.M.; and so on. Modify the program to print not only the high and low temperatures but also the time at which the low temperature was first recorded and the time at which the high temperature was first recorded.

3. Modify the procedure PUTDATA so that the data is printed in the following form:

```
DEMOCRAT        REPUBLICAN      INDEPENDENT
   253               75               24
    40              370              107
    98              150              228
```

4. Modify the version of PUTDATA written in Excercise 3 so that it prints the data in the following form:

```
        DEMOCRAT     REPUBLICAN    INDEPENDENT
JOHNSON    253           75            24
ROBERTS     40          370           107
SAXON       98          150           228
```

5. Using the techniques discussed in this chapter, write a program for processing the results of a political poll. The program should read the responses obtained from the persons questioned. It should print the number of people questioned, the number of people with each combination of party affiliation and candidate preference, the number of and percentage of people who prefer each candidate, and the number of people who belong to each party. All printouts should be labeled with the names of the parties and candidates, where appropriate.

6. Generalize the program of Exercise 5 to handle an arbitrary number of parties and candidates (up to some reasonable limit). The program should begin by reading the number of parties, the names of the parties, the number of candidates, and the names of the candidates. It should then proceed as in Exercise 4.

7. A *magic square* is a square array of numbers such that the numbers in each row, column, and diagonal have the same sum. Write a program to input a square array of numbers and determine whether or not it is a magic square.

8. A company has four salespeople and five products. Let the salespeople be denoted by numbers from 1 to 4 and the products by numbers from 1 to 5. Suppose we are given as data the yearly sales of each product by each salesperson. For example, the data item

3   5   750.00

means that salesperson number 3 sold $750 worth of product number 5. Write a program to input such data items and output the following:

(a)   the total amount sold by each person

(b)   the total amount sold of each product

(c)   the people who sold the largest and smallest amounts of each product

(d)   the products for which each person sold the largest and smallest amounts

If a particular combination of salesperson and product does not occur in the data, assume that the person in question did not sell any of that product.

9. Rewrite the name-printing procedures from Exercises 4 and 5 of Chapter 8 to use arrays of strings. The index type for each array will be an enumerated type and the components of the array will be the names of the enumerated values. For example, we might represent the names of the places in Exercise 4 with an array PLACES such that the value of PLACES[CHURCH] is 'CHURCH', the value of PLACES[WILLEY] is 'WILLEY', and so on. (If you use fixed-length strings, some of the names will have to be padded with blanks to make all the strings the same length.)

10. Add single-letter variables to the desk calculator simulation that you wrote for Exercise 10 of Chapter 6. The operator > is introduced to mean "store the current value of the accumulator in the variable whose name follows." Also, whenever an integer is expected, a variable that has been given a value is permitted instead. To make reading variables and integers easier, an integer is guaranteed to be preceded by a blank, whereas a variable is never preceded by any blanks. For example, the input

```
25 / 10 >A * 13 +A +A =
```

causes the program to print 30.

Print an error message if something other than a variable follows >
or if a variable is used with another operator without having been given
a value. The easiest way to store the values of variables is in an array
indexed by the names of the variables. (What should the index type
be?) Another, separate array will be necessary to record whether each
variable has been given a value.

Chapter 10

SEARCHING AND SORTING

Searching and sorting are two operations frequently carried out on arrays. *Searching* is finding the position of a given value in an array. *Sorting* is arranging the components of an array in some desired order (usually alphabetical or numerical order).

Sorting is often done to aid later searching. For example, we would find it nearly impossible to look up a word in the dictionary or a name in a telephone directory if the entries were not in alphabetical order. Likewise, a computer can search an array much more rapidly if the components of the array are in alphabetical or numerical order.

Searching

Have you ever found an item on a list by running your finger down the list until you come to the item you wanted? This kind of search is called *sequential search*. You start at the beginning of the list and examine the entries one after another until you either find the entry you are looking for or run off the end of the list.

Let's see how to use this method to search a one-dimensional array of integers for a given value. We begin by declaring the following variables;

```
VAR
   LIST: ARRAY[1..100] OF INTEGER;    (* LIST TO BE SEARCHED *)
   SIZE,                              (* NUMBER OF ENTRIES ON LIST *)
   VFIND,                             (* VALUE BEING SEARCHED FOR *)
   I: INTEGER;                        (* "FINGER" THAT KEEPS PLACE IN
                                         LIST *)

   FOUND: BOOLEAN                     (* INDICATES WHETHER OR NOT THE
                                         VALUE BEING SOUGHT WAS
                                         ACTUALLY FOUND *)
```

The components LIST[1] through LIST[SIZE] hold the list to be searched; LIST[SIZE + 1] through LIST[100] are currently unused but allow for future expansion of the list. We require that there be at least one unused component, which we will put to temporary use during the search.

We start by setting I to 1, so that it designates the first position on the list. We then examine the entries on the list one after another. If a particular entry is the value we are seeking, we stop the search. Otherwise, we go on to the next entry:

```
I := 1;
WHILE LIST[I] <> VFIND DO
   I := I + 1
```

If the value we are searching for is on the list, the repetition will terminate with the value of I equal to the index of the value sought. That is, when the repetition stops, the value of the Boolean expression

```
LIST[I] = VFIND
```

is TRUE.

Unfortunately, if the value we are looking for is not on the list, the statements just given will not work. When the value of I exceeds the value of SIZE, the search continues into the unused part of the array. The program may find a spurious value equal to VFIND somewhere in the unused part of LIST. If not, it will eventually try to refer to LIST[101], which does not exist, and the program will terminate with an error message.

In short, we need some way to keep the program from running off the end of the list when the sought-after value is not present. One of the simplest ways of doing this is to store the value of VFIND in the first unused component, LIST[SIZE + 1], before beginning the search:

```
LIST[SIZE + 1] := VFIND
```

This component acts as a sentinel. If the program reaches LIST[SIZE + 1], it finds the sought-after value there, and so the repetition terminates.

After the repetition stops, we have to determine whether the value found is on the part of LIST currently in use or whether the search was stopped by the sentinel. We can do this by evaluating the Boolean expression

```
I <= SIZE
```

If the value of this expression is TRUE, the value found is on the part of the LIST currently in use. If the value of the expression is FALSE, then the value found is not on the part of the list currently in use, hence the search was stopped by the sentinel.

The following statements search the value of LIST for the value of VFIND. If the search concludes successfully, the value of FOUND is TRUE and the value of I is the index of the value that was found. If the search stops because the sentinel was encountered, the value of FOUND is FALSE and the value of I (which equals SIZE + 1—why?) has no significance:

```
LIST[SIZE + 1] := VFIND;
I := 1;
WHILE LIST[I] <> VFIND DO
    I : = I + 1;
FOUND := (I <= SIZE)
```

(Note the use of the Boolean expression I <= SIZE on the right-hand side of the assignment operator. The parentheses are not required, but they make the statement easier to read.)

The program in Figure 10-1 uses sequential search to look up a price on a price list. The price list is stored as two parallel arrays. ITEMNO and PRICE, which have the following form:

ITEMNO	PRICE
1132	32.75
2345	12.99
3724	15.49
5921	5.64
8740	125.43
sentinel	

If ITEMNO[I] is the number of a particular item, then PRICE[I] (for the same value of I) is the price of the item. To find the price of an item given its number, we use sequential search to find the value of I such that ITEMNO[I] is the number of the item in question. With I equal to this value, the value of PRICE[I] is the price we are seeking.

The search is carried out by a procedure:

```
SEARCH(ITEMNUMBER: INTEGER; VAR ITEMPRICE: REAL;
       VAR FOUND: BOOLEAN)
```

Isolating the search statements in a procedure allows us to change the method of search without affecting the rest of the program, something we will presently do. The value of ITEMNUMBER is the item number to be found; if the item number *is* found, ITEMPRICE is used to return the corresponding price. The value of FOUND is set to TRUE or FALSE depending on whether or not the value of ITEMPRICE was found. ITEMNUMBER is a value parameter, since it is used only to pass data to the procedure. ITEMPRICE and FOUND are variable parameters, since they are used to return results. ITEMNO, PRICE, and SIZE are global variables.

The sentinel is installed and the search carried out in the way we have previously discussed:

```
ITEMNO[SIZE + 1] := ITEMNUMBER;
I := 1;
WHILE ITEMNO[I] <> ITEMNUMBER DO
    I := I + 1
```

```
PROGRAM PRICES;
(* LOOK UP PRICES IN PRICE LIST *)
CONST
   LIMIT = 100;
   LIMIT1 = 101;
VAR
   ITEMNO: ARRAY[1..LIMIT1] OF INTEGER;
   PRICE: ARRAY[1..LIMIT] OF REAL;
   SIZE, ITEMNUMBER, I: INTEGER;
   ITEMPRICE: REAL;
   FOUND: BOOLEAN;

PROCEDURE SEARCH(ITEMNUMBER: INTEGER; VAR ITEMPRICE: REAL;
                 VAR FOUND: BOOLEAN);
VAR
   I: INTEGER;
BEGIN
   ITEMNO[SIZE + 1] := ITEMNUMBER;
   I := 1;
   WHILE ITEMNO[I] <> ITEMNUMBER DO
      I := I + 1;
   IF I <= SIZE THEN
      BEGIN
         ITEMPRICE := PRICE[I];
         FOUND := TRUE
      END
   ELSE
      FOUND := FALSE
END; (* SEARCH *)

BEGIN (* MAIN PROGRAM *)
   (* GET PRICE LIST *)
   WRITELN('ENTER PRICE LIST');
   WRITE('HOW MANY ENTRIES? ');
   READLN(SIZE);
   FOR I := 1 TO SIZE DO
      BEGIN
         WRITE('ENTER ITEM NUMBER AND PRICE: ');
         READLN(ITEMNO[I], PRICE[I]);
      END;
   (* LOOK UP PRICES *)
   WRITELN;
   WRITELN('PRICE LOOKUP:  ENTER ITEM NUMBER OF 0 TO STOP');
   WRITE('ITEM NUMBER? ');
   READLN(ITEMNUMBER);
```

FIGURE 10-1. This program uses sequential search to look up items in a price list.

(FIGURE 10-1 continued)

```
WHILE ITEMNUMBER <> 0 DO
   BEGIN
      SEARCH(ITEMNUMBER, ITEMPRICE, FOUND);
      IF FOUND THEN
         WRITELN('PRICE IS ', ITEMPRICE:8:2)
      ELSE
         WRITELN('REQUESTED ITEM NOT FOUND');
      WRITELN;
      WRITE('ITEM NUMBER? ');
      READLN(ITEMNUMBER)
   END
END.
```

Checking whether the sought-after value was found is handled slightly differently. If the sought-after item number was found, we need to do two things: set ITEMPRICE to the corresponding price and set FOUND to TRUE. If the sought-after item number was not found, we set FOUND to FALSE and leave the value of ITEMPRICE unchanged. The following IF statement selects the proper action:

```
IF I <= SIZE THEN
   BEGIN
      ITEMPRICE := PRICE[I];
      FOUND := TRUE
   END
ELSE
   FOUND := FALSE
```

In the main program the item to be looked up—the value of ITEM-NUMBER—is obtained from the user, after which the procedure SEARCH is called:

```
SEARCH(ITEMNUMBER, ITEMPRICE, FOUND);
IF FOUND THEN
   WRITELN('PRICE IS ', ITEMPRICE:8:2)
ELSE
   WRITELN('REQUESTED ITEM NOT FOUND')
```

(Note that the variables ITEMNUMBER, ITEMPRICE, and FOUND, declared in the main program, are not the same as formal parameters with the same names.)

Binary Search. Sequential search is suitable only for short lists. For long ones it is hopelessly inefficient. For example, imagine trying to look up a name in the telephone directory by starting on the first page and examining every name until you find the one you want. If the names in the directory were in random order, sequential search would be our only alternative. But in fact the names are in alphabetical order, and we use this fact to locate quickly the name we want.

One of the most efficient methods of searching an ordered list is *binary search*. Let's illustrate binary search by seeing how we might use it to look up a name in the telephone directory. We start by opening the directory to the middle and dividing the directory into two parts, which we will call the left-hand part and the right-hand part. Now examine the first name on the first page of the right-hand part. If the name we are looking for precedes (in alphabetical order) the name we are examining, then the name we are looking for, if present in the directory at all, is in the left-hand part. If the name we are looking for follows the name we are examining, then the name we are looking for, if present in the directory at all, is in the right-hand part. If the name we are looking for is the same as the one we are examining, then we have found the name we are looking for and our search is over.

If the name we examined was not the one we were looking for, we nevertheless know which half of the directory possibly contains the name we are looking for and which half cannot contain it. We can forget about the half that cannot contain the sought-after name and concentrate on the half that does contain it, if it is present in the directory at all.

We continue the search in the same way, at each step dividing in half the part of the directory that remains to be searched and then narrowing down the search to either the left half or the right half. After surprisingly few halvings, the search narrows down to a single page that contains the desired name (or that would contain it if it were present). This is as far as it is practical to carry a binary search of a telephone directory. But with an array, we can keep going until the part remaining to be searched consists of only a single component.

Figure 10-2 shows a binary-search version of the procedure SEARCH. This procedure is intended to be substituted for the sequential-search version in Figure 10-1 without requiring any changes to the rest of the program.

As a binary search proceeds, we repeatedly narrow down the part of the array that remains to be searched. We use two variables, LOW and HIGH, to keep track of the part of the array that remains to be searched. LOW is the index of the first yet-to-be-searched component, and HIGH is the index of the last such component. Thus, at any time, the components that remain to be searched are

`ITEMNO[LOW] through ITEMNO[HIGH]`

As before, SIZE is the number of components of ITEMNO that are in use. Initially, the entire part of ITEMNO that is in use

`ITEMNO[1] through ITEMNO[SIZE]`

is to be searched. Therefore, we begin by setting LOW to 1 and HIGH to SIZE:

```
PROCEDURE SEARCH(ITEMNUMBER: INTEGER; VAR ITEMPRICE: REAL;
                VAR FOUND: BOOLEAN);
VAR
   HIGH, MID, LOW: INTEGER;
BEGIN
   LOW := 1;
   HIGH := SIZE;
   REPEAT
      MID := (LOW + HIGH) DIV 2;
      IF ITEMNUMBER < ITEMNO[MID] THEN
         HIGH := MID - 1
      ELSE IF ITEMNUMBER > ITEMNO[MID] THEN
         LOW := MID + 1
   UNTIL (ITEMNUMBER = ITEMNO[MID]) OR (LOW > HIGH);
   IF LOW <= HIGH THEN
      BEGIN
         ITEMPRICE := PRICE[MID];
         FOUND := TRUE
      END
   ELSE
      FOUND := FALSE
END; (* SEARCH *)
```

FIGURE 10-2. A procedure for binary search. This procedure can be substituted for the sequential-search procedure in Figure 10-1. If binary search is used, the price list must, of course, be in numerical order according to item numbers.

```
LOW := 1;
HIGH := SIZE;
```

We begin by examining a component that lies approximately in the middle of the part ITEMNO that remains to be searched. The index of the middle element is:

```
MID := (LOW + HIGH) DIV 2
```

We now compare the item number we are searching for with the middle item number, ITEMNO[MID]. If the value of

```
ITEMNUMBER < ITEMNO[MID]
```

is TRUE, then the value of ITEMNUMBER, if present at all, must lie in the first half of the part of ITEMNO that remains to be searched. That is, the sought-after item number must lie in:

```
ITEMNO[LOW] through ITEMNO[MID - 1]
```

Therefore, we narrow down the not-yet-searched part of ITEMNO by setting HIGH to MID − 1:

```
HIGH := MID - 1
```

On the other hand, if the value of

```
ITEMNUMBER > ITEMNO[MID]
```

is TRUE, then the value of ITEMNUMBER, if present at all, must lie in the second half of the part of ITEMNO that remains to be searched. That is, the sought-after item number must lie in

```
ITEMNO[MID + 1] through ITEMNO[HIGH]
```

Therefore, we narrow down the not-yet-searched part of ITEMNO by setting LOW to MID + 1:

```
LOW := MID + 1
```

    There are two conditions under which any search should terminate —when the sought-after item has been found and when the sought-after item is known not to be present. If the value of

```
ITEMNUMBER = ITEMNO[MID]
```

is TRUE then the sought-after item number has been found. If the value of

```
LOW > HIGH
```

is TRUE, then the values of LOW and HIGH have passed each other. The part of ITEMNO remaining to be searched has been reduced to "less than nothing," hence the item number sought is not present.
    After the search has been completed, the values of ITEMPRICE and FOUND must be set. If the value of

```
LOW <= HIGH
```

is TRUE, then ITEMNO[MID] is the item number sought, and PRICE[MID] is the corresponding price. FOUND should be set to TRUE and ITEMPRICE to PRICE[MID]. Otherwise, the item number sought was not found, and FOUND should be set to FALSE:

```
IF LOW <= HIGH THEN
   BEGIN
      ITEMPRICE := PRICE[MID];
      FOUND := TRUE
   END
ELSE
   FOUND := FALSE
```

For large lists binary search is dramatically faster than sequential search. Consider searching a list of one million items. For sequential search we must, on the average, examine half the items on the list, or 500 thousand, before finding the one we are searching for. For a binary search we must examine at most 20 items. The latter statement can be made plausible by entering one million on a pocket calculator and dividing by two 20 times. The result is less than one, indicating that starting with a million-item list and dividing the not-yet-searched part of the list in half 20 times is sufficient to narrow the search down to a single item.

Sorting

If we are to use some form of searching that is more efficient than sequential search, the items on the list being searched must be in some specified order. It is this order that lets us quickly find the desired item. Therefore, computers are often called upon to arrange values in order, not only so that searching routines can work more efficiently, but so that humans can better find their way around in computer printouts.

There are two kinds of sorting: *internal* sorting and *external* sorting. Internal sorting is used when the values to be sorted are stored in arrays in main memory. External sorting is used when the values are sorted in files in auxiliary memory.

For internal sorting we assume that any one of the values to be sorted can be accessed as quickly as any other. For instance, if A is a 1000-component array, then we assume that the same amount of time is required to access A[1], A[500], A[1000], or any other component of A. Internal sorting routines make use of this fact in that they frequently "jump around" in the array, so that A[1], A[500], A[1000], for example, may all be accessed in rapid succession.

But when the values to be sorted are stored in auxiliary memory, the time required to access the value in one location depends on which location was accessed last. After location 1 has been accessed, it is likely to be much quicker to access location 2 than location 500 or location 1000. This is true even for so-called random access devices such as disks. Consequently, internal sorting routines, when they will work at all with auxiliary memory devices, do so very inefficiently.

In this chapter we will confine ourselves to internal sorting routines, of which we will look at three: the *bubble sort*, the *Shell sort*, and *Quicksort*. These will be taken up in order of increasing efficiency and complexity. The bubble sort is easy to program but not very efficient. Quicksort lives up to its name but is the most complex to program. The Shell sort falls between the bubble sort and Quicksort in both efficiency and complexity.

The Bubble Sort.   To see how the bubble sort works, let's try it out on the following list of numbers:

9   8   7   6

We begin by looking at the first two numbers, 9 and 8. Since they are out of order, we exchange them. The list now looks like this:

8   9   7   6

Next, we move forward one position in the list and again compare two adjacent numbers, 9 and 7 this time. Since they are out of order, we exchange them:

8   7   9   6

We continue through the list in this way, comparing adjacent values and exchanging them if they are out of order. We will call one such pass over the list a *compare-and-exchange pass*. To display a compare-and-exchange pass in a convenient way, let's use asterisks to show which values are being compared. Thus, we begin with

9*   8*   7   6

to show that 9 and 8 are being compared. We exchange them and move forward one position. This situation is displayed as follows:

8   9*   7*   6

The values 9 and 8 have been exchanged, and we are now comparing 9 and 7. With the help of this notation, we can display a complete compare-and-exchange pass:

```
9*   8*   7    6
8    9*   7*   6
8    7    9*   6*
8    7    6    9
```

Notice how the 9 moved all the way to the right. In a compare-and-exchange pass, the largest value that is out of order always moves as far to the right as possible. We say that it "bubbles" to the right, like a bubble rising in a container of liquid, hence the name "bubble sort."

The list is not yet in order, although its order has been improved. We can improve the order still further by carrying out additional compare-and-exchange passes:

```
8*   7*   6    9
7    8*   6*   9
7    6    8*   9*
7    6    8    9
```

Now it's 8's turn to bubble up to its proper position. Notice that the last comparison did not produce an exchange, since the values compared (8 and 9) were already in order.

The order of the list is now much improved, but it is not yet perfect. We still need another compare-and-exchange pass:

```
7*  6*  8   9
6   7*  8*  9
6   7   8*  9*
6   7   8   9
```

Now 7 has bubbled into position and the list is sorted.

But how is the program to know that the list is sorted? Suppose we make another compare-and-exchange pass:

```
6*  7*  8   9
6   7*  8*  9
6   7   8*  9*
6   7   8   9
```

No exchanges are made, since all the values are in order. If any of the values were out of order, at least one exchange would have been made. Therefore, when the program can get through a compare-and-exchange pass without making any exchanges, it knows that the list is sorted.

Let's use a Boolean variable NOEXCHANGES to indicate whether or not any exchanges have been made on a particular compare-and-exchange pass. If NOEXCHANGES is TRUE when the pass is completed, no exchanges were made during the pass, hence the list is in order. We can outline the bubble sort routine as follows:

```
REPEAT
    "Do one compare-and-exchange pass.  Set
    NOEXCHANGES to TRUE if no exchanges were
    made and to FALSE otherwise"
UNTIL NOEXCHANGES
```

A compare-and-exchange pass goes through the list comparing adjacent values and exchanging them if they are out of order. The number of values on the list is SIZE. Before each pass begins NOEXCHANGES is set to TRUE. When an exchange is made, NOEXCHANGES is set to FALSE. If no exchanges are made, NOEXCHANGES will retain its initial value of TRUE throughout the pass. Otherwise, it will be set to FALSE:

```
NOEXCHANGES := TRUE;
FOR I := 1 TO SIZE - 1 DO
    IF LIST[I] > LIST[I + 1] THEN
        "Exchange values of LIST[I] and LIST[I + 1].
        Set NOEXCHANGES to FALSE"
```

Figure 10-3 shows the complete procedure BUBBLESORT. Note that to exchange the values of LIST[I] and LIST[I + 1], the variable TEMPORARY is needed to temporarily store the value of LIST[I]:

```
IF LIST[I] > LIST[I + 1] THEN
   BEGIN
      TEMPORARY := LIST[I];
      LIST[I] := LIST[I + 1];
      LIST[I + 1] := TEMPORARY;
      NOEXCHANGES := FALSE
   END
```

Figure 10-4 shows a program for "exercising," or testing, a sorting procedure. The program fills an array with random integers. It prints the contents of the array before sorting, calls the sorting procedure, and prints the contents of the sorted array. This program can be used to test each of the sorting procedures we will develop. The variables STACK and TOP are for one version of Quicksort and are not used by the other sorting procedures.

We can approach the organization of a bubble-sort routine in another way. Let's go back to our example list:

9   8   7   6

After the first compare-and-exchange pass, the largest value, 9, has moved into the last position:

8   7   6   9

```
PROCEDURE BUBBLESORT;
VAR
   I, TEMPORARY: INTEGER;
   NOEXCHANGES: BOOLEAN;
BEGIN
   REPEAT
      NOEXCHANGES := TRUE;
      FOR I := 1 TO SIZE - 1 DO
         IF LIST[I] > LIST[I + 1] THEN
            BEGIN
               TEMPORARY := LIST[I];
               LIST[I] := LIST[I + 1];
               LIST[I + 1] := TEMPORARY;
               NOEXCHANGES := FALSE
            END
   UNTIL NOEXCHANGES
END;
```

FIGURE 10–3. A procedure for sorting the components of the array LIST using a bubble sort.

```
PROGRAM SORTTEST;
(* TEST PROGRAM FOR SORTING ROUTINES *)
VAR
   SEED: REAL;
   I, FIRST, LAST, SIZE: INTEGER;
   LIST: ARRAY[1..1000] OF INTEGER;
   STACK: ARRAY[1..50] OF INTEGER;
   TOP: 0..50;
   CONTINUE: CHAR;

FUNCTION RANDOM(N: INTEGER): INTEGER;
BEGIN
   SEED := SQR(SEED + 3.1415927);
   SEED := SEED - TRUNC(SEED);
   RANDOM := TRUNC(N * SEED) + 1
END; (* RANDOM *)

PROCEDURE BUBBLESORT;
VAR
   I, TEMPORARY: INTEGER;
   NOEXCHANGES: BOOLEAN;
BEGIN
   REPEAT
      NOEXCHANGES := TRUE;
      FOR I := 1 TO SIZE - 1 DO
         IF LIST[I] > LIST[I + 1] THEN
            BEGIN
               TEMPORARY := LIST[I];
               LIST[I] := LIST[I + 1];
               LIST[I + 1] := TEMPORARY;
               NOEXCHANGES := FALSE
            END
   UNTIL NOEXCHANGES
END; (* BUBBLESORT *)

BEGIN (* MAIN PROGRAM *)
   REPEAT
      WRITE('NUMBER OF VALUES TO BE SORTED (2-1000)? ');
      READLN(SIZE);
      WRITE('SEED FOR RANDOM NUMBER GENERATOR? ');
      READLN(SEED);
      WRITELN('FILLING ARRAY');
```

(Continued on page 188.)

FIGURE 10-4. A program for testing or "exercising" a sort procedure. The program fills the array LIST with random one- and two-digit integers, prints the unsorted components, calls the sorting procedure, and then prints the sorted components. The declarations for STACK and TOP are used only by one version of Quicksort.

(FIGURE 10–4 continued)

```
    FIRST := 1;
    LAST := SIZE;
    FOR I := FIRST TO LAST DO
        BEGIN
            LIST[I] := RANDOM(99);
            WRITE(LIST[I]:4)
        END;
    WRITELN;
    WRITELN('SORTING');
    BUBBLESORT;
    WRITELN('SORTED ARRAY');
    FOR I := FIRST TO LAST DO
        WRITE(LIST[I]:4);
    WRITELN;
    WRITE('SORT AGAIN (Y/N)? ');
    READ(CONTINUE); WRITELN
  UNTIL CONTINUE <> 'Y'
END.
```

Therefore, we can forget the last value and concentrate on the first three values. A compare-and-exchange pass over the first three values gives us:

7   6   8

Again, the largest value has bubbled into the last position. Therefore, we can concentrate on the first two values:

7   6

A compare-and-exchange pass bubbles 7 into the final position, giving

6   7

and we are done.

   Thus, we are assured of sorting the entire list if we do one compare-and-exchange pass over

LIST[1] through LIST[SIZE]

then another over

LIST[1] through LIST[SIZE - 1]

then another one

LIST[1] through LIST[SIZE - 2]

and so on until the final pass, which is over

```
LIST[1] and LIST[2]
```

We can outline this version of the bubble sort as follows:

```
FOR LIMIT := SIZE DOWNTO 2 DO
    "Do a compare-and-exchange pass over the
    portion of LIST from LIST[1] through
    LIST[LIMIT]"
```

The compare-and-exchange pass has the same form as before except that LIMIT is used in place of SIZE and the flag NOEXCHANGES is no longer needed:

```
FOR I := 1 TO LIMIT - 1 DO
    IF LIST[I] > LIST[I + 1] THEN
        BEGIN
            TEMPORARY := LIST[I];
            LIST[I] := LIST[I + 1];
            LIST[I + 1] := TEMPORARY
        END
```

Figure 10–5 shows the complete procedure for this version of the bubble sort.

Which version of the bubble sort is best? BUBBLESRT does SIZE − 1 compare-and-exchange passes, even if the first pass happened to put the list in order. The original BUBBLESORT will stop as soon as it can make a pass without having to do any exchanges.

This argument seems to favor BUBBLESORT; however, we can raise this question: For an arbitrary list, how likely is it that BUB-BLESORT will be able to stop before doing SIZE − 1 passes? This turns

---

```
PROCEDURE BUBBLESRT;
VAR
    I, TEMPORARY, LIMIT: INTEGER;
BEGIN
    FOR LIMIT := SIZE DOWNTO 2 DO
        FOR I := 1 TO LIMIT - 1 DO
            IF LIST[I] > LIST[I + 1] THEN
                BEGIN
                    TEMPORARY := LIST[I];
                    LIST[I] := LIST[I + 1];
                    LIST[I + 1] := TEMPORARY
                END
END
```

FIGURE 10–5. An alternate version of the bubble sort.

out not to be very likely. Unless we know in advance that none of the values are very far from their final positions, the chances are that BUBBLESORT will have to run for close to SIZE − 1 passes.

Given that both versions will probably make about the same number of compare-and-exchange passes, which version is the more efficient? BUBBLESORT requires that we keep track of a Boolean variable NOEXCHANGES, which must be set to TRUE at the beginning of each pass, set to FALSE after each exchange, and tested after each pass. BUBBLESRT controls the number of passes with a FOR statement. Most computers can execute the FOR statement more efficiently than they can manipulate the Boolean variable, so BUBBLESRT will often execute faster than BUBBLESORT (although the difference may be marginal). Also, BUBBLESRT saves some time in that, after the first pass, each succeeding pass is over only a part of the list, a part whose size decreases with each pass.

Manipulations that are necessary to control the operation of a program are known as *overhead* or *bookkeeping*. For small lists—10 or 11 components, say—a bubble sort will often outperform more sophisticated routines because the bubble sort does less bookkeeping. But when the lists to be sorted become longer, the extra bookeeping done by the other routines pays off, making them more efficient than the bubble sort.

The Shell Sort. A problem with the bubble sort is that while values move toward their proper positions rapidly in one direction, they move slowly in the other. Again going back to our example

9   8   7   6

after one compare-and exchange pass we have:

8   7   6   9

The value 9 has moved all the way to its proper position at the end of the list; however, 6 has only moved one step toward its final position. We see that the largest out-of-place value moves rapidly to its final position, but other values move much more slowly, often only one position per pass.

The Shell sort (named after its inventor, Donald Shell) improves matters as follows. A series of compare-and-exchange passes are made, but instead of comparing adjacent items, there is a fixed gap between the items that are compared and (if necessary) exchanged. When no more exchanges can be made for a given gap, the gap is narrowed, and the compare-and-exchange passes continue. The final passes are made with a gap of 1, just as in the bubble sort*.

---

*Shell's basic idea—comparing items separated by a gap that is narrowed on successive passes—is often applied to improve two sorting methods—the bubble sort and the insertion sort. Thus, you can get different Shell-sort routines depending on whether you start with the bubble sort (as we do here) or the insertion sort (as is perhaps more common).

What happens is that the earlier passes with large gaps allow values to take giant steps toward their final positions. Thus, the later passes, with narrower gaps, have less work to do.

For example, let's take the list we have been using all along and make a compare-and-exchange pass with a gap of 2. That is, we compare LIST[1] with LIST [3] and LIST[2] with LIST[4]:

```
9*   8    7*   6
7    8*   9    6*
7    6    9    8
```

Notice how far 6 has moved toward its final position. A second compare-and-exchange pass with a gap of 2 makes no exchanges:

```
7*   6    9*   8
7    6*   9    8*
7    6    9    8
```

Since we can make no more exchanges with a gap of 2, we divide the gap in half and continue with a gap of 1:

```
7*   6*   9    8
6    7*   9*   8
6    7    9*   8*
6    7    8    9
```

The list is now in order, although the program will have to make another compare-and-exchange pass (with a gap of 1) to discover this. Since the program can make a compare-and-exchange pass with a gap of 1 without making any exchanges, the list is sorted and the Shell sort can terminate.

The larger the list to be sorted, the greater the advantage of the Shell sort over the bubble sort. For the four-component list in our examples, the Shell sort requires just as many compare-and-exchange passes as the bubble sort. For lists of more than 10 or 11 components, the Shell sort will usually be faster, and for lists of more than 100 components, the difference in speed becomes substantial. For very large lists, the Shell sort is dramatically faster than the bubble sort—about ten times faster for a list of 1000 components.

We start off with a gap equal to one-half the size of the list. Each time we need a new gap, we divide the old gap in half (ignoring any remainder). The final gap used is always 1. We can outline the Shell-sort routine as follows:

```
GAP := SIZE DIV 2;
REPEAT
    "Do a modified bubble sort that compares and
    (if necessary) exchanges LIST[I] and LIST[I + GAP]
    instead of LIST[I] and LIST[I + 1]"
    GAP := GAP DIV 2
UNTIL GAP < 1
```

Figure 10-6 shows the complete procedure SHELLSORT, which can be tested using the program in Figure 10-4. Note that in the "bubble sort" part of the procedure, the value of GAP plays the same role that was played by 1 in the procedure BUBBLESORT.

Quicksort.   When lists are very long or speed is of the essence, we can use a routine called Quicksort, which is even faster than a Shell sort. In fact, Quicksort is one of the fastest known internal sorting routines. As you might expect, Quicksort is more complicated than either the bubble sort or the Shell sort.

Let's begin by considering a list of numbers to be sorted:

3 9 6 5 7 4 1 2 8

We want to divide this list into two sublists in such a way that all the values on the first sublist are less than or equal to all the values on the second sublist. To do this, we choose one of the numbers to serve as a dividing line between the two sublists. All numbers less than the dividing-line value go on the first sublist; all those greater than the dividing-line value go on the second sublist. The dividing-line value itself may end up on either sublist.

```
PROCEDURE SHELLSORT;
VAR
    I, TEMPORARY, GAP: INTEGER;
    NOEXCHANGES: BOOLEAN;
BEGIN
    GAP := SIZE DIV 2;
    REPEAT
      REPEAT
        NOEXCHANGES := TRUE;
        FOR I := 1 TO SIZE - GAP DO
          IF LIST[I] > LIST[I + GAP] THEN
            BEGIN
              TEMPORARY := LIST[I];
              LIST[I] := LIST[I + GAP];
              LIST[I + GAP] := TEMPORARY;
              NOEXCHANGES := FALSE
            END
      UNTIL NOEXCHANGES;
      GAP := GAP DIV 2
    UNTIL GAP < 1
END
```

FIGURE 10-6. This version of the Shell sort essentially does repeated bubble sorts with smaller and smaller gaps between the components being compared and exchanged. The final bubble sort is done with a gap of 1.

For example, let's make the dividing-line value 7, the value at the mid-point of the original list. Then we can divide the list into sublists as follows:

```
3 2 6 5 1 4    7 9 8
```

All values less than 7 are on the first sublist, and all those greater than 7 (together with 7 itself) are on the second sublist.

Now if each of the two sublists is sorted separately

```
1 2 3 4 5 6    7 8 9
```

the entire list is in order and the sorting is complete. Our plan for the Quicksort routine, then, is this: Divide the list to be sorted into two sublists as just illustrated. Then call the Quicksort routine recursively to sort each of the sublists. When the recursive calls return, both the sublists and the original list will be sorted, and the Quicksort routine can terminate.

Going back to the division of the original list into two sublists

```
3 2 6 5 1 4    7 9 8
```

each of the sublists will itself be sorted using the Quicksort routine. Therefore, the sublists will be divided into smaller sublists, which will be divided into still smaller sublists, and so on. Let's follow through this process and see exactly how the original list gets sorted.

We continue with the second sublist:

```
7 9 8
```

We take the middle value, 9, as the dividing line. The list can be divided as follows:

```
7 8    9
```

Since the "list" 9 contains only one value, it can be divided no further. The list

```
7 8
```

can be divided in only one way:

```
7    8
```

This is as far as we can go with the second sublist of the original division. Now let's apply the same process to the first sublist of the original division:

```
3 2 6 5 1 4
```

If we take 6 as the dividing-line value, we get the division

3 2 4 5 1   6

The second of these cannot be divided any further. Using 4 as the dividing-line value, the first can be divided as follows:

3 2 1   5 4

Of the two sublists, the second can only be divided into

4   5

and the first can be divided into:

1   2   3

(Quicksort occassionally divides a list into three sublists, the middle sublist always consisting of a single value. Since the middle sublist cannot be further subdivided and needs no further sorting, it can be ignored.)

Now let's see how these repeated divisions into sublists have put the original list in order:

```
                      3 9 6 5 7 4 1 2 8

            3 2 6 5 1 4                      7 9 8

       3 2 4 5 1                6          7 8        9

     3 2 1        5 4                      7     8

  1  2  3      4  5
```

In this illustration the first line shows the original list, the second line the two sublists of the original list, the third line the sublists of the sublists of the original list, and so on. The end results of the repeated division into sublists are the one-component lists, which cannot be divided any further. The values on the one-component lists, read from left to right (even though they appear on different levels in the diagram) are in the desired numerical order.

Now let's look at the things we have to do to bring about this division of the original list into successively smaller sublists:

1. Choose the dividing-line value.

2. Rearrange the values on the original list so that all those less than the dividing-line value are to the left of a certain point and all those greater than the dividing-line value are to the right of the same point, dividing the list into two sublists.

3. Repeat the same process for each sublist containing more than one item. (A one-item sublist cannot be further sorted.) We do this by calling the Quicksort routine recursively for each sublist to be sorted.

Our first job is to find the dividing-line value. Quicksort works most efficiently when the two sublists are nearly the same size. They will be most nearly the same size if the dividing-line value is the *median* of the values on the original list—the value such that there are as many values less than or equal to it as there are greater than or equal to it. For example, the median of the original list that we used to illustrate Quicksort is 5.

Unfortunately, finding the median of a list of values is almost as hard as sorting the values, so finding and using the median is not practical. We must choose one of the values on the list and hope that it is close to the median. If the values are in random order, then one choice is just as good as another, since any value is as likely as any other to be close to the median.

However, there is an argument for taking a value near the middle of the list. Often we are called on to sort a list that is almost in order—only a small number of values are out of order. In fact, a list that is supposed to be in order may be sorted again just to make sure. In these cases a value near the middle of the list has a good chance of being close to the median. Therefore, we will choose the middle value for the dividing-line value.

Thus, for the list

3 9 6 5 7 4 1 2 8

we chose the middle value 7 for the dividing-line value, and this wasn't too bad a choice, since 7 is not too far from the median, 5. On the other hand, for the sublist

3 2 6 5 1 4

we chose 6, a terrible choice. Since 6 is the largest value on the list, using it as the dividing-line value produces the very unequal subdivision:

3 2 4 5 1   6

It turns out that, on the average, the terrible choices are few enough so that they do not seriously affect the efficiency of the routine.

The next step is to rearrange the values so as to produce the two sublists. We start with two arrows, one at each end of the list.

```
3 9 6 5 7 4 1 2 8
↑               ↑
I               J
```

The two arrows are labeled I and J, since I and J are the array indices that we will use to represent the arrows in Pascal.

The arrow I is moved forward through the list as long as it points to a value less than the dividing-line value. When it reaches a value greater than or equal to the dividing-line value, it stops. The arrow J is moved backward through the list as long as it points to a value greater than the dividing-line value. When it reaches a value less than or equal to the dividing-line value, it stops. Since the dividing-line value for the example is 7, moving arrow I gives us

```
3 9 6 5 7 4 1 2 8
  ↑           ↑
  I           J
```

and moving arrow J gives us:

```
3 9 6 5 7 4 1 2 8
  ↑         ↑
  I         J
```

The values pointed to by I and J are exchanged

```
3 2 6 5 7 4 1 9 8
  ↑         ↑
  I         J
```

after which I is moved forward one position and J is moved backward one position:

```
3 2 6 5 7 4 1 9 8
    ↑       ↑
    I       J
```

This process is repeated: I is moved forward until it encounters a value too large for the first sublist, and J is moved backward until it encounters a value too small for the second sublist.:

```
3 2 6 5 7 4 1 9 8
        ↑ ↑
        I J
```

(Note that J does not move since it is already pointing to a value too small for the second sublist.) Again, we exchange the values:

```
3 2 6 5 1 4 7 9 8
        ↑ ↑
        I J
```

and move I forward one place and J backward one place:

```
3 2 6 5 1 4 7 9 8
          ↑
          I
          J
```

Once more, we move I forward and J backward in search of out-of-place values. Again, the position of J doesn't change since it is already pointing to a value too small for the second sublist:

```
3 2 6 5 1 4 7 9 8
          ↑ ↑
          J I
```

But at this point, the two arrows have passed each other, which signals that our job is done. Everything from the beginning of the list through the value pointed to by J constitutes the first sublist, and everything from the value pointed to by I through the end of the list constitutes the second sublist. Thus we divide our original list as follows:

```
3 2 6 5 1 4     7 9 8
          ↑     ↑
          J     I
```

Finally, the same process is applied to each of the sublists, which we do by calling the Quicksort routine recursively.

Figure 10–7 shows the procedure QUICKSORT. The parameters FIRST and LAST are the indices of the first and last components of the list or sublist to be sorted. Corresponding to the arrows in our examples, the indices I and J are used to locate out-of-place values. DIVIDINGLINE holds the dividing-line value. We begin by setting I to point to the first component of the list to be sorted and J to the last component:

```
I := FIRST;
J := LAST
```

DIVIDINGLINE is set to the middle value on the list to be sorted:

```
DIVIDINGLINE := LIST[(FIRST + LAST) DIV 2];
```

We can outline the rest the procedure as follows:

```
REPEAT
    "Move I forward as long as LIST[I] is
    less than DIVIDINGLINE"
    "Move J backward as long as LIST[J] is
    greater than DIVIDINGLINE"
    IF I <= J THEN
        "Exchange the values of LIST[I] and LIST[J].
        Move I forward one place and J backward one
        place"
UNTIL I > J;
"If FIRST is less than J, call QUICKSORT to sort the
 sublist LIST[FIRST] through LIST[J]. If I is less
 than LAST, call QUICKSORT to sort the sublist LIST[I]
 through LIST[LAST]"
```

```
PROCEDURE QUICKSORT(FIRST, LAST: INTEGER);
VAR
   I, J, DIVIDINGLINE, TEMPORARY: INTEGER;
BEGIN
   I := FIRST;
   J := LAST;
   DIVIDINGLINE := LIST[(FIRST + LAST) DIV 2];
   REPEAT
      WHILE LIST[I] < DIVIDINGLINE DO
         I := I + 1;
      WHILE LIST[J] > DIVIDINGLINE DO
         J := J - 1;
      IF I <= J THEN
         BEGIN
            TEMPORARY := LIST[I];
            LIST[I] := LIST[J];
            LIST[J] := TEMPORARY;
            I := I + 1;
            J := J - 1
         END
   UNTIL I > J;
   IF FIRST < J THEN QUICKSORT(FIRST, J);
   IF I < LAST THEN QUICKSORT(I, LAST)
END
```

FIGURE 10-7. This Quicksort procedure calls itself recursively in two places.

This version of Quicksort contains two recursive calls to QUICK-
SORT. Recursion is less efficient than repetition, because for each
procedure call there is the overhead of passing parameter values and
setting up a memory area for the local variables. Also, some languages
do not permit recursion. Therefore, we will improve the usefulness of
Quicksort if we can reduce the amount of recursion or eliminate it altogether. We can eliminate one of the recursive calls in QUICKSORT easily; eliminating the other will take more work.

A recursive call made by the last statement of a procedure is called
a *tail recursion*. We can always eliminate a tail recursion by repeating
the body of the procedure instead of calling the procedure recursively.
In QUICKSORT we can replace

```
"Everything up to the last line of QUICKSORT"
IF I < LAST THEN QUICKSORT(I, LAST)
```

by

```
REPEAT
   "Everything up to the last line of QUICKSORT"
   FIRST := I
UNTIL FIRST >= LAST
```

That is, instead of calling QUICKSORT with I as the actual parameter corresponding to the formal parameter FIRST, we just set FIRST to the value of I and repeat the statements of QUICKSORT. The condition FIRST >= LAST in the REPEAT statement serves the same purpose as the condition I < LAST in the IF statement. Both make sure that the procedure does not attempt to sort one-component sublists.

Figure 10-8 shows the procedure QUICKSRT, which is QUICK-SORT with the tail recursion eliminated. The statement

```
I := FIRST
```

was moved out of the repetition, since at the end of each repetition the values of I and FIRST are equal (why?). Therefore, this statement only needs to be executed once, at the beginning of the procedure.

Eliminating the remaining recursion takes more work. The problem is this. At the point where the recursive call is made, the values of FIRST and J are the limits of a sublist that needs to be sorted. If we go on with the procedure and do not make the recursive call, the values of

```
PROCEDURE QUICKSRT(FIRST, LAST: INTEGER);
VAR
    I, J, DIVIDINGLINE, TEMPORARY: INTEGER;
BEGIN
    I := FIRST;
    REPEAT
        J := LAST;
        DIVIDINGLINE := LIST[(FIRST + LAST) DIV 2];
        REPEAT
            WHILE LIST[I] < DIVIDINGLINE DO
                I := I + 1;
            WHILE LIST[J] > DIVIDINGLINE DO
                J := J - 1;
            IF I <= J THEN
                BEGIN
                    TEMPORARY := LIST[I];
                    LIST[I] := LIST[J];
                    LIST[J] := TEMPORARY;
                    I := I + 1;
                    J := J - 1
                END
        UNTIL I > J;
        IF FIRST < J THEN QUICKSRT(FIRST, J);
        FIRST := I
    UNTIL FIRST >= LAST
END
```

FIGURE 10-8. This Quicksort procedure was obtained from the one in Figure 10-7 by eliminating the tail recursion—the recursive call at the end of the procedure.

FIRST and J will be changed. Therefore, the values of FIRST and J have to be saved so the sublist can be sorted later.

We can save the values of FIRST and J using a data structure known as a *stack*. As with ordinary stacks, such as stacks of books or papers, we place items on top of the stack and remove items from the top. The stack is represented by a list of values together with the index of the last value on the list. The last value on the list is the top value on the stack. If we place a new value on top of the stack, it is added to the end of the list and becomes the new last value. If we remove an item from the top of the stack, the last value on the list is removed.

Figure 10–4, the program for testing sorting routines, contains declarations for an array STACK to hold the values on a stack and an index TOP to designate the current top value on the stack:

```
STACK: ARRAY[1..50] OF INTEGER;
TOP: 0..50;
```

We can visualize a stack containing four values like this:

```
      1
      10
      11
TOP → 18
```

To put a new value on top of the stack, we add it to the end of the list. First, we move TOP forward one place so that it points to an unused position:

```
TOP := TOP + 1
```

Now, we assign the value we want to put on the stack to STACK[TOP]:

```
STACK[TOP] := 19
```

The stack now looks like this:

```
      1
      10
      11
      18
TOP → 19
```

To remove a value from the top of the stack, we first assign the value of STACK[TOP] to the variable that is to receive the value removed:

```
I := STACK[TOP]
```

The value assigned to I is 19. Now, we move TOP back one position so that it points to the current top value:

```
TOP := TOP - 1
```

These operations leave the stack looking like this:

```
        1
       10
       11
TOP →  18
```

Figure 10-9 shows the procedure QUIKSORT, a nonrecursive version of Quicksort. The stack declared in the testing program (Figure 10-4) is used to hold the indices delimiting the sublists that have yet to be sorted. Thus, at the beginning of the procedure, 1 and SIZE, which delimit the entire list, are placed on the stack:

```
STACK[1] := 1;
STACK[2] := SIZE;
TOP := 2
```

At the point in QUICKSRT where QUICKSRT is called recursively to sort a sublist:

```
IF FIRST < J THEN QUICKSRT(FIRST, J)
```

QUIKSORT saves the values of FIRST and J on the stack so the procedure can come back and sort the sublist later:

```
IF FIRST < J THEN
    BEGIN
        TOP := TOP + 1;
        STACK[TOP] := FIRST;
        TOP := TOP + 1;
        STACK[TOP] := J
    END
```

The procedure operates in a cycle, each repetition of which removes a pair of indices from the stack and processes the corresponding sublist. The repetition continues until the stack is empty (the value of TOP equals 0), thus assuring that all sublists whose limits are saved on the stack are eventually processed:

```
REPEAT
    LAST := STACK[TOP];
    TOP := TOP - 1;
    FIRST := STACK[TOP];
    TOP := TOP - 1
    "Process the list or sublist
    LIST[FIRST] through LIST[LAST]"
UNTIL TOP = 0
```

This example illustrates another use of recursion—as a step in designing a program. Our first recursive version of Quicksort was straightforward to construct and to understand. The final nonrecursive version

```
PROCEDURE QUIKSORT;
VAR
   I, J, DIVIDINGLINE, TEMPORARY,
   FIRST, LAST: INTEGER;
BEGIN
   STACK[1] := 1;
   STACK[2] := SIZE;
   TOP := 2;
   REPEAT
      LAST := STACK[TOP];
      TOP := TOP - 1;
      FIRST := STACK[TOP];
      TOP := TOP - 1;
      I := FIRST;
      REPEAT
         J := LAST;
         DIVIDINGLINE := LIST[(FIRST + LAST) DIV 2];
         REPEAT
            WHILE LIST[I] < DIVIDINGLINE DO
               I := I + 1;
            WHILE LIST[J] > DIVIDINGLINE DO
               J := J - 1;
            IF I <= J THEN
               BEGIN
                  TEMPORARY := LIST[I];
                  LIST[I] := LIST[J];
                  LIST[J] := TEMPORARY;
                  I := I + 1;
                  J := J - 1
               END
         UNTIL I > J;
         IF FIRST < J THEN
            BEGIN
               TOP := TOP + 1;
               STACK[TOP] := FIRST;
               TOP := TOP + 1;
               STACK[TOP] := J
            END;
         FIRST := I
      UNTIL FIRST >= LAST
   UNTIL TOP = 0
END
```

FIGURE 10-9. This Quiksort procedure was obtained from the one in Figure 10-8 by eliminating the remaining recursion.

is much more complex and would be hard to construct from scratch. But by starting with the recursive version and modifying it to remove the recursion, we didn't have too much trouble arriving at the nonrecursive version. To put it another way, recursion is a useful way of *thinking* about algorithms even if the function or procedure that we finally arrive at turns out to be nonrecursive.

Exercises

1. In Exercise 6 of Chapter 6 we considered a business supply house that priced typewriter ribbons as follows:

Quantity Ordered	Price per Dozen Ribbons
1 dozen	$27
2–4 dozen	$26
5–9 dozen	$24
10 dozen or more	$21

Our task was to write a program that would input how many dozen ribbons a customer orders and output the price per dozen ribbons and the total cost of the order. This differs from the price-list-lookup problem considered in this chapter in that each entry in the column to be searched consists of a range of values instead of a single value.

We can represent the information in this table in two parallel arrays, QUANTITY and PRICE:

```
QUANTITY      PRICE
    1          27
    4          26
    9          24
 sentinel      21
```

QUANTITY gives the upper limit of each quantity range. The lower limit of a range need not be given, since it is just one more than the upper limit of the preceding range. The last component of QUANTITY is used to store a sentinel, which is simply the value being searched for —the number of dozens of ribbons actually ordered. Modify the sequential search procedure so that it will search this kind of table. Given the number of dozens ordered, the procedure will return the price per dozen. Rewrite the program called for in Exercise 6 of Chapter 6 to use arrays and sequential search.

2. When you went to Switzerland last year you visited a chocolate factory and fell helplessly in love with their praline chocolates. You brought back with you an input file containing their recipes, and you have since added to the file the numbers of each kind of praline that you would like to make. Write a program to calculate and print your shopping list for the ingredients.

The format of the first part of the input file is one line per kind of praline. (Some of the pralines made are gianduja, hazelnut, almond, nougat, and truffles—milk chocolate and dark.) Each line contains the name of a kind of praline in twelve characters, followed by eight real numbers, each representing the quantity in grams of each of the ingredients required to make one praline of a particular kind. The ingredients are sugar, chocolate liqueur, cocoa butter, cream, lecithin, hazelnuts, almonds, and nougat. The first part of the input file is terminated by a line that contains only one blank. Then comes another series of lines, each containing the name of a praline, but this time with only one integer following the name. The integer represents the number of pralines of a particular kind that you want to make.

3. When binary search is used with the price-list program of Figure 10-1, the item numbers must be in numerical order. Modify the program to read a price list with the item numbers in any order and then sort the price list so that the item numbers are in numerical order. Use the Shell sort. Don't forget that when you exchange two components of ITEMNO, you must also exchange the corresponding components of PRICE.

4. To compute the *median* of a list of numbers, we first arrange the values in numerical order. If the number of values is odd, the middle value of the sorted list is the median. If the number of values is even, the median is the average of the two middle values. Write a program to read in a list of numbers and print out its median.

5. The *percentile rank* of a student in a class in the percentage of students in the class who received lower grades than the student in question. Write a program to read in the names and grades of the students in a class and print the names, grades, and percentile ranks. Note that students who receive the same grade must have the same percentile rank; your data should include some students with identical grades.

6. Modify the program of Exercise 5 so that when it prints the names, grades, and percentile ranks, the names of the students are in alphabetical order.

7. When the sublist being sorted contains less than ten values, Quicksort becomes inefficient because of the overhead of calling procedures or manipulating the stack. For short lists a low-overhead sorting method such as the bubble sort would do a better job. Therefore, modify Quicksort (any version) as follows: (a) the Quicksort routine will not attempt to sort sublists of less than ten components—these will be treated as the present routines treat one-component sublists. (b) After Quicksort finishes, the sorting will be completed by making nine compare-and-exchange passes over the entire list. Why can we be sure that nine compare-and-exchange passes are sufficient?

8. Many computer systems allow a Pascal program to read the computer's internal clock. Modify the sort-testing routine (Figure 10-4) so that it reads the clock immediately before and after calling the sorting procedure. After the sorted values have been printed, the program should calculate and print the time required by the sort. Use this program to explore the relative speeds of the bubble sort, the Shell sort, and the three versions of Quicksort. How do these speeds depend on the length of the list being sorted?

9. Write a recursive binary-search procedure. After the procedure divides the not-yet-searched part of the list in half and selects one of the halves for further searching, it should call itself to search the selected half.

10. Using the techniques discussed in this chapter, remove the tail recursion from the procedure we wrote in Chapter 7 to solve the Towers of Hanoi problem. Describe how the modified procedure manipulates the disks.

Chapter 11

STRUCTURED TYPES: RECORDS

Arrays have two outstanding characteristics (1) All the components of an array are of the same data type. (2) The index used to refer to particular component of an array can be computed during the execution of the program—at "execution time."

A *record* is the opposite of an array in both these respects. The components of a record (known as *fields*) can be of different data types and usually are. And the *field identifiers* by which record components are referenced cannot be computed at execution time but must be specified when the program is written.

We use words such as "list," "table", and "book" to help us visualize arrays. For records the word "record" itself should suffice, for it brings to mind the collections of diverse information found in school records, employment records, medical records, and the like. A record in Pascal is just such a collection of different kinds of data.

Record Definitions

The following example illustrates the definition of a record type:

```
TYPE
   WEATHER = RECORD
                SKY: (CLOUDY, PTLYCLDY, CLEAR);
                PRECIP: (RAIN, SNOW, SLEET, HAIL, NONE);
                LOW,
                HIGH: INTEGER
             END;
```

WEATHER is the record type being defined. The identifiers SKY, PRECIP, LOW, and HIGH are the field identifiers, which are used to refer to the components of a value of type WEATHER.

For example, suppose U, V, and W are variables of type WEATHER:

```
VAR
    U, V, W: WEATHER;
```

W names a memory location that holds a value of type WEATHER. This memory location is made up of four smaller locations, one for each component of a value of type WEATHER:

W

CLOUDY
RAIN
50
75

We can refer to particular components of the value of W as follows. The variable name W is followed by a period and the appropriate field identifier. The result, known as a *field designator*, names the location holding the corresponding component. Thus the locations making up W are named as follows:

W.SKY	CLOUDY
W.PRECIP	RAIN
W.LOW	50
W.HIGH	75

The field designators can be used just like any other variables. For instance,

```
W.SKY := PTLYCLDY
```

changes the contents of W. SKY to PTLCLDY,

```
WRITELN(W.LOW)
```

causes the computer to print 50, and

```
I := W.HIGH - W.LOW
```

assigns 25 to I.

Note that the field designator

```
W.SKY
```

is similar to the indexed variable

```
A[3]
```

The record variable W corresponds to the array variable A. The period in the field designator corresponds to the brackets in the indexed variable. And the field identifier SKY corresponds to the index 3.

On the other hand, keep in mind the differences between field designators and indexed variables. The indexed variables of an array all have the same type. The field designators of a record generally have different types. The index of an indexed variable can be computed by the program. The field identifier of a field designator must be specified when the program is written.

As was the case for array variables, the value of one record variable can be assigned to another record variable provided the two record variables are of the same type. Thus,

```
V := W
```

is valid and equivalent to:

```
V.SKY := W.SKY;
V.PRECIP := W.PRECIP;
V.LOW := W.LOW;
V.HIGH := W.HIGH
```

The following are other examples of record type definitions:

```
EMPLOYEE = RECORD
              SSNUMBER: PACKED ARRAY[1..9] OF CHAR;
              NAME,
              ADDRESS: PACKED ARRAY[1..40] OF CHAR;
              PAYRATE: REAL;
              MSTATUS: (SINGLE, MARRIED, DIVORCED);
              NUMDEPENDENTS: INTEGER
           END;
CAR = RECORD
         MAKE,
         MODEL,
         BODYTYPE,
         COLOR: PACKED ARRAY[1..10] OF CHAR;
         WEIGHT: INTEGER
      END;
BOOK = RECORD
          TITLE: PACKED ARRAY[1..80] OF CHAR;
          AUTHOR,
          PUBLISHER,
          CITY: PACKED ARRAY[1..20] OF CHAR;
          YEAR: INTEGER;
          PRICE: REAL
       END;
```

```
PASSENGER = RECORD
                NAME: PACKED ARRAY[1..20] OF CHAR;
                FLIGHT,
                SEAT: PACKED ARRAY[1..4] OF CHAR;
                PHONENO: PACKED ARRAY[1..10] OF CHAR
            END;
DATE = RECORD
            MONTH: (JAN, FEB, MAR, APR, MAY, JUNE,
                    JULY, AUG, SEPT, OCT, NOV, DEC);
            DAYOFWEEK: (MON, TUE, WED, THURS, FRI, SAT, SUN);
            DAYOFMONTH: 1..31;
            YEAR: INTEGER
        END;
FRACTION = RECORD
                NUMERATOR,
                DENOMINATOR: INTEGER
            END;
COMPLEX = RECORD
                REALPT,
                IMAGPT: REAL
            END;
```

Nested Records

It's possible for a field of a record to itself be another record. For example, suppose we define the record type DAY as follows:

```
DAY = RECORD
          DT: DATE;
          WX: WEATHER
      END;
```

A value of type DAY has as its fields values of type DATE and WEATHER. Since DATE and WEATHER are themselves record types, a record of type DAY contains records of types DATE and WEATHER.

For example, suppose we declare:

```
VAR
    TODAY: DAY;
```

Then TODAY.DT and TODAY.WX are variables of types DATE and WEATHER. To refer to the fields of the values of TODAY.DT and TODAY.WX, we must append an additional field identifier:

```
TODAY.DT.MONTH
TODAY.DT.DAYOFMONTH
TODAY.DT.DAYOFWEEK
TODAY.DT.YEAR
```

```
TODAY.WX.SKY
TODAY.WX.PRECIP
TODAY.WX.LOW
TODAY.WX.HIGH
```

We can use these field designators to assign values to the fields of TO-
DAY. For example:

```
TODAY.DT.MONTH := MAY;
TODAY.DT.DAYOFMONTH := 24;
TODAY.DT.DAYOFWEEK := THURS;
TODAY.DT.YEAR := 1982;
TODAY.WX.SKY := CLOUDY:
TODAY.WX.PRECIP := RAIN;
TODAY.WX.LOW := 55;
TODAY.WX.HIGH := 75
```

We can think of TODAY as being laid out in memory as follows:

TODAY.DT.MONTH	MAY
TODAY.DT.DAYOFMONTH	24
TODAY.DT.DAYOFWEEK	THURS
TODAY.DT.YEAR	1982
TODAY.WX.SKY	CLOUDY
TODAY.WX.PRECIP	RAIN
TODAY.WX.LOW	55
TODAY.WX.HIGH	75

It isn't necessary for nested records to be defined as separate data
types. For example, declarations like the following are permitted:

```
VAR
    PERSON: RECORD
                NAME: RECORD
                        FIRST,
                        MIDDLE,
                        LAST: PACKED ARRAY[1..20] OF CHAR
                    END;
                ADDR: RECORD
                        STREET,
                        CITY: PACKED ARRAY[1..40] OF CHAR;
                        STATE: PACKED ARRAY[1..2] OF CHAR;
                        ZIP: PACKED ARRAY[1..5] OF CHAR
                    END
            END;
```

We can use the following field designators to refer to the fields of the
value of PERSON:

```
PERSON.NAME
PERSON.ADDR
PERSON.NAME.FIRST
PERSON.NAME.MIDDLE
PERSON.NAME.LAST
PERSON.ADDR.STREET
PERSON.ADDR.CITY
PERSON.ADDR.STATE
PERSON.ADDR.ZIP
```

The WITH Statement. Field designators can get to be rather cumbersome, particularly when the fields of one record are themselves records, forcing us to use a long string of field identifiers to specify the field that we want to refer to.

Another problem arises when we refer to different fields of the same record. For example, suppose the array REPORT is declared as follows:

```
REPORT: ARRAY[1..7] OF WEATHER;
```

When we refer to REPORT[I], the computer has to do a calculation to determine which memory location holds the record corresponding to the value of I. When we refer to

```
REPORT[I].SKY
REPORT[I].PRECIP
REPORT[I].LOW
REPORT[I].HIGH
```

the computer will probably do the calculation for locating REPORT[I] four times, once to refer to the SKY field, once to refer to the PRECIP field, and so on. We need some way of telling the computer to locate a record once and then remember its location while referring to its fields.

The WITH statement allows us to refer to the fields of a record using the field identifiers alone. We can refer to a field deep within a nested set of records without having to write a long string of field identifiers. And the computer only needs to locate a record once, no matter how many references we make to its fields. For example, let's use a WITH statement to assign values to the fields of W:

```
WITH W DO
   BEGIN
      SKY := CLOUDY;
      PRECIP := RAIN;
      LOW := 55;
      HIGH := 75
   END
```

Putting the assignments in the WITH statement takes the place of prefixing every field identifier with

W.

We can use the same technique for REPORT[I]:

```
WITH REPORT[I] DO
    BEGIN
        SKY := CLEAR;
        PRECIP := NONE;
        LOW := 28;
        HIGH := 45
    END
```

The WITH statement tells the computer to locate the record REPORT[I] and remember its location. The record does not have to be located again each time a value is assigned to one of its fields.

We can list more than one record variable in a WITH statement and then refer to the fields of all the record variables listed. This feature is particularly useful when dealing with nested records. For example, consider the record variable TODAY of type DAY, which we discussed earlier. To refer to the fields of TODAY, TODAY.DT, and TODAY.WX, we use a WITH statement beginning with:

```
WITH TODAY, DT, WX DO
```

Notice that once TODAY has been listed, the computer will place the prefix TODAY. before field identifiers when necessary. Therefore, we need only list DT and WX instead of TODAY.DT and TODAY.WX. The assignments illustrated in the previous section can be made as follows:

```
WITH TODAY, DT, WX DO
    BEGIN
        MONTH := MAY;
        DAYOFMONTH := 24;
        DAYOFWEEK := THURS;
        YEAR := 1982;
        SKY := CLOUDY;
        PRECIP := RAIN;
        LOW := 55;
        HIGH := 75
    END
```

Record Variants

Sometimes we want to consider record values to be of the same type even though they have different structures. Pascal allows a record to have a *variant part*, which can have different structures for different records of the same type.

For example, a bibliography usually contains references to both books and magazine articles. But references to books have a different form than references to articles. For a book the author, title, city of publication, publisher, and year of publication are given. For an article we need the author, the title of the article, the name of the magazine, the month and year of publication, and the pages on which the article begins and ends.

Since the author, title, and year of publication are the same for both books and articles, they will always be present. But the city of publication and the publisher will be present only in references to books. The magazine name, the month of publication, and the beginning and ending pages will be present only in references to articles.

We also need some way of distinguishing references to books from references to articles, so the program can determine the structure of the value it is dealing with. For this purpose, let's define a type

```
REFTYPE = (BOOK, ARTICLE);
```

whose values we will use to distinguish the two kinds of references.

We define a type REFERENCE, which includes references to both books and articles, as follows:

```
REFERENCE = RECORD
              AUTHOR: PACKED ARRAY[1..40] OF CHAR;
              TITLE: PACKED ARRAY[1..80] OF CHAR;
              YEAR: INTEGER;
              CASE KIND: REFTYPE OF
                BOOK: (CITY: PACKED ARRAY[1..20] OF CHAR;
                       PUBLISHER: PACKED ARRAY[1..10] OF CHAR);
                ARTICLE: (NAME PACKED ARRAY[1..20] OF CHAR;
                          MONTH: (JAN, FEB, MAR, APR, MAY, JUN,
                                  JULY, AUG, SEPT, OCT, NOV, DEC);
                          PAGES: PACKED ARRAY[1..7] OF CHAR)
            END;
```

The record has a *fixed part*, which is the same for every value of type REFERENCE, and a *variant part*, which is different for different values of type REFERENCE. The fixed part always comes first in the record definition, followed by the variant part, if any. Everything through

```
CASE KIND: REFTYPE OF
```

belongs to the fixed part of the record. Everything following belongs to the variant part.

All values of type REFERENCE have fields AUTHOR, TITLE, YEAR, and KIND. But some values have fields CITY and PUBLISHER, and others have fields NAME, MONTH, and PAGES. The field KIND, the one that occurs between CASE and OF, is called the *tag field*. Its value determines which structure a particular value has. If the value of KIND is BOOK, a program processing the record knows it is dealing with a reference to a book. If the value of KIND is ARTICLE, the program knows it is dealing with a reference to a magazine article.

The possible values of the tag field are used to label the variant parts of a record:

```
BOOK: ("Variant part for a book reference");
ARTICLE: ("Variant part for an article reference")
```

Each variant part is enclosed in parentheses.

Thus, for a reference to a book the value of KIND is BOOK, and the record has the same structure as if it had been defined as

```
RECORD
    AUTHOR: PACKED ARRAY[1..40] OF CHAR;
    TITLE: PACKED ARRAY[1..80] OF CHAR;
    YEAR: INTEGER;
    KIND: REFTYP;
    CITY: PACKED ARRAY[1..20] OF CHAR;
    PUBLISHER: PACKED ARRAY[1..10] OF CHAR
END
```

For a reference to a magazine article the value of KIND is ARTICLE, and the record has the same structure as if it had been defined as

```
RECORD
    AUTHOR: PACKED ARRAY[1..40] OF CHAR;
    TITLE: PACKED ARRAY[1..80] OF CHAR;
    YEAR: INTEGER;
    KIND: REFTYPE;
    NAME: PACKED ARRAY[1..20] OF CHAR;
    MONTH: (JAN, FEB, MAR, APR, MAY, JUN,
            JULY, AUG, SEPT, OCT, NOV, DEC);
    PAGES: PACKED ARRAY[1..7] OF CHAR
END
```

It's not necessary for the record to contain a tag field. If there is no tag field, no field of the record specifies what structure the record has, and a program processing the record must get this information elsewhere. For example, we could define the type REFERENCE without the tag field KIND:

```
REFERENCE = RECORD
        AUTHOR: PACKED ARRAY[1..40] OF CHAR;
        TITLE: PACKED ARRAY[1..80] OF CHAR;
        YEAR: INTEGER;
        CASE REFTYPE OF
            BOOK: (CITY: PACKED ARRAY[1..20] OF CHAR;
                    PUBLISHER: PACKED ARRAY[1..10] OF CHAR);
            ARTICLE: (NAME: PACKED ARRAY[1..20] OF CHAR;
                    MONTH: (JAN, FEB, MAR, APR, MAY, JUN,
                            JULY, AUG, SEPT, OCT, NOV, DEC);
                    PAGES: PACKED ARRAY[1..7] OF CHAR)
    END;
```

With this definition a value of type REFERENCE can consist of the fields AUTHOR, TITLE, YEAR, CITY, and PUBLISHER or the fields AUTHOR, TITLE, YEAR, NAME, MONTH, and PAGES. It's up to the program to know which structure a particular value has. The line

```
CASE REFTYPE OF
```

indicates that values of type REFTYPE are used to label the variant parts in the record definition. However, no field is declared to be of type REFTYPE.

The Scopes of Field Identifiers

The scope of a field identifier is the record in which the corresponding field is defined. When record definitions are nested, the scope of each field identifier is the *smallest* record containing the definition of the corresponding field.

This means that the same field identifier can be used in different records:

```
VAR
    U: RECORD
           A,
           B: INTEGER
       END;
    V: RECORD
           A,
           B: REAL
       END;
```

There is no difficulty in distinguishing the field identifiers of the different records:

```
U.A := 5;
U.B := 25;
V.A := 7.2;
V.B := 6.3
```

The integer values are assigned to the fields of the record variable U; the real values are assigned to the fields of the record variable V. The same statements could also have been written:

```
WITH U DO
   BEGIN
      A := 5;
      B := 25
   END;
```

```
WITH V DO
   BEGIN
      A := 7.2;
      B := 6.3
   END
```

It's also possible to use the same identifiers for variable names and field identifiers:

```
VAR
   A, B: BOOLEAN;
   U: RECORD
         A, B: INTEGER
      END;
   V: RECORD
         A, B: REAL
      END;
```

With these declarations, the following statements are valid:

```
A := TRUE;      B := FALSE;
U.A := 5;       U.B := 25;
V.A := 7.2;     V.B := 6.3
```

These statements could also be written:

```
A := TRUE;      B := FALSE;
WITH U DO
   BEGIN
      A := 5;      B := 25
   END;
WITH V DO
   BEGIN
      A := 7.2;      B := 6.3
   END
```

Note that the field identifiers in the variant part of a record all have the same scope. Therefore, it is *not* permissible to use the same identifier in different variants. For example, we are sometimes tempted to make incorrect declarations like the following:

```
U: RECORD
      A: INTEGER;
      CASE B: BOOLEAN OF
         TRUE: (C: INTEGER);
         FALSE: (C: REAL)
   END;
```

The idea is to let C be an integer field when the value of B is TRUE and a real field when the value of B is FALSE. But this doesn't work since both Cs have the same scope, so their definitions conflict. We must use different identifiers for the integer field and the real field:

```
U: RECORD
       A: INTEGER;
       CASE B: BOOLEAN OF
           TRUE: (CI: INTEGER);
           FALSE: (CR: REAL)
   END;
```

This way, the computer always knows that U.CI represents an integer value and U.CR represents a real value. If our previous declaration had been allowed, the computer would not have been able to tell whether U.C represented an integer or a real value.

It's worth repeating here what has already been said in connection with functions and procedures: Just because Pascal sometimes allows us to use the same name for different things does not mean that we should do so without good reason.

Pointer Types

The variables we have dealt with so far are said to be *static*, since they are declared when the program is written and remain in existence throughout the execution of the block in which they are declared. Although the values of such variables can be changed as the program executes, no program statement can create a new static variable or dispose of one that is no longer needed.

The problem with static variables is that we often don't know in advance how much memory a program will need. We would like to write the program in such a way that it can create new variables when they are needed. It should also be able to dispose variables that are no longer needed, leaving the corresponding memory locations free to be reused when new variables are created. Variables that can be created and disposed of as a program executes are called *dynamic variables*.

Since a dynamic variable is not declared when the program is written, there is no identifier that we can use to refer to it. Instead, the procedure that creates a dynamic variable returns the address of the corresponding memory location. Such a memory address is called a *pointer*, since it designates or "points to" a particular memory location. To deal with dynamic variables, we need two things: (1) data types whose values are pointers, and (2) a mechanism for referring to a memory location designated by the value of a pointer.

We denote a pointer type by prefixing a type identifier with an upward arrow. The type identifier gives the type of variables that can be pointed to by values of the pointer type. Thus

```
↑INTEGER
```

is the type whose values are pointers to integer variables, and

↑REAL

is the data type whose values are pointers to real variables. On some systems a circumflex is used in place of the upward arrow.

The declaration

```
VAR
    P: ↑INTEGER;
```

specifies that the value of P is a pointer to a variable of type *integer*. To denote the variable pointed to, we follow the pointer variable by an upward arrow, so

```
P↑
```

denotes the variable pointed to by the value of P. Thus,

```
P↑ := 25
```

assigns 25 to the variable pointed to by the value of P, and

```
I := P↑
```

assigns to I the value of the variable pointed to by the value of P.

It's often convenient to draw diagrams in which a pointer value is represented by an arrow extending from the pointer variable to the variable being pointed to. Figure 11–1 uses such a diagram to illustrate the relationship between P and P↑.

A standard procedure NEW creates new dynamic variables. For example,

```
NEW (P)
```

creates a new integer variable and assigns its address to P. The statement

```
P↑ := 5
```

assigns the value 5 to the newly created variable.

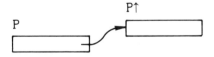

FIGURE 11–1. **In diagrams a pointer value is represented by an arrow. The arrow extends from inside the variable holding the pointer value to the variable being pointed to. If P is the variable holding the pointer variable, then P↑ denotes the variable pointed to.**

When a dynamic variable is no longer needed, we can use the procedure DISPOSE to free the memory space allocated to the variable. The statement

```
DISPOSE(P)
```

informs the system that the variable pointed to by the value of P is no longer needed. We must take care never to attempt to use a pointer value after the variable to which it points has been disposed of.

UCSD Pascal does not have the proceduure DISPOSE but provides instead a less general and less useful method of reusing memory locations that are no longer needed. Since the method used in UCSD Pascal is not used in most other versions of Pascal, it will not be discussed here.

We sometimes need a pointer value that does not point to any variable. Such a value is represented by the reserved word NIL. After the assignment

```
P := NIL
```

the value of P does not point to any variable. The expression P↑ is meaningless when the value of P is NIL. NIL is often used as a sentinel value in processing dynamic variables.

We rarely use dynamic variables of simple types such as INTEGER and REAL. Usually, dynamic variables are record variables. Each record represents some real-world entity such as a person or an inventory item. A program creates new dynamic variables when it is given new entities to deal with and disposes of dynamic variables that are no longer needed when it is relieved of responsibility for some entities. Frequently, some fields of the value of a dynamic variable contain pointers to other dynamic variables, allowing records for different entities to refer to one another by means of pointers.

Binary Trees.   As an example of the use of pointers and dynamic variables, we will see how to create and process a data structure called a *binary tree*. In Chapter 10 we saw that binary search is highly efficient, but the list to be searched has to be in alphabetical or numerical order. If new values are added to the list, they must be inserted in the proper position in alphabetical or numerical order, and other values must be moved to make room for them. If values are deleted from the list, other values must be moved to close up the gaps left by the deleted values. A binary tree allows us to use a form of the highly efficient binary search but with our data stored in dynamic variables that we can create and dispose of at will.

Figure 11–2 shows a binary tree. The circled numbers are called *nodes;* the lines connecting the nodes are called *branches.* The tree is drawn upside down compared to the trees found in nature, so the topmost node is the *root* of the tree and the bottommost nodes are the *leaves.* The nodes below a given node and connected to it by branches are said to be *children* of the given node. (For example, nodes 430 and

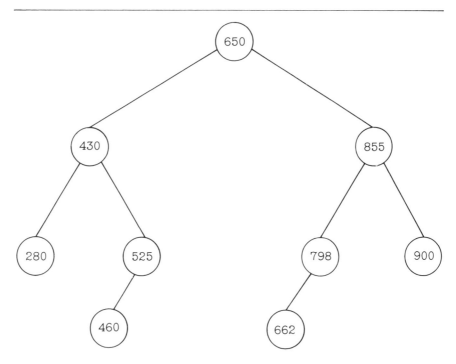

FIGURE 11-2. A binary search tree. At each node, we compare the number we are searching for with the number in the node. If the number we are searching for is less than the number in the node, we follow the left branch leaving the node. If the number we are searching for is greater, we follow the right branch. If the number we are searching for equals the number in the node, then we have found the node we are looking for. If the left or right branch we are to follow does not exist, then the number we are looking for is not in the tree.

855 are the children of node 650.) The child to the lower left of a node is its *left child*; the child to the lower right is its *right child*. No node may have more than two children. On the other hand, one or both of the children may be missing. A leaf can be defined more precisely as a node with no children.

The numbers in the nodes are values to be looked up. That is, we are going to search the tree for the node containing a particular number. To make the search as efficient as possible, the binary tree is constructed so that it has the following property. If we follow the left branch descending from a node, we can only reach nodes with smaller numbers than the node we started from. If we follow the right branch descending from a node, we can only reach nodes with larger numbers than the node we started from.

For example, if we take the left branch from node 650, we can eventually reach nodes 280, 430, 460, and 525, all of which have smaller numbers than node 650. On the other hand, if we follow the right branch from node 650, we can eventually reach nodes 662, 798, 855, and 900, all of which have larger numbers than node 650. The same situation holds for all the other nodes. For example, if we take the left branch from node 430, we reach node 280. If we take the right branch, we can reach nodes 460 and 525.

This property provides us with a simple and efficient method of searching a binary tree. Starting at the root, we compare the number we are searching for with the number of the root. If the two are equal, we have found the node we are searching for and can stop. If the number we are searching for is less than the number of the root, we take the left branch leaving the root, the branch that leads to lower-numbered nodes. If the number we are searching for is greater than the number of the root, we take the right branch, the one that leads to higher-numbered nodes. We repeat this process for each node we encounter until we reach the node we are looking for. If we try to take a left or right branch and find that no such branch exits, then the number we are looking for is not in the tree.

For example, suppose we are trying to find node 460. Starting from the root, we take the left branch, since 460 is less than 650. From node 430 we take the right branch, since 460 is greater than 430. From node 525 we take the left branch, since 460 is less than 525. The left branch from node 525 leads to node 460, the node we are seeking.

On the other hand, suppose we are trying to find node 300. Again, we take the left branch from the root, since 300 is less than 650. From node 430 we take the left branch, since 300 is less than 430. From 280 we try to take the right branch, since 300 is greater than 280. However, there is no right branch leaving node 280, so node 300 is not in the tree.

Let's see how to store a price list as a binary tree. Each entry on the price list will be stored in a separate node. Each node will contain the number of an item, its price, and pointers to the node's two children. If a particular child is not present, the value of the corresponding pointer will be NIL. We define two types, LINK and NODE:

```
TYPE
    LINK = ↑NODE;
    NODE = RECORD
              ITEMNO: INTEGER;
              PRICE: REAL;
              LEFT,
              RIGHT: LINK
           END;
```

Values of type LINK are pointers to nodes. These values will be used to link nodes to their children, hence the name of the type. Each node is a record containing four fields. ITEMNO is the number of a particular item, and PRICE is its price. LEFT is the pointer to the left child of a node, and RIGHT is the pointer to the right child of the node. ITEMNO and PRICE contain the useful information stored in a node; LEFT and RIGHT are needed to link the nodes into a binary tree.

Note one unusual feature of these definitions. Normally, Pascal does not allow us to refer to an identifier until after it has been defined. If that rule held for pointer types, the definitions just given would be impossible: LINK refers to NODE and NODE refers to LINK, so we would be at a loss as to which definition to put first. To avoid this problem, Pascal allows us to refer to a pointer type before the type to be pointed to is defined. That is, we can refer to ↑NODE before NODE is defined.

The Program BINARYTREE.   Now let's write a program to look up prices in a price list stored as a binary tree. Our program will also be able to add new prices to the price list—that is, add new nodes to the binary tree. We will construct the program in top-down fashion, writing the main program first and then the procedures that it calls. Figure 11-3 shows the main program.

The program begins by defining the types LINK and NODE. The variable ROOT, declared to be of type LINK, will point to the ROOT of the binary tree. We will always access the tree via the value of ROOT. If, due to a program error or computer malfunction, invalid data were stored in ROOT, the entire tree would be lost.

To simplify the program listings, and to emphasize the top-down method of program construction, the procedure declarations are given in separate figures (Figures 11-4 and 11-5). Of course, before actually compiling the program, the procedure declarations must be inserted in the main program at the point indicated by the comment.

It's convenient to provide the tree with a dummy root that does not contain valid data. The root of the tree is pointed to by the value of ROOT, whereas every other node is pointed to by the LEFT or RIGHT field of some other node. Because of this difference, if the root were an ordinary data node some operations would have to treat it as a special case. By providing the tree with a dummy root that does not contain valid data, all data nodes are pointed to by the LEFT or RIGHT fields of other nodes, and none has to be treated as a special case.

The statement part of the main program begins, then, by creating the dummy root. The statement

```
NEW(ROOT)
```

creates a dynamic variable of type NODE and assigns to ROOT a pointer to the newly created variable. ROOT↑ now denotes the newly created variable, so we can refer to the fields of the variable using ROOT↑.ITEMNO, ROOT↑.PRICE, ROOT↑.LEFT, and ROOT↑.RIGHT. To keep from having to repeat ROOT↑., we can use a WITH statement:

```
WITH ROOT↑ DO
   BEGIN
      ITEMNO := −MAXINT;
      LEFT := NIL;
      RIGHT := NIL
   END
```

Since the root is a dummy node, we want to assign ITEMNO a value that is not a valid item number, so that no search for a valid item number

```
PROGRAM BINARYTREE;
(* INFORMATION STORAGE AND RETRIEVAL USING A BINARY TREE *)
TYPE
   LINK = ↑NODE;
   NODE = RECORD
                ITEMNO: INTEGER;
                PRICE: REAL;
                LEFT,
                RIGHT: LINK
           END;
VAR
   ROOT: LINK;
   ITEMNUMBER: INTEGER;
   ITEMPRICE: REAL;
   RESPONSE: CHAR;
   FOUND: BOOLEAN;

(* PROCEDURE DECLARATIONS WILL BE FILLED IN HERE *)

BEGIN
   (* INITIALIZE TREE WITH DUMMY ROOT *)
   NEW(ROOT);
   WITH ROOT↑ DO
      BEGIN
         ITEMNO := −MAXINT;
         LEFT := NIL;
         RIGHT := NIL
      END;
   (* STORE AND RETRIEVE DATA *)
   REPEAT
      WRITE('R(ETRIEVE, S(TORE, Q(UIT? ');
      READ(RESPONSE); WRITELN;
      CASE RESPONSE OF
         'R': BEGIN
                 WRITE('ENTER ITEM NUMBER: ');
                 READLN(ITEMNUMBER);
                 FIND(ITEMNUMBER, ITEMPRICE, FOUND);
                 IF FOUND THEN
                     WRITELN('PRICE IS ', ITEMPRICE:8:2)
                 ELSE
                     WRITELN('REQUESTED ITEM NOT FOUND')
              END;
```

FIGURE 11–3. A program for storing information in and retrieving information from a binary tree. This figure shows the main program only; the procedures are shown in separate figures.

(FIGURE 11-3 continued)

```
    'S': BEGIN
            WRITE('ENTER ITEM NUMBER AND PRICE: ');
            READLN(ITEMNUMBER, ITEMPRICE);
            INSERT(ITEMNUMBER, ITEMPRICE)
         END
    END: (* CASE *)
    WRITELN
  UNTIL RESPONSE = 'Q'
END.
```

will ever find the root. Assuming all valid item numbers are positive, we assign ITEMNO the value -MAXINT. The PRICE field of the root is not used, so no value is assigned to it. The LEFT and RIGHT fields are assigned the value NIL, indicating that the root currently has neither a left child nor a right child.

The remainder of the main program is concerned with accepting commands and data from the user and calling the proper procedures to carry out the commands. Only a few points about this part of the program will be discussed here, with the study of the remaining details being left as an exercise.

The statement

```
WRITE('R(ETRIEVE, S(TORE, Q(UIT? ');
```

requests the user to enter R to retrieve information, S to store information, and Q to terminate the program. The user's response is accepted by

```
READ(RESPONSE); WRITELN;
```

where RESPONSE is a character variable. In UCSD Pascal the READ statement accepts a single character from the keyboard. The user need only hit the R, S, or Q key; it isn't necessary to press the carriage return or enter key. The WRITELN statement provides the carriage return automatically. Some other versions of Pascal, however, may require the user to press the carriage return or enter key in order to get the R, S, or Q accepted by the program.

The value of RESPONSE is used as the selector in a CASE statement. In UCSD Pascal if there is no case corresponding to the value of the selector, the CASE statement takes no action, and the computer goes on to the statement following the CASE statement. This has several advantages. First, invalid characters, such as blank spaces, are automatically ignored. Second, we do not have to provide a case for the response Q. This response is ignored by the CASE statement but causes the REPEAT statement to terminate. Some versions of Pascal, however, give an error message if there is no case corresponding to the value of the selector. The program must be modified for these versions. (So modifying it is a good exercise.)

If the user enters R to retrieve information, the program obtains the item number to be looked up and assigns it to ITEMNUMBER. The procedure FIND is called to find the price of the requested item:

```
FIND(ITEMNUMBER, ITEMPRICE, FOUND)
```

If the requested item number is found, ITEMPRICE is set to the price of the item, and FOUND is set to TRUE. If the requested item number is not found, FOUND is set to FALSE.

If the user enters S to store information, the program requests the number and price of an item and assigns these to ITEMNUMBER and ITEMPRICE. The procedure INSERT is called to insert in the tree a new node having the given item number and price.

```
INSERT(ITEMNUMBER, ITEMPRICE)
```

Note that at this point we have organized our entire program without concerning ourselves with the details of searching the tree or inserting new nodes in it. We will take care of those details when we write the procedures FIND and INSERT. The ability to postpone consideration of details while we work out the overall structure of our program is an important advantage of top-down construction.

The Procedure FIND.   Figure 11-4 shows the procedure FIND. The variable CURRENT is used to point to the node with which the program is currently working. Since we always start a search at the root, we begin by setting CURRENT to the value of ROOT, so that current points to the root of the tree. Since the desired node has not yet been found, FOUND is set to FALSE:

```
CURRENT := ROOT;
FOUND := FALSE
```

The search continues as long as the value of CURRENT is not NIL and the value of FOUND is FALSE. If the value of CURRENT becomes NIL, then we have tried to reach a nonexistent node, hence the item number we are looking for is not in the tree. If the value of FOUND becomes TRUE, then a node having the desired item number has been found:

```
WHILE (CURRENT <> NIL) AND (NOT FOUND) DO
    "Process node pointed to by CURRENT"
```

To process a node, we compare ITEMNUMBER, the item number we are looking for, with CURRENT↑.ITEMNO, the item-number field of the current node. If the two are equal, we have found the node we are

```
PROCEDURE FIND(ITEMNUMBER: INTEGER; VAR ITEMPRICE: REAL;
               VAR FOUND: BOOLEAN);
(* FIND AND GET PRICE FROM RECORD WITH GIVEN ITEM NUMBER *)
VAR
   CURRENT: LINK;
BEGIN
   CURRENT := ROOT;
   FOUND := FALSE;
   WHILE (CURRENT <> NIL) AND (NOT FOUND) DO
      IF ITEMNUMBER = CURRENT↑.ITEMNO THEN
         BEGIN
            ITEMPRICE := CURRENT↑.PRICE;
            FOUND := TRUE
         END
      ELSE IF ITEMNUMBER < CURRENT↑.ITEMNO THEN
         CURRENT := CURRENT↑.LEFT
      ELSE (* ITEMNUMBER > CURRENT↑.ITEMNO *)
         CURRENT := CURRENT↑.RIGHT
END;
```

FIGURE 11–4. **This procedure searches a binary tree for the node having a given item number.**

looking for. ITEMPRICE is set to the value of the PRICE field of the current node, and FOUND is set to TRUE.

If the item number we are looking for is less than the item number of the current node, CURRENT is set to the value of the LEFT field of the current node, so that CURRENT now points to that node's left child, if any. If the item number we are looking for is greater than the item number of the current node, then we set CURRENT to the value of the RIGHT field of the current node, so that CURRENT now points to that node's right child, if any. If a left or right child doesn't exist, the LEFT or RIGHT contains the value NIL, which is assigned to CURRENT, causing node processing to terminate.

The following IF statement processes one node:

```
IF ITEMNUMBER = CURRENT↑.ITEMNO THEN
   BEGIN
      ITEMPRICE := CURRENT↑.PRICE;
      FOUND := TRUE
   END
ELSE IF ITEMNUMBER < CURRENT↑.ITEMNO THEN
   CURRENT := CURRENT↑.LEFT
ELSE (* ITEMNUMBER > CURRENT↑.ITEMNO *)
   CURRENT := CURRENT↑.RIGHT
```

The Procedure INSERT.   Figure 11–5 shows the procedure INSERT. Our strategy for inserting a new node is to search the tree for a node with the given item number. If such a node is found, we assume that the user merely wants to update the PRICE field of an existing node, hence the PRICE field of the node found is set to ITEMPRICE.

If a node with the given item number does not exist, eventually we will attempt to move to the left or right child of a node and find that the child in question doesn't exist. When that happens we create a new node and insert it in the position that would have been occupied by the

```
PROCEDURE INSERT(ITEMNUMBER: INTEGER; ITEMPRICE: REAL);
(* INSERT NEW RECORD INTO TREE *)
VAR
    CURRENT: LINK;
    FINISHED: BOOLEAN;

FUNCTION MAKENODE(ITEMNUMBER: INTEGER; ITEMPRICE: REAL): LINK;
(* CONSTRUCT RECORD WITH GIVEN ITEMNUMBER AND PRICE *)
VAR
    NEWREC: LINK;
BEGIN
    NEW(NEWREC);
    WITH NEWREC↑ DO
        BEGIN
            ITEMNO := ITEMNUMBER;
            PRICE := ITEMPRICE;
            LEFT := NIL;
            RIGHT := NIL
        END;
    MAKENODE := NEWREC
END; (* MAKENODE *)

BEGIN (* INSERT *)
    CURRENT := ROOT;
    FINISHED := FALSE;
    WHILE NOT FINISHED DO
        IF ITEMNUMBER = CURRENT↑.ITEMNO THEN
            BEGIN
                CURRENT↑.PRICE := ITEMPRICE;
                FINISHED := TRUE
            END
        ELSE IF ITEMNUMBER < CURRENT↑.ITEMNO THEN
            IF CURRENT↑.LEFT <> NIL THEN
                CURRENT := CURRENT↑.LEFT
```

FIGURE 11–5. If a node having the specified item number is present in the tree, this procedure updates the corresponding price. Otherwise, a new node with the specified item number and price is inserted into the tree.

(FIGURE 11-5 continued)

```
    ELSE
       BEGIN
          CURRENT↑.LEFT := MAKENODE(ITEMNUMBER, ITEMPRICE);
          FINISHED := TRUE
       END
  ELSE (* ITEMNUMBER > CURRENT↑.ITEMNO *)
     IF CURRENT↑.RIGHT <> NIL THEN
        CURRENT := CURRENT↑.RIGHT
     ELSE
        BEGIN
           CURRENT↑.RIGHT := MAKENODE(ITEMNUMBER, ITEMPRICE);
           FINISHED := TRUE
        END
END; (* INSERT *)
```

missing child. The ITEMNO and PRICE fields of the new node are set to the item number and price provided by the user; the LEFT and RIGHT fields are set to NIL, since the new node currently has no children. Note that if a search for the same item number is now carried out, the search will not stop in attempting to reach a nonexistent node, but will reach the newly inserted node instead.

(For example, suppose we want to insert a node with the number 600 in Figure 11-2. Searching for node 600, we go left from the root and right from node 430. We try to go right from node 525 but cannot, since node 525 has no right child. Therefore, we insert node 600 as the right child of node 525. If the search for node 600 is repeated, the newly inserted node will be found.)

The INSERT procedure uses two local variables: CURRENT, which points to the node the procedure is currently working with, and FINISHED, which has the value TRUE if the procedure has completed its work and the value FALSE, otherwise. INSERT uses a function, MAKENODE, which creates a node having a given item number and price and returns a pointer to that node. In accordance with the top-down approach, we will look at the statement part of INSERT before considering the details of MAKENODE.

Like FIND, INSERT starts at the root of the tree, so it begins by setting CURRENT to the value of ROOT. At this point the procedure cannot be finished processing nodes, so FINISHED is set to FALSE. Nodes are processed as long as the value of FINISHED remains FALSE:

```
CURRENT := ROOT;
FINISHED := FALSE;
WHILE NOT FINISHED DO
   "Process node pointed to by CURRENT"
```

Node processing is done with a giant IF statement that handles three cases, depending on whether the value of ITEMNUMBER (the item number being sought) is equal to, less than, or greater than the value of CURRENT↑.ITEMNO (the item-number field of the current node).

• *Case 1:* ITEMNUMBER equals CURRENT↑.ITEMNO. The search has found a node with the item number being searched for. Therefore, no new node will be inserted. Instead, the PRICE field of the node found is updated, after which FINISHED is set to TRUE to indicate that processing is complete:

```
CURRENT↑.PRICE := ITEMPRICE;
FINISHED := TRUE
```

• *Case 2:* ITEMNUMBER is less than CURRENT↑.ITEMNO. If the current node has a left child, we set CURRENT to point to that left child. If the current node does not have a left child, then we insert a new node (created by MAKENODE) as the left child of the current node. If a new node is inserted, FINISHED is set to TRUE to indicate that processing is complete:

```
IF CURRENT↑.LEFT <> NIL THEN
   CURRENT := CURRENT↑.LEFT
ELSE
   BEGIN
      CURRENT↑.LEFT := MAKENODE(ITEMNUMBER, ITEMPRICE);
      FINISHED := TRUE
   END
```

• *Case 3:* ITEMNUMBER is greater than CURRENT↑.ITEMNO. If the current node has a right child, we set CURRENT to point to that right child. If the current node does not have a right child, then we insert a new node (created by MAKENODE) as the right child of the current node. If a new node is inserted, FINISHED is set to TRUE to indicate that processing is complete:

```
IF CURRENT↑.RIGHT <> NIL THEN
   CURRENT := CURRENT↑.RIGHT
ELSE
   BEGIN
      CURRENT↑.RIGHT := MAKENODE(ITEMNUMBER, ITEMPRICE);
      FINISHED := TRUE
   END
```

The Function MAKENODE.   MAKENODE creates and returns a pointer to a node whose ITEMNO and PRICE fields have specified values and whose LEFT and RIGHT fields are set to NIL. Note that a Pascal function cannot return a structured value, but it can return a pointer to a structured value. Pointers, then, are one way of letting Pascal functions, in effect, return array and record values. Note also that, although nested function and procedure declarations were discussed in Chapter 7, MAKENODE is the first example of a nested declaration that we have encountered.

MAKENODE begins by creating a new node and storing a pointer to it in the local variable NEWREC:

```
NEW(NEWREC)
```

A WITH statement is used to assign values to the fields of the newly created node:

```
WITH NEWREC↑ DO
    BEGIN
        ITEMNO := ITEMNUMBER;
        PRICE := ITEMPRICE;
        LEFT := NIL;
        RIGHT := NIL
    END
```

A pointer to the new node is returned as the value of the function:

```
MAKENODE := NEWREC
```

Exercises

1. Figure 11-6 illustrates a *linked list*, which is made up of records called *cells*. Each cell has two fields, VALUE and NEXT. The VALUE field of each cell holds an integer value; the NEXT field holds a pointer to the next cell on the list. The NEXT field of the last cell on the list contains the value NIL, which is indicated by a diagonal line in Figure 11-6. The first cell of the list is pointed to by a global variable FIRST. It is convenient to make the first cell of the list a dummy cell that contains no useful data and is never processed by the routines for inserting and deleting cells. The types CELL and LINK are declared as follows:

```
TYPE
    LINK = ↑CELL;
    CELL = RECORD
                VALUE: INTEGER;
                NEXT: LINK
            END;
```

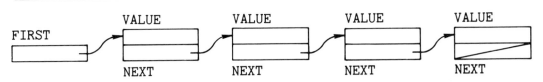

FIGURE 11-6. A linked list. The NEXT field for the last item on the list contains NIL, which is indicated in diagrams by a diagonal line through the field.

Write a function

```
FIND(V)
```

that searches the list for the first cell containing the value V and returns a pointer to the cell found. Since the first cell on the list is a dummy, the search should skip over it.

2. For the linked list described in Exercise 1, write a procedure

```
INSERT(P, V)
```

to insert a new cell containing the value V immediately following the cell pointed to by P. (Hint: The new cell must be linked to the cell now pointed to by P↑.NEXT, and P↑.NEXT must be set to point to the new cell.)

3. For the linked list described in Exercise 1, write a procedure

```
DELETE(P)
```

to delete the cell following the cell pointed to by P. The deleted cell should be disposed of with DISPOSE. (Hint: P↑.NEXT now points to the cell to be deleted; it must be set to point to the cell following the cell to be deleted.)

4. The idea of a stack was introduced in Chapter 10. Let's define a data type STACK by

```
STACK = RECORD
            TOP: 0..50;
            CONTENTS: ARRAY[1..50] OF INTEGER
        END
```

and declare:

```
S: STACK;
```

When S is empty, the value of S.TOP is 0. Otherwise, CONTENTS[S.TOP] contains the top value on the stack. When the value of S.TOP is 50, the stack is said to be full. Write the following two predicates:

> EMPTY(S)   Returns TRUE if S is empty; otherwise returns FALSE.
>
> FULL(S)   Returns TRUE if S is full; otherwise returns FALSE.

Now write the following three procedures for manipulating stacks:

> CLEAR(S)   Produces an empty stack by setting S.TOP to 0.

PUSH(S, I)   If FULL(S) is FALSE, places the value of I on top of the stack. Otherwise, leaves the value of S unchanged.

POP(S, I)   If EMPTY(S) is FALSE, removes the top value from the stack and assigns that value to I. Otherwise, leaves S and I unchanged.

All valid manipulations of the stack can be carried out using the two predicates and the three procedures. When using those predicates and procedures, we do not have tc know how the stack is implemented —that is, we do not have to know how the data type STACK is defined.

5. To illustrate the remark made at the end of Exercise 4, let's implement a stack as a linked list and write the same predicates and procedures for this implementation. Although the internal workings of the predicates and procedures will be vastly different, they can be used in exactly the same way. We use the type definitions in Exercise 1 with the addition of

```
STACK = LINK;
```

and declare the variable:

```
S: STACK;
```

The value of S points to the top item on the stack. Each item is linked to the one immediately below it on the stack. The NEXT field of the bottom item is NIL. When the stack is empty, the value of S is NIL. New values of type CELL are created by NEW when values are pushed on the stack and disposed of by DISPOSE when values are popped off. Write the predicates FULL and EMPTY and the procedures CLEAR, PUSH, and POP. (FULL should always return FALSE, since a linked list cannot become full unless all the memory available for dynamic variables is exhausted.)

6. This problem is for readers familiar with complex numbers. Define a data type:

```
COMPLEX = RECORD
             REALPT,
             IMAGPT: REAL
          END
```

and variables:

```
X, Y, Z: COMPLEX;
```

We intend for X.REALPT to be the real part of the value of X and X.IMAGPT to be the imaginary part. Write the following procedures:

SUM(X, Y, Z)   Sets Z equal to the sum of the complex numbers X and Y.

DIFF(X, Y, Z)   Sets Z equal to the difference of the complex numbers X and Y.

PROD(X, Y, Z)   Sets Z equal to the product of the complex numbers X and Y.

QUOT(X, Y, Z)   Sets Z equal to the quotient of the complex numbers X and Y.

7. Modify Exercise 6 to work with pointers to complex numbers rather than with the complex numbers themselves. Each procedure in Exercise 6 is to be replaced by a function that takes two pointers to complex numbers as parameters and returns a pointer to the result of carrying out the operation in question. Thus the value of SUM(P, Q) is a pointer to a complex number that is the sum of the complex numbers pointed to by P and Q.

8. Rewrite the price-list-lookup program so that the price list is maintained as a linked list rather than a binary tree. In addition to looking up prices and inserting new entries on the price list, the program should be able to delete entries that are no longer needed.

9. Provide the program BINARYTREE with a command that prints out the entire price list with the item numbers in numerical order. The procedure for carrying out the command should be organized as follows:

(1) Print all entries that can be reached by following the left branch from the root.

(2) Print the entry corresponding to the root.

(3) Print all entries that can be reached by following the right branch from the root.

The procedure should call itself recursively for steps 1 and 3.

10. In a doubly linked list, each cell contains not only a pointer to the cell that follows it but also a pointer to the cell that precedes it. A doubly linked list can be based on the following type definitions:

```
LINK = ↑CELL;
CELL = RECORD
          VALUE: INTEGER;
          LEFT,
          RIGHT: LINK
       END;
```

LEFT points to the preceding cell and RIGHT points to the following one. The value of LEFT for the first cell on the list is NIL, as is the value of RIGHT for the last cell on the list. Write versions of INSERT and DE-LETE (as defined in Exercises 2 and 3) for doubly linked lists. The parameter for this version of DELETE should point to the cell to be deleted rather than to the cell preceding the one to be deleted. Why can the parameter be a pointer to the cell to be deleted (the most desirable situation) for doubly linked lists but not for singly linked ones?

Chapter 12

STRUCTURED TYPES: FILES

A *file* is a sequence of values stored in auxiliary memory. All the values belong to the same data type. The number of values stored is not fixed but can vary as the file is manipulated.

There are two ways to access the values stored in a file: *sequential access* and *random access*. In sequential access the values can only be accessed in the order in which they are stored in the file. In random access the values can be accessed in whatever order the programmer desires. Standard Pascal provides only sequential access. Since random access is required in many real-world applications, however, many versions of Pascal provide random access as a nonstandard feature. As with all nonstandard features, the implementation of random access varies from one version of Pascal to another.

Sequential Access

Values stored in a file must be transferred one by one to main memory for processing. At any time we have access only to the value that is currently in main memory. It's as if we had a window into the file through which we could reach in and get just one value. We can move the window around, so at different times we can get different values, but at any one time the only value we can access is the one that can be seen through the file window.

In Pascal we can define a file type and declare a variable to be of that type as follows:

```
TYPE
    DATA = FILE OF INTEGER;
VAR
    F: DATA;
```

Each value of type DATA is a sequence of integers. The number of integers in the sequence is not fixed, but varies from one sequence to another. The empty sequence, which contains no values, is included. Some typical values of type DATA are

```
  2    4    8    6    4   -2    0   -5   25
  7    3    1    8
100
```
                                                        (empty sequence)

F is a variable of type DATA. Therefore, the value of F is a sequence of integers. For example, let's assume the value of F to be

```
9    5    4    7    2
```

At any time we have access to only one of these values, the one currently in main memory. The area of main memory in which the accessible value is stored is called the file *buffer*. Associated with F is another variable F↑, called the *buffer variable*, whose value is the currently accessible value of the file, the value stored in main memory in the file buffer.

We can indicate the position of the window into the file with an arrow:

```
9    5    4    7    2
          ↑
```

The currently accessible value is 4, and 4 is the value of F↑. Thus

```
I := F↑
```

assigns the value 4 to I, and

```
WRITE(F↑)
```

prints the value 4.

Sequential File Processing: Input.   For sequential processing we start at the beginning of the file, process values until we come to the end, then stop. The first step in processing a sequential file is to call the procedure RESET, which positions the file window over the first component of the file and transfers that component to main memory. Thus, after executing

```
RESET(F)
```

the file window of F is positioned over the first component

```
9    5    4    7    2
↑
```

and that component is transferred to main memory. The value of F↑ is 9, and this value is available for processing.

When we are ready to process the next value in the file, we use the built-in procedure GET to move the file window forward one position and transfer the next value into main memory. After executing

```
GET(F)
```

the file F looks like this

```
9   5   4   7   2
    ↑
```

The value of F↑ is 5, and this value is available for processing.

If we execute GET(F) enough times, eventually the file window will move beyond the end of the file:

```
9   5   4   7   2
                  ↑
```

In this situation the value of F↑ is undefined, and the effect of any further calls to GET is unpredictable.

The program must be able to detect this situation so it won't attempt to manipulate meaningless values or make invalid calls to GET. For this purpose, Pascal provides a Boolean function (or predicate) EOF(F), whose value is TRUE if the window into file F has moved beyond the end of the file and FALSE if it has not.

As an example of processing input from a sequential file, the following statements compute the sum of all the values in F:

```
SUM := 0;
RESET(F);
WHILE NOT EOF(F) DO
    BEGIN
        SUM := SUM + F↑;
        GET(F)
    END
```

Sequential File Processing: Output.   To begin with, we need an empty file to hold the data we are going to store. We obtain an empty file by calling the built-in procedure REWRITE:

```
REWRITE(F)
```

F now looks like this

```
                          (empty sequence)

↑
```

and is ready to receive values.

If we want to store the value 5, say, in the file, we first assign this value to F↑:

```
F↑ := 5
```

The value 5, however, is still in main memory. The built-in procedure PUT transfers the value of F↑ to auxiliary memory and advances the file window one position. After executing

```
PUT(F)
```

F looks like this:

```
5
   ↑
```

The value 5 has been transferred to the file and the window is now over the next unused position. Executing

```
F↑ := 7;
PUT(F)
```

puts 7 in the file

```
5   7
       ↑
```

and so on.

As an example of output to a sequential file, the following statements store the integers 1 through 100 in F:

```
REWRITE(F);
FOR I := 1 TO 100 DO
   BEGIN
      F↑ := I;
      PUT(F)
   END
```

Text Files.   Text can be stored as files of characters. However, text is normally divided into lines for convenience in printing. To recognize this division into lines in a way that is independent of the conventions of any particular computer system, Pascal has a predefined type TEXT. We can think of TEXT as defined by

```
TEXT = FILE OF CHAR;
```

with additional provisions for grouping the characters into lines.

Suppose we declare F by:

```
F: TEXT;
```

The value of F is a sequence of characters. The characters include not only the ordinary ones but a special line-separator character that divides the file into lines. Let's represent the line-separator character by a bar, |. Then the value of F might look like this:

ABCD | EFG | HIJKL

If the contents of F were sent to a video display or printer, the output would look like this:

```
ABCD
EFG
HIJKL
```

Pascal does not allow the user's program to access the line-separator character. The reason is that different computer systems use different characters to separate lines. A program written to recognize the line-separator character used by one system wouldn't work properly on another system that uses a different line-separator character. To prevent programs from depending on a particular line-separator character, Pascal does two things:

1. When the file window is positioned over a line separator, the value of the buffer variable is a blank space, not the line-separator character.

2. Pascal provides a Boolean function EOLN(F) whose value is TRUE when the file window of F is positioned over a line-separator character and FALSE when it is not. The program uses EOLN to recognize the end of a line.

READ, READLN, WRITE, WRITELN, and PAGE.   Pascal defines some additional procedures for manipulating text files. We have been using most of these procedures all along, but with our present knowledge of files we can define them more precisely.
Let C be a character variable and F a text-file variable. Then

```
READ(F, C)
```

is equivalent to

```
C := F↑;
GET(F)
```

and

```
WRITE(F, C);
```

is equivalent to

```
F↑ := C;
PUT (F)
```

If V is a variable of type REAL, INTEGER, or CHAR, then

```
READ(F, V)
```

reads a sufficient number of characters to make up a value of the type of V and assigns to V the value so obtained.

If E is an expression yielding a value of type REAL, INTEGER, BOOLEAN, CHAR, or packed array of character, then

```
WRITE(F, E)
```

converts the value of E into a string of characters and writes those characters to F. As we already know, field-width parameters can be supplied to specify how the values will be written.

(In UCSD Pascal values of type STRING can be both read and written. Values of type BOOLEAN cannot be written.)

The READ and WRITE procedures can read and write more than one value on a single call. The statement

```
READ(F, V1, V2, ..., VN)
```

is defined to be equivalent to

```
READ(F, V1); READ(F, V2); ... READ(F, VN)
```

and

```
WRITE(F, V1, V2, ..., VN)
```

is defined to be equivalent to

```
WRITE(F, V1); WRITE(F, V2); ... WRITE(F, VN)
```

The procedure READLN moves the file window to the character following the next line separator. Thus,

```
READLN(F)
```

is equivalent to:

```
WHILE NOT EOLN(F) DO
   GET(F);
GET(F)
```

The procedure WRITELN appends a line separator to the file being written. After

```
WRITELN(F)
```

the next character written to F will start a new line.

The procedures READLN and WRITELN can be combined with READ and WRITE. Thus,

```
READLN(F, V1, V2, ..., VN)
```

is equivalent to

```
READ(F, V1, V2, ..., VN);
READLN(F)
```
and
```
WRITELN(F, E1, E2, ..., EN)
```

is equivalent to

```
WRITE(F, E1, E2, ..., EN);
WRITELN
```

If the text file F is associated with a printer, then

```
PAGE(F)
```

causes the printer to advance to the top of a new page.

The Files INPUT and OUTPUT. Pascal has two standard files, INPUT and OUTPUT, to which the following rules apply:

1. The files INPUT and OUTPUT are already declared when the program begins execution. Declarations for these files must not be included in the program.

2. Before a program begins execution, the computer system executes the following:

```
RESET(INPUT);
REWRITE(OUTPUT)
```

The program must not attempt to apply RESET to INPUT or REWRITE to OUTPUT.

3. If the file parameter is omitted for READ, READLN, EOF, or EOLN, then INPUT is assumed. If the file parameter is omitted for WRITE, WRITELN, or PAGE, OUTPUT is assumed. In the following each statement on the left is equivalent to the corresponding one on the right:

```
READ(V1, V2, ..., VN)           READ(INPUT, V1, V2, ..., VN)
READLN(V1, V2 ..., VN)          READLN(INPUT, V1, V2, ..., VN)
EOF                             EOF(INPUT)
EOLN                            EOLN(INPUT)
WRITE(E1, E2, ..., EN)          WRITE(OUTPUT, E1, E2, ..., EN)
WRITELN(E1, E2, ..., EN)        WRITELN(OUTPUT, E1, E2, ..., EN)
PAGE                            PAGE(OUTPUT)
```

Thus the input and output statements that we have been using all along, such as

```
WRITE('AMOUNT IN YOUR ACCOUNT NOW? ');
READLN(AMOUNT)
```

read from the standard file INPUT and write to the standard file OUT-PUT.

Lazy Evaluation and Interactive Files.   A problem arises when an input file corresponds to the user's keyboard. Since RESET transfers the first component of a file to main memory, RESET waits for the user to type a character before returning. For the standard file INPUT, RESET is called automatically before execution of the program begins, so the user must type one character before any of the statements the program can be executed. What's more, since READ(F, C) is defined as

```
C := F↑;
GET(F)
```

it assigns to C the last character typed by the user but waits for the user to type another character before returning. The user must always type the next character before the program will process the current one.

This behavior makes interactive processing impossible. In general, our future input to the computer depends on the computer's response to our current input. It's absurd to have to begin typing the next command or data item before the current one is processed. For example, if we were playing chess with the computer, we would have to start typing our next move before the computer replied to our current one! There are two ways around this problem: *lazy evaluation* and *interactive files*.

Lazy evaluation refers to not carrying out an operation when it is requested but putting it off until it is actually needed. Applying lazy evaluation to the operation of obtaining a character from the keyboard solves the problem just discussed, since the user is not required to type a character until the program is ready to process it.

For example, suppose file F corresponds to the keyboard and the program executes

```
RESET(F)
```

The computer system is requested to transfer a character from the key-board to main memory. But because of lazy evaluation, action on the re-quest is postponed until the value of F↑ is actually needed. RESET re-turns as soon as the request has been entered, instead of hanging up waiting for the user to type a character.

Suppose the program now executes

```
READ(F, C)
```

which is equivalent to:

```
C := F↑;
GET(F)
```

The statement C := F↑ makes use of the value of F↑, so the system must get to work and obtain a character from the keyboard. After the character typed by the user has been transferred to F↑ and assigned to C, the statement GET(F) requests the system to read another character. But this request will not be acted on until the character is actually needed. Therefore, GET(F) returns as soon as the request is entered, instead of hanging up waiting for another character to be typed. READ(F, C) returns the current character typed by the user.

For future calls to READ, C := F↑ causes the system to actually get the character requested during the previous call to READ. GET(F) requests the system to get still another character but doesn't wait around until another character is actually typed. The advantage of lazy evaluation is that the desired behavior is obtained without changing any of the definitions of standard Pascal.

UCSD Pascal does not use lazy evaluation but provides a file type INTERACTIVE for which the definitions of standard Pascal are modified. Interactive files are the same as text files except:

1. Executing RESET does not obtain the first character from the file.

2. READ(F, C) is defined to be equivalent to

```
GET(F);
C := F↑
```

Thus a character is delivered to the program as soon as GET(F) obtains it from the keyboard.

3. EOF(F) becomes TRUE when the user presses a special end-of-file key.

In UCSD Pascal the standard file INPUT is an interactive file corresponding to the user's keyboard.

External Files.   If we declare a file F by a declaration such as

```
F: FILE OF INTEGER;
```

but do nothing else to establish any connection between F and some existing file, then F represents a *local* or *internal* file. An internal file exists during the execution of the program in which it is declared but vanishes when the program terminates. Internal files are suitable only for temporary storage during the execution of a program.

Ordinarily, however, we want to input data from an existing disk file or to create a new file for storing output, a file that will continue to exist on disk after the execution of the program terminates. Or we may want a file to correspond to some input or output device, such as a printer. We need some way to establish a connection between files declared in Pascal and actual disk files, input devices, and output devices.

In standard Pascal this is achieved by listing external files as parameters in the program heading. For instance, if a program uses the file F in addition to the standard files INPUT and OUTPUT, the program heading looks like this:

```
PROGRAM PROCESSFILES(INPUT, OUTPUT, F);
```

When we request the computer's operating system to execute this program, we inform it what actual disk files, input devices, or output devices correspond to the file parameters listed in the program heading.

This approach is often not convenient for interactive programs. We would like the program itself to be able to get the necessary file names from the user, rather than having to rely on the operating system for this task. That way, the program can prompt the user for each file name so that even an untrained user will know what file names are required. The program can supply default file names if the user doesn't enter names for some files. And in some situations the user may decide, as a result of interacting with the program, to process a certain file even though the need to process that file was not clear when the execution of the program was requested.

For these reasons many versions of Pascal provide alternative or additional methods of associating file names in Pascal programs with the names under which the files are stored externally. Unfortunately, the methods vary substantially from one version of Pascal to another. We will look here at the method used by UCSD Pascal, since it is employed in the example programs for this chapter.

UCSD Pascal uses nonstandard versions of RESET and REWRITE to assign external names to files. Parameters in the program header cannot be used for this purpose; UCSD Pascal ignores any parameters in the program header. In UCSD Pascal

```
RESET(F, 'TESTDATA')
```

resets F and establishes a correspondence between it and the existing disk file TESTDATA. The statement

```
REWRITE(F, 'RESULTS')
```

makes F correspond to an empty, newly created disk file named RESULTS.

Instead of writing file names into the program we can get them from the user. If S is a variable of type STRING, we can get the name of an already existing file as follows:

```
WRITE('NAME OF INPUT FILE? ');
READLN(S);
RESET(F, S)
```

To get the name of a file to be used for output, we can use

```
WRITE('NAME OF OUTPUT FILE? ');
READLN(S);
REWRITE(F, S)
```

In UCSD Pascal any disk file to which output has been sent must be closed after use. Closing a file assures that all the data has been transferred from main memory to the file and that all necessary information about the file has been entered in the directory for the disk on which the file is stored. In UCSD Pascal

```
CLOSE(F, LOCK)
```

causes the file corresponding to F to be stored permanently on disk, while

```
CLOSE(F, PURGE)
```

causes the file to be deleted from disk.

The File-Update Problem

A good exercise in sequential file processing is writing a program to update a file. Suppose we have a disk file, such as a file of customer accounts, which has to be updated every month. We call this file the *master file*. Every month certain transactions take place. Customers make new purchases, for instance, or make payments on their accounts. New customers are added to the master file, and inactive customers are removed. We assume that records for all the transactions have been stored in another file, called the *transaction file*.

Each month we want to run to a program that will use the data in the transaction file to update the master file. The inputs to the program are the old master file (the file to be updated) and the transaction file. The output from the program is the new (updated) master file. Note that we do not attempt to change the old master file, but rather produce a new file containing the updated records. If something should go wrong during the processing, the old master file will not have been changed, and the program can be run again after the problem has been corrected.

During the update we need some way of matching records in the transaction file with records to be updated in the master file. We must be able to tell when a transaction record and a master record refer to the same entity—the same customer, for example.

We can achieve this by giving each record a *key* component, which uniquely identifies the entity to which the record refers. Typically, the key is an account number, a customer number, an employee number, a social security number, or some similar identifying number. (Although people may complain that computers are turning them into numbers, names make bad keys; different people have the same name, and people don't always write their names the same way.) We will match a record in the transaction file with the record in the master file having the same key.

Since both the master and transaction files are to be processed sequentially, records will be read from them only in the order in which they are stored in the files. To be able to match the records in one file with the corresponding records in the other, the records in each file must be in alphabetical or numerical order according to their key values.

Note that the records in the master and transaction files will not correspond one to one. Many records in the master file will not be updated on a particular run, so there will be no corresponding records in the transaction file. And the transaction file may contain some new records that are to be added to the master file.

To test our file-update program after it is written, we need programs to create a master file, create a transaction file, and list (print the contents of) a master file. Looking at these programs first will provide us with some elementary examples of file processing and will familiarize us with the structure of the master and transaction files.

The Program CREATEMASTER. Figure 12-1 shows the program CREATEMASTER, which is intended to create a master file for testing

```
PROGRAM CREATEMASTER;
(* CREATE A MASTER FILE *)
CONST
    SENTINEL = 9999;
TYPE
    MASTER = RECORD
                  KEY: INTEGER;
                  BALANCE: REAL
              END;
VAR
    MASTERFILE: FILE OF MASTER;
    FILENAME: STRING;
BEGIN
    WRITE('FILE NAME? ');
    READLN(FILENAME);
    REWRITE(MASTERFILE, FILENAME);
    WHILE NOT EOF(INPUT) DO
        BEGIN
            WRITE('KEY AND BALANCE? ');
            READLN(MASTERFILE↑.KEY, MASTERFILE↑.BALANCE);
            PUT(MASTERFILE)
        END;
    MASTERFILE↑.KEY := SENTINEL;
    PUT(MASTERFILE);
    CLOSE(MASTERFILE, LOCK)
END.
```

FIGURE 12-1. A program to create a master file.

the file-update program. For simplicity each record in the master file
has just two fields, KEY and BALANCE:

```
MASTER = RECORD
             KEY: INTEGER:
             BALANCE: REAL
         END;
```

The value of KEY identifies a particular record; we will assume
that the keys are four-digit numbers such as 3751, 4862, and 5234. The
last record in the master file is a special sentinel record with a key of
9999.

The BALANCE field contains a value that can be updated. It might
be the amount a customer owes to a company, which will change as
purchases and payments are made. It could be the amount in a person's
bank account, which will change with deposits and withdrawals. Or it
could refer to something having nothing to do with money, such as the
number of items of a particular kind that are in stock.

The program is in UCSD Pascal, the idiosyncracies of which should
be kept in mind. MASTERFILE is declared as the name of the file in the
Pascal program. The string variable FILENAME will hold the external
name that the user provides for the file:

```
VAR
    MASTERFILE: FILE OF MASTER;
    FILENAME: STRING;
```

The program begins by obtaining the external name of the file from
the user:

```
WRITE('FILE NAME? ');
READLN(FILENAME);
RESET(MASTERFILE, FILENAME)
```

The program reads values for KEY and BALANCE and writes records with these values to the file being created. Processing continues
until the user presses the end-of-file key, which causes EOF(INPUT) to
return TRUE:

```
WHILE NOT EOF(INPUT) DO
    BEGIN
        WRITE('KEY AND BALANCE? ');
        READLN(MASTERFILE↑.KEY, MASTERFILE↑.BALANCE);
        PUT(MASTERFILE)
    END
```

To simplify the operation of the file-update program, the last record
of the master file is a special sentinel record with a key of 9999. The
constant SENTINEL is defined by

```
SENTINEL = 9999;
```

The following statements write the sentinel record and close the file:

```
MASTERFILE↑.KEY := SENTINEL;
PUT(MASTERFILE);
CLOSE(MASTERFILE, LOCK)
```

The Program CREATETRANS. Figure 12–2 shows the program CREATETRANS, which creates a transaction file. A transaction record can request one of three operations: add a new record to the file, update an existing record, or delete a record from the file. The kind of

---

```
PROGRAM CREATETRANS;
(* CREATE TRANSACTION FILE *)
CONST
   SENTINEL = 9999;
TYPE
   TRANSTYPE = (ADD, UPDATE, DELETE);
   TRANSACTION = RECORD
                    KEY: INTEGER;
                    KIND: TRANSTYPE;
                    AMOUNT: REAL
                 END;
VAR
   TRANSFILE: FILE OF TRANSACTION;
   FILENAME: STRING;
   TYPECODE: 1..3;
BEGIN
   WRITE('FILE NAME? ');
   READLN(FILENAME);
   REWRITE(TRANSFILE, FILENAME);
   WHILE NOT EOF(INPUT) DO
      BEGIN
         WRITE('KEY, TYPE CODE, AMOUNT? ');
         READLN(TRANSFILE↑.KEY, TYPECODE, TRANSFILE↑.AMOUNT);
         CASE TYPECODE OF
            1: TRANSFILE↑.KIND := ADD;
            2: TRANSFILE↑.KIND := UPDATE;
            3: TRANSFILE↑.KIND := DELETE
         END;
         PUT(TRANSFILE)
      END;
   TRANSFILE↑.KEY := SENTINEL;
   PUT(TRANSFILE);
   CLOSE(TRANSFILE, LOCK)
END.
```

FIGURE 12–2. A program to create a transaction file.

transaction—add, update, or delete—is specified by a value of the enumerated type TRANSTYPE:

```
TRANSTYPE = (ADD, UPDATE, DELETE);
```

The records in the transaction file have the following structure:

```
TRANSACTION = RECORD
                KEY: INTEGER;
                KIND: TRANSTYPE;
                AMOUNT: REAL
              END;
```

As usual, the value of KEY is the identifying number of the record. The value of KIND specifies the kind of transaction—add, update or delete. When a record is added, the value of AMOUNT is the balance for the new record. When a record is updated, the value of AMOUNT—which can be either positive or negative—is added to the balance of the record being updated. When a record is deleted, the value of AMOUNT is not used.

The program for creating the transaction file is similar to the corresponding program for the master file, so we will not go through it in detail. Note, however, that values of the enumerated type TRANSTYPE cannot be read from a text file. Therefore, a type code of 1 for ADD, 2 for UPDATE, and 3 for DELETE is read instead. A CASE statement assigns the appropriate value to TRANSFILE↑.KIND based on the value of the type code.

Note that the transaction file also ends with a sentinel record having a key of 9999.

The Program LISTMASTER. Figure 12-3 shows the program LISTMASTER, which prints a listing of a master file so we can see whether the file has been updated properly. Since the master file has a sentinel record, LISTMASTER uses the sentinel rather than EOF(MASTERFILE) to determine when the end of file has been reached.

The Program FILEUPDATE. Figure 12-4 shows the file-update program. Proceeding in top-down fashion, we will discuss the main program and then the procedures that it calls. To emphasize this, and to reduce the program listings to manageable size, the procedures are given in separate listings (Figures 12-5 through 12-8). A comment in Figure 12-4 shows where the procedures are to be inserted.

The program begins by defining the constant SENTINEL and the types TRANSTYPE, MASTER, and TRANSACTION. It then declares the integer variable CURRENTKEY, which holds the key value being processed. OLDFILE (the old master file) and NEWFILE (the new master file) are declared as files of master records. TRANSFILE is declared as a file of transaction records. The Boolean variable FILLED is a flag whose value is TRUE only if NEWFILE↑—the buffer variable for the new master file—contains a record to be written to the new master file.

```
PROGRAM LISTMASTER;
(* PRINT LISTING OF MASTER FILE *)
CONST
   SENTINEL = 9999;
TYPE
   MASTER = RECORD
               KEY: INTEGER;
               BALANCE: REAL
            END;
VAR
   MASTERFILE: FILE OF MASTER;
   FILENAME: STRING;
BEGIN
   WRITE('FILE NAME? ');
   READLN(FILENAME);
   RESET(MASTERFILE, FILENAME);
   WRITELN('KEY':10, 'BALANCE':10);
   WHILE MASTERFILE↑.KEY <> SENTINEL DO
      BEGIN
         WRITELN(MASTERFILE↑.KEY:10, MASTERFILE↑.BALANCE:10:2)
         GET(MASTERFILE)
      END
END.
```

FIGURE 12-3. A program to print a listing of a master file.

Processing begins by calling the procedure OPENFILES, which obtains the external names of the three files from the user. RESET is executed for the two input files, OLDFILE and TRANSFILE, and REWRITE is executed for the output file, NEWFILE. Executing RESET for OLDFILE and TRANSFILE reads the first record of each file into the corresponding buffer variable.

Processing continues until both the old master file and the transaction file are exhausted. Therefore, processing continues while neither OLDFILE↑.KEY nor TRANSFILE↑.KEY is equal to the sentinel. The procedure GETNEXTKEY is called to get the next key value to be processed. The procedure PROCESSTRANSACTIONS is called to process all transaction records whose keys have the value found by GETNEXTKEY. This processing may or may not produce a record to be written to the new master file. If the value of FILLED (set by GETNEXTKEY or PROCESSTRANSACTIONS) is TRUE, then the buffer variable NEWFILE↑ contains a record to be written to the new master file:

```
IF FILLED THEN
   PUT(NEWFILE);
```

```
PROGRAM FILEUPDATE;
(* UPDATE MASTER FILE FROM TRANSACTION FILE *)
CONST
   SENTINEL = 9999;
TYPE
   TRANSTYPE = (ADD, UPDATE, DELETE);
   MASTER = RECORD
               KEY: INTEGER;
               BALANCE: REAL
            END;
   TRANSACTION = RECORD
                    KEY: INTEGER:
                    KIND: TRANSTYPE;
                    AMOUNT: REAL
                 END;
VAR
   CURRENTKEY: INTEGER;
   OLDFILE, NEWFILE: FILE OF MASTER;
   TRANSFILE: FILE OF TRANSACTION;
   FILLED: BOOLEAN;

(* PROCEDURES WILL BE FILLED IN HERE *)

BEGIN
   OPENFILES;
   WHILE    (OLDFILE↑.KEY <> SENTINEL)
         OR (TRANSFILE↑.KEY <> SENTINEL) DO
      BEGIN
         GETNEXTKEY;
         PROCESSTRANSACTIONS;
         IF FILLED THEN
            PUT(NEWFILE)
      END;
   NEWFILE↑.KEY := SENTINEL;
   PUT(NEWFILE);
   CLOSE(NEWFILE, LOCK)
END.
```

FIGURE 12-4. A program to update a master file using a transaction file. This figure shows only the main program; the procedures are shown in separate figures.

The main program finishes up by writing a sentinel record to NEW-FILE and closing the file.

Figure 12-5 shows the procedure OPENFILES, which gets the external names of the files, executes RESET for OLDFILE and TRANS-FILE, and executes REWRITE for NEWFILE.

```
PROCEDURE OPENFILES;
(* GET FILE NAMES, RESET OLDFILE AND TRANSFILE,
   REWRITE NEWFILE.  RESETTING OLDFILE AND NEWFILE
   GETS THE FIRST RECORD OF EACH FILE *)
VAR
    OLDMASTER, NEWMASTER, TRANS: STRING;
BEGIN
    WRITE('OLD MASTER FILE? ');
    READLN(OLDMASTER);
    WRITE('TRANSACTION FILE? ');
    READLN(TRANS);
    WRITE('NEW MASTER FILE? ');
    READLN(NEWMASTER);
    RESET(OLDFILE, OLDMASTER);
    RESET(TRANSFILE, TRANS);
    REWRITE(NEWFILE, NEWMASTER)
END;
```

FIGURE 12–5. This procedure gets the external names of the old master file, the new master file, and the transaction file. RESET is applied to the old master file and the transaction file; REWRITE is applied to the new master file.

Figure 12–6 shows the procedure GETNEXTKEY, which selects the next key value to be processed. If there is a record in the old master file with the selected key value, the record is moved to NEWFILE↑, the buffer variable for the new master file, and FILLED is set to TRUE, indicating that NEWFILE↑ contains a valid record whose key is equal to the current key. If there is no record in the old master file with the selected key value, no record is moved to NEWFILE↑, and FILLED is set to FALSE, indicating that NEWFILE↑ does not contain valid data.

GETNEXTKEY has two key values to select from: OLDFILE↑.KEY, the key of the last record read from the old master file, and TRANSFILE↑.KEY, the key of the last record read from the transaction file. Since the records in NEWFILE are to have their keys in numerical order, smaller keys should be processed before larger ones. Therefore, GETNEXTKEY selects the smaller of the two keys available to it and assigns this key to CURRENTKEY.

If OLDFILE↑.KEY is less than or equal to TRANSFILE↑.KEY, the procedure selects OLDFILE↑.KEY, which is the key of a record in the old master file. The record in question is moved to NEWFILE↑ for processing. FILLED is set to TRUE, indicating that NEWFILE↑ contains valid data, and another record is read from OLDFILE:

```
CURRENTKEY := OLDFILE↑.KEY;
NEWFILE↑ := OLDFILE↑;
FILLED := TRUE;
GET(OLDFILE)
```

```
PROCEDURE GETNEXTKEY;
(* SET CURRENTKEY TO NEXT KEY TO BE PROCESSED.  IF CURRENTKEY IS
   THE KEY OF A RECORD IN THE MASTER FILE, THEN PLACE THAT
   RECORD IN NEWFILE↑, SET FILLED TO TRUE, AND READ ANOTHER
   RECORD FROM OLDFILE.  OTHERWISE, SET FILLED TO FALSE *)
BEGIN
    IF OLDFILE↑.KEY <= TRANSFILE↑.KEY THEN
        BEGIN
            CURRENTKEY := OLDFILE↑.KEY;
            NEWFILE↑ := OLDFILE↑;
            FILLED := TRUE;
            GET(OLDFILE)
        END
    ELSE
        BEGIN
            CURRENTKEY := TRANSFILE↑.KEY;
            FILLED := FALSE
        END
END;
```

FIGURE 12-6. This procedure selects the next key value to be processed. If this value is the key of a record in the old master file, that record is moved to NEW-FILE↑, FILLED is set to TRUE, and a new record is read from the old master file.

If OLDFILE↑.KEY is greater than TRANSFILE↑. KEY, the value of TRANSFILE↑. KEY is selected as the current key. Since OLDFILE↑.KEY is greater than the current key, we have already passed the point in the old master file where there could be a record whose key is equal to the current key. Hence FILLED is set to FALSE, indicating that NEWFILE↑ does not contain a record from the old master file whose key is equal to the current key:

```
CURRENTKEY := TRANSFILE↑.KEY;
FILLED := FALSE
```

Figure 12-7 shows the procedure PROCESSTRANSACTIONS, which processes all transaction records whose keys are equal to the current key. The procedure processes each transaction record by calling either ADDRECORD, UPDATERECORD, or DELETERECORD, depending on which kind of transaction the record represents. After processing the current transaction, the procedure gets another record from the transaction file. Processing continues as long as the key of the current transaction record is equal to the value of CURRENTKEY.

Figure 12-8 shows the three procedures ADDRECORD, UPDATERECORD, and DELETERECORD.

ADDRECORD adds a new record to the master file. If the value of FILLED is TRUE, ADDRECORD prints an error message, since the master file already contains a record with the current key, and a new record

```
PROCEDURE PROCESSTRANSACTIONS;
(* PROCESS ALL TRANSACTIONS WHOSE KEYS ARE EQUAL TO
   CURRENTKEY *)
BEGIN
   WHILE TRANSFILE↑.KEY = CURRENTKEY DO
      BEGIN
         CASE TRANSFILE↑.KIND OF
            ADD: ADDRECORD;
            UPDATE: UPDATERECORD;
            DELETE: DELETERECORD
         END;
         GET(TRANSFILE)
      END
END;
```

FIGURE 12-7. This procedure processes all transaction records whose keys are equal to the value of CURRENTKEY.

with that key cannot be added. If the value of FILLED is FALSE, ADDRECORD sets NEWFILE↑.KEY to the key of the transaction record, NEWFILE↑.BALANCE to the AMOUNT field of the transaction record, and FILLED to TRUE to indicate that NEWFILE↑ now contains a valid record.

UPDATERECORD updates the master record having the same key as the transaction record. If the value of FILLED is TRUE, then the AMOUNT field of the transaction record is added to the BALANCE field of NEWFILE↑. If the value of FILLED is FALSE, there is no record in the master file having the same key as the transaction record, so UPDATERECORD prints an error message.

DELETERECORD deletes the record in the master file having the same key as the transaction record. If the value of FILLED is TRUE, it is set to FALSE, deleting the record stored in NEWFILE↑ by asserting that NEWFILE↑ no longer contains valid data. If the value of FILLED is already FALSE, the procedure prints an error message indicating that the record to be deleted is not present in the master file.

Random Access

We will look at how random access is implemented in UCSD Pascal. Several other versions of Pascal use similar methods.

UCSD Pascal assumes the records of a file to be numbered starting with 0. Thus, the first record in a file is record 0, the second record is record 1, the third record is record 2, and so on. The built-in procedure

```
SEEK(FILE, RECORDNUMBER)
```

```
PROCEDURE ADDRECORD;
(* ADD ONE RECORD *)
BEGIN
   IF FILLED THEN
      BEGIN
         WRITE('CANNOT ADD RECORD ', CURRENTKEY);
         WRITELN('--RECORD ALREADY IN MASTER FILE')
      END
   ELSE
      BEGIN
         NEWFILE↑.KEY := TRANSFILE↑.KEY;
         NEWFILE↑.BALANCE := TRANSFILE↑.AMOUNT;
         FILLED := TRUE
      END
END; (*ADDRECORD *)

PROCEDURE UPDATERECORD;
(* UPDATE ONE RECORD *)
BEGIN
   IF FILLED THEN
      NEWFILE↑.BALANCE := NEWFILE↑.BALANCE + TRANSFILE↑.AMOUNT
   ELSE
      BEGIN
         WRITE('CANNOT UPDATE RECORD ', CURRENTKEY);
         WRITELN('--RECORD NOT IN MASTER FILE')
      END
END; (* UPDATERECORD *)

PROCEDURE DELETERECORD;
(* DELETE ONE RECORD *)
BEGIN
   IF FILLED THEN
      FILLED := FALSE
   ELSE
      BEGIN
         WRITE('CANNOT DELETE RECORD ', CURRENTKEY);
         WRITELN('--RECORD NOT IN MASTER FILE')
      END
END; (* DELETE RECORD *)
```

FIGURE 12–8. These three procedures modify the master file by adding a record, updating an existing record, or deleting an existing record. An error message is printed if a given operation cannot be carried out.

specifies that the next GET or PUT statement for FILE will access the record designated by RECORDNUMBER. Thus,

```
SEEK(F, 5)
```

specifies that the next GET or PUT statement for file F will access record number 5.

To get a designated record from a file, we use SEEK followed by GET. Thus,

```
SEEK(F, 5);
GET(F)
```

transfers record 5 of file F to the buffer variable F↑. To store a record in a designated position in the file, we use SEEK followed by PUT. Thus,

```
SEEK(F, 25);
PUT(F)
```

stores the contents of F↑ as record number 25 of the file.

In general, random file processing is similar to sequential file processing, except that every GET or PUT must be preceded by a SEEK specifying the record to be accessed.

Hashing.   Random files present us with the following problem. Given the key of a record—the number or string that uniquely identifies the entity to which the record refers—we need to know the record number under which the record is stored in the random file. There are three basic approaches to solving this problem:

1. Choose the keys equal to the record numbers. This is the simplest approach when it can be used. In most cases it cannot be used, however, since keys are chosen for purposes other than storing the records in a computer, and the resulting key values are not suitable for use as record numbers. For example, the key may have nine digits or more, yet our file is unlikely to contain billions of records.

2. We can maintain an index, or directory, for our file. Given a key, we look it up in the index and find the number of the corresponding record. This method is widely used.

3. Given the key, we carry out a calculation that yields the number of the corresponding record. This method, also widely used, is called *hashing*, since the calculation scrambles, or "makes a hash of," the original key. In the remainder of this chapter we will look at a program that stores and retrieves information using hashing.

As an example, we will use the price list that has been the subject of two previous programs. Each entry on the price list, which contains an item number (the key) and the price of the item, is stored in a separate record in the file. Given an item number, we want to calculate the record number of the corresponding record. That is, we need a function HASH such that

```
RECNO := HASH(ITEMNUMBER)
```

assigns RECNO the record number of the record corresponding to the value of ITEMNUMBER.

Unfortunately, it is usually impractical to devise a function HASH that will yield a different record number for each value of ITEM-NUMBER. Sometimes, HASH will calculate the same record number for two different item numbers—that is, it will assign two different entries on the price list to the same record in the random file. This situation is known as a *collision*.

There are many methods for handling collisions. The simplest is this: Suppose we are storing a price-list entry and find that the record designated by HASH is already occupied. We step through the file until we find an unused record and store our entry in the first unused record found.

Since we cannot rely on HASH absolutely, when we retrieve an entry we must see if the record designated by HASH actually contains the entry we are trying to retrieve. If not, we must step through the file searching for the entry that we want.

Because of collisions, HASH does not always yield the location of an empty record in which to store a price-list entry or the location of the record containing the entry with a given key. What it tells us is where to begin searching in the file for an empty record or for a particular entry. If the hashing scheme is well designed, the search will, on the average, be very short, requiring us to examine only one or two records before finding the one we are looking for.

When searching, we need another function for stepping through the file. Suppose the record whose number is returned by HASH is already occupied (when we are storing information) or does not contain the item number we are looking for (when we are retrieving information). What record should we look at next? And if this record is not the one we are seeking, which one should we look at after that? Given the record currently being examined, NEXT yields the record that should be examined next:

```
RECNO := NEXT(RECNO)
```

Repeated application of NEXT must take us to every record in the file, then bring us back to the record with which the search began.

Suppose the record designated by HASH does not contain the entry we are looking for, so we embark on a search for that entry. How long should the search continue? When can we decide that the entry is not present and call off the search? We recall that when we are storing an entry and a collision occurs, we search for the first empty record and store the entry there. Consequently, when we are searching for an entry and come upon an empty record, we can call off the search, for we know that if the entry were present, the search made when it was inserted would not have passed over an empty record, but would have used the empty record to store the entry. The search for an entry, then, continues until the entry is found or until and empty record is found.

This, however, raises another problem. When a record is deleted, it creates an empty record that was not present when earlier insertions took place, and this new empty record could cause some searches to terminate prematurely. One way to handle this problem is to distinguish between empty records (records that have never had any data stored in them) and deleted records (records whose contents are no longer needed). Deleted records are available for reuse, but encountering a deleted record will not terminate a search.

No more than about 80% of the available records in a hash file should be actually used for data. This assures that enough empty records are available so that when a new entry is inserted, the chances are that only a short search will be needed to find an empty record to hold the new entry. If this *loading factor* of 80% is exceeded, then searches will become lengthly and time-consuming.

With this preliminary sketch of hashing in mind, let's turn to the example programs and see how the details are worked out.

The Program INITIALIZE. Each record in our hash file will contain a field indicating whether it is FULL (in use), DELETED (no longer in use), or EMPTY (never used). When the file is first created, all the records should be marked EMPTY. The program INITIALIZE (Figure 12–9) writes a file of empty records. Note that INITIALIZE uses sequential (rather than random) access, so record 0 is written first; record 1, second; and so on. Since nothing would be gained by storing the empty records in any other order, random access is not needed.

For the method of hashing—the particular functions HASH and NEXT—that we are going to use to work properly, the number of records in the file must be a *prime number*—a number not evenly divisible by any numbers other than 1 and itself. The first few prime numbers are 2, 3, 5, 7, 11, and 13. Larger prime numbers can be looked up in mathematical handbooks or generated by computer programs. We will use the prime number 61 as the size of the small test file we are creating. Both INITIALIZE and our information retrieval program HASHFILE contain the constant definition

```
FILESIZE = 61;
```

To mark a record as FULL, DELETED, or EMPTY, we use the enumerated type STATE defined by:

```
STATE = (FULL, DELETED, EMPTY);
```

We can now define the data type of the records in the file:

```
PRICERECORD = RECORD
                STATUS: STATE;
                ITEMNO: INTEGER;
                PRICE: REAL
              END;
```

Since INITIALIZE uses only sequential access, the rest of the program should be familiar. PRICELIST is declared to be a file of

```
PROGRAM INITIALIZE;
(* INITIALIZE RANDOM FILE WITH EMPTY RECORDS *)
CONST
   FILESIZE = 61;
TYPE
   STATE = (FULL, DELETED, EMPTY);
   PRICERECORD = RECORD
                      STATUS: STATE;
                      ITEM: INTEGER;
                      PRICE: REAL
                  END;
VAR
   FILENAME: STRING;
   PRICELIST: FILE OF PRICERECORD;
   I: INTEGER;
BEGIN
   WRITE('FILE NAME? ');
   READLN(FILENAME);
   REWRITE(PRICELIST, FILENAME);
   FOR I := 1 TO FILESIZE DO
      BEGIN
         WITH PRICELIST↑ DO
            BEGIN
               STATUS := EMPTY;
               ITEM := 0;
               PRICE := 0.0
            END;
         PUT(PRICELIST)
      END;
   CLOSE(PRICELIST, LOCK)
END.
```

FIGURE 12-9. **A program to initialize a hash file with empty records. This program accesses the file sequentially, since the order in which the empty records are stored is unimportant.**

PRICERECORD. The program begins by getting the external name for PRICELIST and calling REWRITE for the file, after which it stores the empty records:

```
FOR I := 1 to FILESIZE DO
   BEGIN
      WITH PRICELIST↑ DO
         BEGIN
            STATUS := EMPTY;
            ITEM := 0;
            PRICE := 0.0
         END;
      PUT(PRICELIST)
   END
```

Only the assignment

```
STATUS := EMPTY
```

is actually required. Note, however, that the assignments must be repeated for each record. The buffer variable may refer to different areas of memory for different records, so we cannot assume that the buffer variable will retain its value after a record has been written to the file.

The Program HASHFILE.   Figures 12-10 through 12-14 show the program HASHFILE, an information storage and retrieval program using hashing. The program begins with definitions and declarations, many of which are duplicates of those in INITIALIZE. The variables ITEM-NUMBER and ITEMPRICE hold an item number and price entered by the user. OK is a Boolean variable whose value is set to indicate whether or not an operation on the file was carried out successfully. As in some previous programs, the functions and procedures are given in separate listings to keep the listings from getting too large and to emphasize the top-down approach to program construction.

The program begins by getting the external name for PRICELIST and applying RESET to the file. The remainder of the main program accepts users' requests and calls the proper procedure to carry out each request. Since this part of the program has nothing directly to do with either random access or hashing, its study will be left as an exercise.

To retrieve information from a particular record, the main program executes the procedure call

```
FIND(ITEMNUMBER, ITEMPRICE, OK)
```

with ITEMNUMBER set to the item number requested by the user. If a record with that item number is in the file, the procedure sets ITEM-PRICE to the corresponding price and OK to TRUE. Otherwise, OK is set to FALSE.

Figure 12-11 shows the procedure FIND. We begin by using the function HASH to compute the record number at which we are to start searching the file for the record whose key is the value of ITEM-NUMBER. This record number must be assigned to two variables: REC-NO, which is number of the record currently being examined, and START, which keeps track of the point in the file at which our search began.

```
START := HASH(ITEMNUMBER);
RECNO := START
```

FOUND, which is to be set to TRUE if the sought-after value was found and FALSE otherwise, is initially set to FALSE:

```
FOUND := FALSE
```

```
PROGRAM HASHFILE;
(* MAINTAIN PRICE FILE USING HASHING *)
CONST
   FILESIZE = 61;
TYPE
   STATE = (FULL, DELETED, EMPTY);
   PRICERECORD = RECORD
                      STATUS: STATE;
                      ITEMNO: INTEGER;
                      PRICE: REAL
                  END;
VAR
   FILENAME: STRING;
   PRICELIST: FILE OF PRICERECORD;
   ITEMNUMBER: INTEGER;
   ITEMPRICE: REAL;
   OK: BOOLEAN;
   RESPONSE: CHAR;

(* FUNCTION AND PROCEDURE DECLARATIONS WILL BE
   FILLED IN HERE *)

BEGIN
   WRITE('FILE NAME? ');
   READLN(FILENAME);
   RESET(PRICELIST, FILENAME);
   REPEAT
      WRITE('R(ETRIEVE, S(TORE, D(ELETE, OR Q(UIT? ');
      READ(RESPONSE); WRITELN;
      CASE RESPONSE OF
         'R': BEGIN
                 WRITE('ENTER ITEM NUMBER: ');
                 READLN(ITEMNUMBER);
                 FIND(ITEMNUMBER, ITEMPRICE, OK);
                 IF OK THEN
                     WRITELN('PRICE IS ', ITEMPRICE:8:2)
                 ELSE
                     WRITELN('REQUESTED ITEM NOT FOUND')
              END;
```

(Continued on page 264.)

FIGURE 12-10. A program for information storage and retrieval using a hash file. This figure shows only the main program; the functions and procedures are shown in separate figures.

(FIGURE 12-10 continued)

```
        'S': BEGIN
                WRITE('ENTER ITEM NUMBER AND PRICE: ');
                READLN(ITEMNUMBER, ITEMPRICE);
                INSERT(ITEMNUMBER, ITEMPRICE, OK);
                IF NOT OK THEN
                    WRITELN('NO ROOM IN FILE')
             END;

        'D': BEGIN
                WRITE('ENTER ITEM NUMBER: ');
                READLN(ITEMNUMBER);
                DELETE(ITEMNUMBER, OK);
                IF NOT OK THEN
                    WRITELN('REQUESTED ITEM NOT FOUND')
             END
     END; (* CASE *)
     WRITELN
  UNTIL RESPONSE = 'Q'
END.
```

The search is controlled by a REPEAT statement. The repeated statements begin by getting the record designated by the value of REC-NO:

```
SEEK(PRICELIST, RECNO);
GET(PRICELIST)
```

If the STATUS field of the record obtained is FULL (the record contains valid data) and the ITEMNO field equals the requested item number, then we have found the desired record. ITEMPRICE is set to the PRICE field of the record and FOUND is set to TRUE:

```
ITEMPRICE := PRICELIST↑.PRICE;
FOUND := TRUE
```

The final repeated statement sets RECNO to the number of the next record to be examined:

```
RECNO := NEXT(RECNO)
```

The search can terminate under any of three conditions:

1. The value of FOUND is TRUE. The sought-after record has been found.

2. The value of the STATUS field of the record being examined is EMP-TY. If we find an empty record, we can call the search off, since the

```
PROCEDURE FIND(ITEMNUMBER: INTEGER; VAR ITEMPRICE: REAL;
                VAR FOUND: BOOLEAN);
(* FIND AND GET PRICE FROM RECORD WITH GIVEN ITEM NUMBER *)
VAR
   START, RECNO: INTEGER;
BEGIN
   START := HASH(ITEMNUMBER);
   RECNO := START;
   FOUND := FALSE;
   REPEAT
      SEEK(PRICELIST, RECNO);
      GET(PRICELIST);
      IF    (PRICELIST↑.STATUS = FULL)
         AND (PRICELIST↑.ITEMNO = ITEMNUMBER) THEN
         BEGIN
            ITEMPRICE := PRICELIST↑.PRICE;
            FOUND := TRUE
         END;
      RECNO := NEXT(RECNO)
   UNTIL FOUND OR (PRICELIST↑.STATUS = EMPTY) OR (RECNO = START)
END;
```

FIGURE 12–11. **This procedure locates the price-list entry having a given item number.**

procedure for inserting entries in the file would not have passed over an empty record.

3. The value of RECNO is equal to START. Having examined every record in the file, we have come back to the one we started with. This situation can occur only if no EMPTY (never used) records remain in the file.

To insert a new entry into the file, the main program executes the procedure call:

```
INSERT(ITEMNUMBER, ITEMPRICE, OK)
```

ITEMNUMBER and ITEMPRICE contain the data that is to be inserted into the file. INSERT sets OK to TRUE if the insertion was successfully made and to FALSE if the file was full.

Figure 12–12 shows the procedure INSERT, which has the same general organization as FIND. Both START and RECNO are set to the starting record number computed by HASH. The Boolean variable INSERTED, which indicates whether or not a successful insertion was made, is initially set to FALSE.

Starting at the record number computed by HASH, INSERT searches for an unused (empty or deleted) record. If such a record is found, it is used for the new entry being inserted. The first two repeated statements read the record designated by the value of RECNO:

```
PROCEDURE INSERT(ITEMNUMBER: INTEGER; ITEMPRICE: REAL
                    VAR INSERTED: BOOLEAN);
(* INSERT NEW RECORD INTO FILE *)
VAR
   START, RECNO: INTEGER;
BEGIN
   START := HASH(ITEMNUMBER);
   RECNO := START;
   INSERTED := FALSE;
   REPEAT
      SEEK(PRICELIST, RECNO);
      GET(PRICELIST);
      IF    (PRICELIST↑.STATUS = EMPTY)
         OR (PRICELIST↑.STATUS = DELETED) THEN
         BEGIN
            PRICELIST↑.STATUS := FULL;
            PRICELIST↑.ITEMNO := ITEMNUMBER;
            PRICELIST↑.PRICE := ITEMPRICE;
            SEEK(PRICELIST, RECNO);
            PUT(PRICELIST);
            INSERTED := TRUE
         END;
      RECNO := NEXT(RECNO)
   UNTIL INSERTED OR (RECNO = START)
END;
```

FIGURE 12–12. **This procedure inserts a new price-list entry in a hash file.**

```
SEEK(PRICELIST, RECNO);
GET(PRICELIST)
```

If the status of the record obtained is DELETED or EMPTY, then the record is available and can be used to store the new entry:

```
PRICELIST↑.STATUS := FULL;
PRICELIST↑.ITEMNO := ITEMNUMBER;
PRICELIST↑.PRICE  := ITEMPRICE;
SEEK(PRICELIST, RECNO);
PUT(PRICELIST);
INSERTED := TRUE
```

Note that when putting a previously gotten record back in the file, SEEK must be executed again before executing the PUT statement.

As in FIND, the final repeated statement computes the record number of the next record to be examined. The search can terminate under two conditions. The value of INSERTED can be TRUE, indicating that a successful insertion was performed. Or the value of RECNO can

```
PROCEDURE DELETE(ITEMNUMBER: INTEGER; VAR FOUND: BOOLEAN);
(* DELETE RECORD WITH GIVEN ITEM NUMBER *)
VAR
    START, RECNO: INTEGER;
    SAVESTATUS: STATE;
BEGIN
    START := HASH(ITEMNUMBER);
    RECNO := START;
    FOUND := FALSE;
    REPEAT
        SEEK(PRICELIST, RECNO);
        GET(PRICELIST);
        SAVESTATUS := PRICELIST↑.STATUS;
        IF    (SAVESTATUS = FULL)
          AND (PRICELIST↑.ITEMNO = ITEMNUMBER) THEN
            BEGIN
                PRICELIST↑.STATUS := DELETED;
                SEEK(PRICELIST, RECNO);
                PUT(PRICELIST);
                FOUND := TRUE
            END;
        RECNO := NEXT(RECNO)
    UNTIL FOUND OR (SAVESTATUS = EMPTY) OR (RECNO = START)
END;
```

FIGURE 12–13. **This procedure deletes a specified price-list entry from a hash file.**

equal the value of START, indicating that after examining every record in the file, we have come back to the one we started with. If this happens, the file is full—it contains no empty or deleted records.

To delete an entry from the file, the main program executes the procedure call

```
DELETE(ITEMNUMBER, OK)
```

where ITEMNUMBER is the item number of the entry to be deleted. The Boolean variable OK is set to TRUE if the designated entry was found and deleted; if the designated entry was not found, OK is set to FALSE. Figure 12–13 shows the procedure DELETE, which will not be discussed in detail since it is similar to FIND. If the designated record is found, it is written back to the file with its STATUS field set to DELETED.

Finally, we come to the functions HASH and NEXT, shown in Figure 12–14, which determine how entries will be placed in the file and the order in which records will be examined during searches. There are many possibilities for these functions, which is why we wrote the rest of the program without assuming specific HASH and NEXT functions.

```
FUNCTION HASH(KEY: INTEGER): INTEGER;
(* COMPUTE HASH CODE FOR GIVEN KEY *)
BEGIN
   HASH := KEY MOD FILESIZE
END;

FUNCTION NEXT(RECNO: INTEGER): INTEGER;
(* COMPUTE NUMBER OF NEXT RECORD TO BE EXAMINED *)
BEGIN
   NEXT := (RECNO + 1) MOD FILESIZE
END;
```

FIGURE 12–14. The function HASH computes the record number in the hash file at which the search for a given item is to begin. During a search the function NEXT computes the record number of the next record to be examined.

We want HASH to distribute the entries as evenly as possible throughout the file, so each record that is in use will be reasonably close to an unused record. If this is true, then collisions will be rare, and when a search must be made, it will be short. On the other hand, a cluster of records that are in use increases the chance of collisions and the length of searches in that region of the file. A reasonably good hashing function is obtained by dividing the key by the number of records in the file and taking the remainder:

```
HASH := KEY MOD FILESIZE
```

For this hashing function to give good results, FILESIZE must be a prime number.

The function NEXT computes the number of the next record to be examined in a search. Repeated applications of NEXT must step through every record in the file, then return to the record with which the search began. The most obvious NEXT function simply advances to the next record in the file:

```
NEXT := (RECNO + 1) MOD FILESIZE
```

The records in the file are numbered 0 through FILESIZE – 1. As long as RECNO + 1 is in this range, the "MOD FILESIZE" has no effect, and NEXT returns the value of RECNO + 1. If, however, we attempt to step beyond the end of the file, then RECNO + 1 is equal to FILESIZE, and the remainder after dividing by FILESIZE is 0. Hence, our search "wraps around" —when we reach the end of the file we go back to the beginning of the file. The file is processed as if the last and first records were adjacent.

This version of NEXT has one drawback. If we start searching for a place for a new entry within a cluster of occupied records, the new entry will be placed at the end of the cluster, making the cluster larger. A simple way to minimize this effect is to use

```
NEXT := (RECNO + STEP) MOD FILESIZE
```

where the value of STEP is greater than 1. If FILESIZE is a prime number, then any value of STEP in the range 1 through FILESIZE – 1 will provide the required property that NEXT step through every record in the file before returning to the starting record.

When the functions and procedures are inserted in the main program, HASH and NEXT must come before FIND, INSERT, and DELETE, since a function or procedure must be declared before it can be referred to by another function or procedure.

Exercises

1. A *listing* results when the contents of a file are printed out for easier reading. For example, we may wish a printout of information that is stored on disk or on punched cards. Write a program to list the file INPUT on OUTPUT—that is, each line read from INPUT should be printed as a line of OUTPUT. The program should work regardless of the number of characters on a line or the number of lines in INPUT.

2. Modify the program of Exercise 1 so that each printed line is preceded by a line number. The line number is printed in a four-character field and separated from the remainder of the line by one blank space. The first printed line is numbered 1, the next line 2, and so on.

3. Modify the program of Exercise 2 to print the listing 60 lines to a page and with a page number in the upper-right-hand corner of each page.

4. Suppose the file CLASS is declared as follows:

```
TYPE
    STUDENT = RECORD
                ID: PACKED ARRAY[1..9] OF CHAR;
                NAME: PACKED ARRAY[1..40] OF CHAR;
                GRADE: INTEGER
              END;
VAR
    CLASS: FILE OF STUDENT;
```

Write a program to print a listing of the file CLASS.

5. The records in the file CLASS are supposed to be in order of increasing values of the ID field. Write a program to check the order of the records in CLASS and print the ID fields of any exceptions. Specifically, the program will print the ID field of any record whose ID field is less than that of the preceding record.

6. Suppose that two classes are to be combined. We want to merge the files CLASS1 and CLASS2 into a single class CLASS3. The records of CLASS1 and CLASS2 are in ascending order according to the ID field, and CLASS3 should be likewise. *Hints:* A merge program is similar to, but much simpler than, the file-update program discussed in this chapter. On each cycle of operation the program compares CLASS1↑.ID and CLASS2↑.ID. If CLASS1↑.ID is less than CLASS2↑.ID, then the value of CLASS1↑ is written to CLASS3. Otherwise, the value of CLASS2↑ is written to CLASS3. When the end of either CLASS1 or CLASS2 is reached, all the records remaining in the other file are transferred to CLASS3.

7. Sometimes we need a listing of only those records that occur in two files. For example, if students are not allowed to take two particular courses at the same time, we might wish to compare the class rolls for the courses to discover any violators. Likewise, we sometimes want to list any record that occurs in only one of two files. If students are required to take two courses simultaneously, we might want a list of students who are taking one course but not the other. Write a program to accept two student files, CLASS1 and CLASS2, as input and produce two text files as output. One text file will contain the names of all students enrolled in both classes, and the other will contain the names of all students enrolled in one class but not the other.

8. Files are sometimes used for temporary storage when a program must deal with more data than will fit into main memory at one time. To demonstrate this, write a program to generate, and then find the sum of, 200,000 random numbers between 0 and 1. The catch is that you must first generate—and store—the numbers and only then start adding. Your program should satisfy the frequent requirement that a large segment of the data should be available at once, so make sure that at least 2000 numbers are simultaneously in main memory. Assume that a file is needed even if your system will allow you to store the 200,000 numbers in main memory.

9. As an aid to understanding hashing, modify the program HASHFILE so that, on receipt of a P (for Print) command, it will list the file PRICELIST. One line should be printed for each record in the file, and the lines should be printed in the order in which the records occur in the file. If a record is empty or deleted, the word EMPTY or DELETED should be printed. For each occupied record, the item number of the record should be printed. (The item price can be omitted, since it is of no interest in studying the way the records are stored in the hash file.) To keep the display or printout from being too unwieldy, use a small file size, such as 11, 13, or 17 records.

10. Write an information storage and retrieval program using an in-memory index—an index that resides in main memory during processing. The database—the body of information maintained by the program—will be stored as two files—an index file containing the index and a data file containing the data of interest. When the program begins execution, it reads the index into an array in main memory. Before terminating, the program writes the (possibly modified) index back to the index file.

Each index entry has the following form:

```
INDEXENTRY = RECORD
                EMPTY: BOOLEAN;
                KEY: INTEGER
             END;
```

In main memory, the index is stored in an array declared by

```
INDEX: ARRAY[0..MAXRECNO] OF INDEXENTRY;
```

where the constant MAXRECNO is the largest record number that occurs in the data file.

There is a one-to-one correspondence between index entries and records in the data file. For any value of I in the range 0 through MAXRECNO, INDEX[I] is the index entry corresponding to record I—the record whose record number is equal to the value of I. INDEX[I].EMPTY is TRUE if record I is currently unused and FALSE if record I is in use. If INDEX[I].EMPTY is FALSE, then INDEX[I].KEY is the key of record I —the value that will be used to look up a particular record.

Use sequential search to find the index entry with a particular key value and to find the first unused index entry. To access the data record having a particular key, find the index entry with that key, then access the corresponding record in the data file. To insert a new data record, find the first unused index entry, set EMPTY to FALSE, set KEY to the key of the record being inserted, and store the data to be inserted in the corresponding record in the data file. To delete the record having a given key, find the index entry with that key and set EMPTY to TRUE.

Chapter 13

STRUCTURED TYPES: SETS

A *set* is a collection of values. For example, the set that contains the values 1, 3, 5, and 9 is denoted in Pascal as

[1, 3, 5, 9]

The values that belong to a set are called its *elements*. The elements of [1, 3, 5, 9] are 1, 3, 5, and 9.

(If you have encountered sets in mathematics courses, you recall that the elements were enclosed in braces, like this:

{1, 3, 5, 9}

In Pascal, however, braces are reserved for enclosing comments. Therefore, square brackets are used for sets.)

Set Declarations

A set type can be declared as follows:

LETTERSET = SET OF 'A'..'Z';

The type 'A'..'Z' is called the *base type* and is the type of the elements of the sets. Suppose we declare the set variable S by:

S: LETTERSET;

Some possible values of S are:

```
['A']  ['A', 'C']  ['A', 'E', 'I', 'O', 'U']  []
```

Note that [] denotes the *empty set*, the set that has no elements. Every set type includes the empty set as a value, regardless of the base type.

Now consider the following definitions:

```
PRIMARY = (RED, YELLOW, BLUE);
PRIMSET = SET OF PRIMARY;
```

The following are all the possible values of PRIMSET:

```
[]   [RED]   [YELLOW]   [BLUE]   [RED, YELLOW]
[RED, BLUE]   [YELLOW, BLUE]   [RED, YELLOW, BLUE]
```

A variable of type PRIMSET must have one of these eight values.

The base type must be an ordinal type. Each version of Pascal places certain additional limitations on the values of set types. These limitations typically take the following form:

1. There is a limit on the number of elements a set can have. This, in turn, imposes a limit on the number of different values in the base type. A type can be the base type of a set type only if the number of different values belonging to it does not exceed a certain limit. This limit invariably excludes INTEGER as a base type and in some cases excludes CHAR as well.

2. Only integers belonging to a certain subrange may be elements of sets. For instance, if the subrange is $0..58$, then $1..5$, $5..10$, and $0..58$ are permissible base types, but $-1..3$ and $98..100$ are not. Also, the set [25, 40] is allowed but [-2, 5] and [59] are not.

3. If CHAR is not allowed as a base type, only character values that belong to some given subrange of CHAR may be elements of sets.

If these restrictions were the same for every version of Pascal, they would not be too much of a problem. But since they are different for different versions, a program using sets may work with one version of Pascal but not with another. This limits the usefulness of sets for programs intended to be *portable*—usable on different computer systems with different versions of Pascal.

In UCSD Pascal, a set can may have up to 4080 elements. Integers in the subrange $0..4079$ can belong to sets. (For UCSD Pascal on the Apple II computer, a set can have at most 512 elements, and only integers in the subrange $0..511$ can belong to sets.) CHAR is allowed as a base type. Some other versions of Pascal place much more severe restrictions on sets, allowing only 58 or 64 elements and not allowing CHAR as a base type.

Operations on Sets

Set values are created by means of *set constructors*. We have been using set constructors all along to display set values:

```
[1, 3, 5, 9]    ['A', 'B', 'C']    [RED, YELLOW]
```

A set constructor is an expression that is evaluated as the program executes. This means it can contain variables as well as constants. For example, suppose the variable I and J have the values 5 and 3. The set constructor

```
[I, J, I + J, I - J, I * J, I DIV J]
```

has the value

```
[5, 3, 8, 2, 15, 1]
```

(The order in which the elements are listed is immaterial.) On the other hand, if the values of I and J were 7 and 2, the same set constructor would have the value:

```
[7, 2, 9, 5, 14, 3]
```

The list of elements in a set constructor can contain subranges as well as the values of individual elements. Thus,

```
[1..5]
```

is equivalent to

```
[1, 2, 3, 4, 5]
```

and

```
['A', 'C'..'F', 'L', 'W'..'Z']
```

is equivalent to

```
['A', 'C', 'D', 'E', 'F', 'L', 'W', 'X', 'Y', 'Z']
```

There are three operations that can be applied to sets to yield other sets. These are *union*, *intersection*, and *difference*, which in Pascal are denoted by +, *, and –. They are defined as follows, where S and T are variables of the same set type:

S + T   The *union* of S and T, which contains those elements that belong to S, to T, or to both S and T.

S * T   The *intersection* of S and T, which contains those elements that belong to both S and T.

S — T   The *difference* of S and T, which contains those elements
             that belong to S but do not belong to T.

The following expressions and their values illustrate the union, intersection, and difference operations:

Expression	Value
[1, 2, 3] + [4, 5, 6]	[1, 2, 3, 4, 5, 6]
[1, 2, 3, 4] + [3, 4, 5]	[1, 2, 3, 4, 5]
[1, 2, 3, 4] * [3, 4, 5]	[3, 4]
[1, 2, 3,] * [4, 5, 6]	[ ]
[1, 2, 3, 4, 5] − [2, 3]	[1, 4, 5]
[1, 2, 3] − [4, 5, 6]	[1, 2, 3]

The priorities of +, *, and − are the same when they are used as set
operators as when they are used as arithmetic operators. Thus, the expression

[1, 2] * [2, 3] + [1, 5] * [5, 6]

is evaluated as follows:

```
[1, 2] * [2, 3] + [1, 5] * [5, 6]    intersections first
           [2] + [5]                 then union
           [2, 5]
```

Parentheses can also be used in set expressions, as the following
evaluation illustrates:

```
[1, 2] * ([2, 3] + [1, 5]) * [5, 6]    parentheses first
[1, 2] * [1, 2, 3, 5] * [5, 6]         left-to-right order
           [1, 2] * [5, 6]
           [ ]
```

The following relational operators apply to sets of the same set type
and yield BOOLEAN values:

```
=      <>
<=     >=
IN
```

If S and T are set variables with the same base type, and the type of I is
the same as the base type of S and T, we can define the relational operators as follows:

S = T   TRUE if S *equals* T; that is, if S and T have the same ele-
             ments

S <> T   TRUE if S is *not equal* to T; that is, if S and T do not have
             the same elements.

S <= T   TRUE if S is a *subset* of T; that is, if every element of S is also an element of T

S >= T   TRUE if S is a *superset* of T; that is, if every element of T is also an element of S.

I IN S   TRUE if I is an element of S

The following expressions and values illustrate the relational operators for sets:

Expression	Value
[1, 2, 3] = [1, 2, 4]	FALSE
[1, 2, 3] <> [1, 2, 4]	TRUE
[2, 3] <= [1, 2, 3]	TRUE
[1, 2, 3] >= [2]	TRUE
[1, 2, 3] <= [1, 2, 4]	FALSE
[1, 2, 3] >= [1, 2, 4]	FALSE
2 IN [1, 2, 3]	TRUE
4 IN [1, 2, 3]	FALSE

The relational operators all have the same priority, and that priority is the same as the priority of the operators

=   <>   <=   >=

when they are applied to numbers. Thus, the relational operators have a lower priority than +, *, or –. This means that in expressions such as

```
S + T <= U * V
I IN S + T - U
```

the set expressions are evaluated before the relational operators are applied.

Using Sets

We often use sets to avoid complex Boolean expressions. For example, suppose that C is a character variable and we want to know whether the value of C is one of the arithmetic operators '+', '–', '*', '/'. One way to determine this would be to evaluate the Boolean expressions:

```
(C = '+') OR (C = '-') OR (C = '*') OR (C = '/')
```

But the much simpler expression

```
C IN ['+', '-', '*', '/']
```

gives the same result.

Or suppose we want to know if the value of C is one of the uppercase letters of the alphabet. The expression

```
('A' <= C) AND (C <= 'Z')
```

would determine this, but the equivalent expression using sets

```
C IN ['A'..'Z']
```

is easier to read and can be evaluated more efficiently by the computer.

In several programs we have used a flag—a Boolean variable that records whether or not a certain condition is true. One part of the program checks the condition and assigns the appropriate value to the flag; another part of the program uses the value of the flag to determine what action the program should take at that point.

In a complex program we can have many conditions whose truth or falsity can influence the behavior of the program. Certain parts of the program check particular conditions and record whether they are true or false. Other parts of the program base their actions on the truth or falsity of various conditions. For a particular action to be taken, certain conditions have to be true and other conditions have to be false. The truth or falsity of still other conditions may be irrelevant to the decision.

Suppose that the behavior of a certain program is influenced by six conditions, which we will denote A, B, C, D, E, F. Let's define a data type whose values are those six conditions:

```
CONDITION = (A, B, C, D, E, F)
```

We will use a set variable T to record which conditions are true. At any time during the program the conditions that are members of the value of T are true, and those that are not members of the value of T are false. We declare T by:

```
T: SET OF CONDITION;
```

At the beginning of the program we assign T the set of conditions that are initially true. If none of the conditions are initially true, we assign T the empty set:

```
T := []
```

If a certain part of the program determines that the condition A is true, then it can place that condition in the set T of true conditions as follows:

```
T := T + [A]
```

If the value of T is [C, F] before this statement is executed, it will be [A, C, F] afterwards. On the other hand, if the value of T is [A, C, F] before the statement is executed, it will still be [A, C, F] afterwards.

Suppose the program later determines that condition A has become false. The program removes A from the set of true conditions as follows:

```
T := T - [A]
```

If the value of T is [A, C, F] before this statement is executed, it will be [C, F] afterwards. On the other hand, if the value of T is [C, F] before the statement is executed, it will still be [C, F] afterwards.

Now, suppose we want to execute a certain statement under the following conditions:

• A and C are true

• F is false

• B, D, and E are irrelevant to the decision

Our first step is to eliminate from T the conditions whose truth is irrelevant to the decision. We can do this using the expression:

```
T * [A, C, F]
```

The set [A, C, F] is sometimes called a *mask*, since intersecting it with T masks or hides any elements of T whose presence is not relevant to the decision at hand.

For the statement to be executed, A and C must be elements of T, and F must not be an element of T. Thus, the statement will be executed if:

```
T * [A, C, F] = [A, C]
```

The following causes the statement to be executed only under the specified conditions:

```
IF T * [A, C, F] = [A, C] THEN
    statement
```

Let's generalize this by introducing set variables M (the mask) and TR (the set of conditions that must be true). Replacing the set constructors by set variables, the controlling IF statement becomes:

```
IF T * M = TR THEN
    statement
```

If the values of M and TR are [A, C, F] and [A, C], then the conditions for the execution of the statement will be the same as the ones previously given. But suppose another part of the program makes the assignments:

```
M := [A, B, C, D];
TR := [A, B]
```

Now the statement will be executed when A and B are true and C and D are false. The conditions E and F are irrelevant. Thus, one part of a program can change the conditions under which a statement in another part of the program will be executed, an effect not easily obtained with Boolean variables.

Now let's look at another application. In Chapter 1 we spoke of a *language processor*, which inputs a program in a higher level language and either executes the program or translates it into a language that is easier to execute.

The input to a translator is a stream of characters. The first step in the processing is to break this stream down into meaningful groupings of characters—reserved words, identifiers, numbers, operators, and the like. These groupings are called *symbols*, and we pick them out automatically when we read a program. For example, when we see the statement

```
NEWVAL := OLDVAL + 32 * I
```

we see not a stream of characters but a sequence of symbols:

```
NEWVAL
:=
OLDVAL
+
32
*
I
```

The part of a language processor that recognizes the individual symbols of a program is called a *scanner*.

Let's write a scanner that will input a simple Pascal program and produce a list of symbols such as the one just shown. To simplify matters, we will assume that the Pascal program deals only with integers —only integer constants, integer variables, and operators applicable to integers appear. There are no arrays, no comments, and the program is typed in all uppercase letters.

Our scanner will distinguish three kinds of symbols:

1. *Identifiers and reserved words.* We do not distinguish between identifiers and reserved words. (In a real language processor, a table of reserved words would be used to make the distinction.) For an identifier or reserved word, the first character must belong to ['A'..'Z'], and the remaining characters must belong to ['A'..'Z', '0'..'9'].

2. *Integer constants.* The characters of an integer constant must belong to ['0'..'9']. A plus or minus sign preceding a constant is considered to be a separate symbol, not part of the constant.

3. *Operators and punctuation marks.* The characters making up these all belong to:

```
[ '+', '-', '*', '/', '=', '<', '>', '(', ')', ':', ';', ',' ]
```

The symbols of a program can be separated by any number of blank spaces. When two or more symbols of the same kind occur in succession, such as in

```
I := J DIV K;
J := +25;
K := (I + J) * (I - J)
```

they *must* be separated by blank spaces. If the blank spaces in the above statements were omitted, the scanner would consider JDIVK, :=+, and)*(to be symbols.

Figure 13-1 shows the scanner program. We assume that CHAR can be used as a base type for sets. Input is from the UCSD Pascal predefined file KEYBOARD. KEYBOARD is similar to INPUT except that the characters typed on the keyboard are not "echoed"—they do not automatically appear on the screen as typed. What appears on the screen is the output produced by the scanner program. When you type a stream of characters, the screen will show the stream broken down into symbols, with each symbol on a different line.

```
PROGRAM SCAN;
(* EXTRACT SYMBOLS FROM STREAM OF CHARACTERS *)
VAR
   C: CHAR;
   SPECIAL: SET OF CHAR;
   SCANNING: BOOLEAN;
BEGIN
   SPECIAL := ['+', '-', '*', '/', '=', '<', '>', '(',
               ')', ':', ';', ','];
   SCANNING := TRUE;
   READ(KEYBOARD, C);
   WHILE SCANNING DO
      BEGIN
         WHILE C = ' ' DO
            READ(KEYBOARD, C);
         IF C IN ['A'..'Z'] THEN
            BEGIN
               REPEAT
                  WRITE(C);
                  READ(KEYBOARD, C)
               UNTIL NOT (C IN ['A'..'Z', '0'..'9']);
               WRITELN
            END
```

(Continued on page 282.)

FIGURE 13-1. This program extracts identifiers, numbers, and special symbols from a stream of characters. Each symbol extracted is printed on a separate line.

(FIGURE 13-1 continued)

```
      ELSE IF C IN ['0'..'9'] THEN
         BEGIN
            REPEAT
               WRITE(C);
               READ(KEYBOARD, C)
            UNTIL NOT (C IN ['0'..'9']);
            WRITELN
         END
      ELSE IF C IN SPECIAL THEN
         BEGIN
            REPEAT
               WRITE(C);
               READ(KEYBOARD, C)
            UNTIL NOT (C IN SPECIAL);
            WRITELN
         END
      ELSE IF C = '.' THEN
         BEGIN
            WRITELN(C);
            SCANNING := FALSE
         END
      ELSE
         BEGIN
            WRITELN('ILLEGAL CHARACTER: ', C);
            READ(KEYBOARD, C)
         END
   END
END.
```

Exercises

1. Modify SCAN so that it ignores comments. When a '{' is encountered, everything through the next '}' is ignored. (This problem is slightly harder if '(*' and '*)' are used for comments.)

2. Modify SCAN so that it will recognize string constants as separate ymbols and print each string constant on a separate line. Assume that single quote marks cannot occur inside string constants.

3. Same as Exercise 2, but assume that a single quote mark is represented inside a string by two single quote marks in succession. Thus

```
Y'ALL COME
```

is represented as

'Y' 'ALL COME'

Hint: For this kind of problem, it's often helpful to look ahead one character, and Pascal provides a simple means of doing this. If the characters are being read from file F using READ, the value of F↑ is the next character that will be read. *Warning:* The preceding statement does not apply to UCSD Pascal interactive files. (Why?)

4. Modify SCAN so it will recognize real as well as integer constants. A numeric constant has the following general form: an integer part, such as

254

followed by an optional fractional part, such as

.75

followed by an optional exponent part, such as

E+25   or   E-25   or   E25

5. Most versions of Pascal represent sets internally in much the same way that the compact coded number in Exercise 7 of Chapter 7 represented neighbors who were at home. Define your neighbors as (for example):

```
TYPE
   NEIGH = (JONES, GIVAUD, HENDRIKS, VEREY, KROSS);
```

and then rewrite the function HOME to look at the value of a set variable to decide how many neighbors are at home.

6. Taking the same situation as in Exercise 5 (and in Exercise 7 of Chapter 7) write a program that reads a series of lines reporting on the movements of your neighbors, where each line has a person's initial followed by O (meaning "just gone out") or I (meaning "just come in"). Keep an up-to-date record in two set variables, ATHOME and AWAY, and at end-of-file, print who is available to help mow the village green, who is out, and who has managed to keep his or her movements secret. How difficult would it be to change your program if the names and number of all your neighbors changed?

7. Write a simple interpreter—a program that reads and executes other programs—for a Pascal-like minilanguage. An example of a program in the minilanguage is:

```
PROGRAM
CONST
   A= 25
   X='F'
VAR
   I:INTEGER
   C:CHAR
   J:INTEGER
BEGIN
   J:= 5+ 3* 2
   C:=X
   C:='.'
   WRITE C
   WRITELN J/ 5
END
```

This program does nothing useful; it is merely supposed to illustrate all the elements of the minilanguage. The language has many limitations in comparison with Pascal, all designed to make it easier to process. The principal one is that each number is preceded by a blank, so that your program will know when to read the next item into an integer variable. Not all blanks indicate that a number follows—only those in an expression or on the right-hand side of a constant definition. Further limitations on the language are:

• Each definition, declaration, and statement must be on a separate line, as in the example.

• Only one-character identifiers are allowed.

• The only types are INTEGER and CHAR.

• Expressions (integer only) have the same precedence rules and limitations as for the calculator in Exercise 10 of Chapter 6 and Exercise 10 of Chapter 9.

• No more than one variable can be declared in each declaration (not, for example, I,J:INTEGER);

• WRITE, WRITELN, and assignment are the only allowed statements.

• WRITE and WRITELN take only one argument—a character variable or constant, or an integer expression not beginning with a number.

You will need an identifier table to keep track of identifiers such as A, X, I, C, and J above. Each entry in the table should be a record showing whether that identifier has been declared, whether it is a constant identifier or a variable, its type, whether it has a value, and its value. For this exercise, an array of such records, indexed by the names of the variables, is suitable. Your interpreter must do the following:

• Record information in the identifier table as it reads the CONST and VAR parts of an input program.

- Check the following aspects of the program: syntax (each definition, declaration, or statement occurs in the proper part of the program and has the form expected—for example, a constant definition occurs in the constant-definition part of the program and consists of an identifier followed by an equal sign, which in turn is followed by a constant), same type for right-hand and left-hand sides of assignment statement, left-hand side of assignment statement must not be constant identifier, variables have been assigned values when values are needed. Note that checking is usually done as the program is interpreted, rather than as a separate step.

- Evaluate expressions and carry out the specified assignments.

- Produce output as requested by WRITE and WRITELN statements.

8. Rewrite the interpreter from the previous exercise so as to use an identifier table in the form of a linked list instead of an array. Records will be created only for those identifiers that are actually defined and used in the program.

9. Rewrite the interpreter from the previous exercises to read all its input as characters, even items intended to be integers. For instance, '254+J' would be read initially as five characters. Digit strings such as '254' must be converted to integer values by the interpreter. If each digit character read is assigned to C, and the integer value is accumulated in I, then the conversion can be performed by initializing I to 0 and executing

```
I := 10 * I + ORD(C) - ORD('0')
```

for each character in the digit string. In this version of the interpreter numbers no longer have to be preceded by blank spaces, and an integer expression in a WRITE or WRITELN statement can begin with a number. Blank spaces can be used anywhere except inside an identifier or reserved word, inside a number, or between the : and = of :=.

10. Rewrite your interpreter from the previous exercises to accept identifiers of any length. Only the first eight characters of an identifier are significant—that is, any two identifiers with the same first eight characters are considered identical. Consequently, only the first eight characters of an identifier need to be stored in the identifier table.

PASCAL RESERVED WORDS

The following are the reserved words in standard Pascal. Note that each version of Pascal may have a small number of additional reserved words for special features available in that version.

AND	END	NIL	SET
ARRAY	FILE	NOT	THEN
BEGIN	FOR	OF	TO
CASE	FUNCTION	OR	TYPE
CONST	GOTO	PACKED	UNTIL
DIV	IF	PROCEDURE	VAR
DO	IN	PROGRAM	WHILE
DOWNTO	LABEL	RECORD	WITH
ELSE	MOD	REPEAT	

THE GOTO STATEMENT

Programming in Pascal is done with constructions intended to accomplish specific purposes, such as the IF and CASE statements for selection, the FOR, WHILE, and REPEAT statements for repetition, and function and procedure declarations for providing building blocks from which to construct a program.

On rare occasions we may want the computer to leave one of these constructions before reaching its end. For this purpose Pascal provides the GOTO statement, which causes the computer to jump to a specified point in the program. Execution continues from the point to which the computer jumps.

The following example illustrates a GOTO statement:

```
    GOTO 25;
    . . .
25: I := 5;
    . . .
```

The integer 25 is a *label*. A colon separates the label from the statement it labels.

When the computer executes

```
GOTO 25
```

it immediately goes to the statement labeled 25, executes that statement, and continues execution with the following statement.

A label must be declared in the block in which it is used to label a statement. The declaration has the following form:

```
LABEL 25;
```

Including the label declaration in our example gives us

```
LABEL 25;
...
BEGIN
   ...
   GOTO 25;
   ...
25: I := 5;
   ...
END
```

A label can only be used to label one statement (otherwise, the computer would not know which statement to go to). A label is an unsigned integer constant of up to four digits. Do not confuse the labels used with GOTO statements with the labels for the different cases in a CASE statement. The two kinds of labels are completely different. It is not permitted to jump *into* a structure such as an IF, CASE, FOR, WHILE, or REPEAT statement or a function or a procedure. It is permissible to jump *out* of such a structure, however.

Label declarations precede all the other declarations and definitions at the beginning of a block. The following shows the order of all the declarations and definitions permitted in Pascal:

- label declarations

- constant definitions

- type definitions

- variable declarations

- function and procedure declarations

GOTO statements make a program harder to read, understand, and debug. They are almost never required in a properly designed program, and their use is emphatically not recommended. People used to programming in BASIC or FORTRAN are in the habit of using GOTO statements, which are required in those languages. The "GOTO habit" must be broken, however, if one is to become competent in Pascal or any other modern programming language.

DECLARATIONS ASSUMED IN THE TEXT

Except where explicitly stated otherwise, the variables X, Y, Z, I, J, K, P, Q, and C are assumed to have the following declarations:

```
VAR
    X, Y, Z: REAL;
    I, J, K: INTEGER;
    P, Q: BOOLEAN;
    C: CHAR;
```

FOR FURTHER READING

A textbook is often not the most convenient reference when you are writing and debugging your programs. If at all possible, you should get a copy of the reference manual for the version of Pascal you are using. The following are two good general reference books on Pascal:

Tiberghien, Jacques. *The Pascal Handbook.* Berkeley: SYBEX, Inc., 1981.

Watt, David. *Addison-Wesley Pocket Guide to Pascal.* Reading, Mass: Addison-Wesley Publishing Company, 1982.

The following can be used for additional reading on Pascal and its applications:

Bowles, Kenneth L. *Microcomputer Problem Solving Using PASCAL.* New York: Springer-Verlag, 1977.

Conway, R.; Gries, D.; and Zimmerman, E. C. *A Primer on PASCAL.* Cambridge, Mass.: Winthrope Publishers, 1976.

Grogono, Peter. *Programming in PASCAL.* Reading, Mass.: Addison-Wesley Publishing Company, 1978.

Jensen, Kathleen; and Wirth, Niklaus. *PASCAL User Manual and Report.* Berlin: Springer-Verlag, 1974.

Schneider, G. M.; Weingart, S. W.; and Perlman, D. M. *An Introduction to Programming and Problem Solving with PASCAL.* New York: John Wiley & Sons, 1978.

Wirth, Niklaus. *Systematic Programming.* Englewood Cliffs, N. J.: Prentice-Hall, 1973.

_____. *Algorithms + Data Structures = Programs.* Englewood Cliffs, N. J.: Prentice-Hall, 1976.

INDEX

A

ABS (standard function), 55
Access
  random, 4, 7, 256–69
  sequential, 6, 237–56
Accumulating totals, 37
Accumulator, 37
Actual parameters, 54, 110
Addition operator, 24, 50–52
ADDRECORD (procedure), 255–57
Address, 4
ALARM (procedure), 141
Algorithm, blackjack dealer's, 93–96
AND (operator), 61–63
Applications software, 7
Arguments, 54
Arithmetic expressions, 24–25
Arithmetic in Pascal, 23–25
Arithmetic operators, 24
  priorities of, 50–52, 61–62
ARITHMETIC (program), 25
ARRAY (reserved word), 145ff
Arrays, 145–71
  assignment of, 151
  components of, 145ff
  dimensions of, 166
  input of, 151–52, 168–69
  multidimensional, 165–71
  one-dimensional, 145–53
  output of, 151–52, 168–69
  packed, 153–54
  parallel, 157
  use of FOR statement with, 149–51
Array variables, 146
Arrow
  in buffer variable, 238
  in pointer type definitions, 218–19
  in pointer variable references,
    219
ASCII character code, 5
  collating sequence for, 60
Assembly language, 8
Assignment
  of arrays, 151
  of records, 209
Assignment operator, 32
Assignment statement, 32–37
Assumed declarations, 32, 291

B

Base type, 273
  limitations, on, 274
BASIC, 8–9
Becomes (assignment operator), 32
BEGIN (reserved word), 23, 68
Binary digits, 5
Binary search, 179–83
BINARYTREE (program), 223–31
Binary trees, 220–31
Binary tree search, 220–31
Bits, 5
Blackjack dealer's algorithm, 93–96
Block, 118–23
Bookkeeping, 190

BOOK (record), 209
Boole, George, 15
BOOLEAN (standard data type), 12,
    15, 31, 135
Boolean expressions, 58–63
    in IF statement, 91ff
    in REPEAT statement, 84, 85
    in WHILE statement, 76, 77
Boolean operators, 61–63
    priorities of, 62
BOXES (program), 117–18
BOX (procedure), 116–18
Braces (curley brackets)
    for enclosing comments, 22
    for enclosing sets in mathematics,
        273
Brackets
    for enclosing array indices, 146ff
    for enclosing sets, 273ff
Branch, of binary tree, 220
Bubble sort, 183–90
BUBBLESORT (procedure), 185–86
BUBBLESRT (procedure), 188-90
Buffer variable, 238
Building blocks, 109
Byte, 5

C

Card readers, 5–6
CAR (record), 209
CASE
    in record definition, 214–16
    statement, 97, 102–5, 143
Central processing unit, 4–5
CHANGE2 (program), 163–65
CHAR (standard data type), 15, 31,
    135, 140–42
CHESSMAN (data type), 136
Children, of node, 220–21
CHR (standard function), 141–42
CLOSE (procedure), 247
CLR (function), 142–43
COBOL, 8–9
Collating sequence, 60
Collision, 259
Colon
    in declarations, 31
    in output statements, 17ff
COLOR (data type), 136
Columns, of two-dimensional array,
    165–66
Comments, 22–23
Compare-and-exchange pass, 184
Compiler, 9

COMPLEX (record), 210
Components
    of array, 145ff
    of computer, 4–7
    of file, 237ff
    of record, 207ff
    of set, 273ff
Component type, 146
Compound statement, 23, 68–69
Computer, 1, 4–7
    components of, 4–7
    general purpose, 3
    special purpose, 3
Computer firmware, 3
Computer hardware, 3–7
Computer portraits, 2
Computer programming, 2–4
Computer software, 3, 7–10
Computer terminals, 5–6
Concatenation, 161
CONCAT (standard function), 161
Constant definitions, 43–44
Constants
    Boolean, 14
    character, 14
    integer, 12
    real, 13–14
    string, 15–16
    programmer defined, 43–44
CONST (reserved word), 43–44
Constructor, set, 275
CONVERT (program), 52–53
COPY (standard function), 161
CPU, 5
CREATEMASTER (program), 248–50
CREATETRANS (program), 250–51
Curly brackets (braces)
    for enclosing comments, 22
    for enclosing sets in mathematics,
        273
CYLINDER (program), 56–57

D

Data, reading of, 79–84
Data types, 11–16
    definitions of, 136
    enumerated, 136ff
    ordinal, 135–43
    simple, 135–43
    standard, 12–16, 135
    subrange, 138ff
DATE (record), 210
DAY (data type), 136
DAY (record), 210

DEALER (program), 93–96
Declarations
    assumed, 291
    function, 109-12
    nested, 120-23
    procedure, 115
    set, 273-74
    variable, 30-32
Dedicated computer, 3
Definitions
    constant, 43–44
    data type, 136
    of file types, 237–38
    of pointer types, 218–19
    of record types, 207–10
DELETE
    standard procedure, 162–63
    procedure in hash-file program,
      267
DELETERECORD (procedure),
    255–57
Difference, 275–76
Digitizer, 2
Dimension of array, 166
Diskette, 1–2, 6–7
DISPOSE (procedure), 220
Dividing-line value, in Quicksort,
    192ff
Division operators, 24–25, 50–52
DIV operator, 24–25, 50–52
in change-making program, 45–46
DO (reserved word)
    in FOR statement, 67–68
    in WHILE statement, 76
DOWNTO (reserved word), 68
Dynamic variables, 218

E

Elements, of set, 273
ELSE part, of IF statement, 92
    matching with proper IF
      statement, 98–99
EMPLOYEE (record), 209
Empty sequence, 238–39
Empty set, 274
END (reserved word)
    in CASE statement, 102-3
    in record definitions, 207ff
    statement bracket, 23, 68
Enumerated types, 136ff
EOF (standard predicate), 81–82, 239,
    243
EOLN (standard predicate), 241, 243
Exponent, 13

Exponential notation, 13–14
Expressions, 23–25, 49–63
    Boolean, 58–63
    containing sets, 276–77
    operator priorities in, 50–52, 61–62
    parentheses in, 50–52
    variables in, 34–37
    with more than one operator,
      49–52
External files, 245–47
External sorting, 183

F

FACTORIAL (function), 113–15,
    118–19
    recursive version of, 127–28
FALSE (Boolean constant), 15
FIBONACCI (program), 72–73
Fibonacci's problem, 72–73
Field designators, 208
    compared with indexed variables,
      208–9
Field identifiers, 207-8
    scopes of, 216–18
Field-width parameters, 17–19
FILE (reserved word), 237
Files, 237–69
    external, 245–47
    interactive, 244–45
    local, 245
    random, 256-69
    sequential, 237–56
    text, 244–45
File-update problem, 247–56
FILEUPDATE (program), 251–56
File window, 237
FIND (procedure)
    in binary-tree program, 226–27
    in hash-file program, 262–65
Firmware, 3
Fixed-length strings, 155–59
Fixed part, of variant record, 213–16
Floating-point notation, 13–14
Formal parameters, 110ff
    declarations of, 110
FOR statement, 67–76, 143
    nested, 75–76, 168–71
    use of ordinal types in, 143
    use with arrays, 149–51
FORTRAN, 8–9
FRACDEMO (program), 112
FRAC (function), 110–12
FRACTION (record), 210
Function declaration, 109–12

Function designator, 54
Function header, 110
FUNCTION (reserved word), 110
Functions, 109–15
    standard, 54–56

G

GAME (program), 126
GETDATA (procedure), 168
GETNEXTKEY (procedure), 254–255
GET (standard procedure), 239
Global variables, 123–26
GOTO statement, 289–90
GRADE (data type), 136

H

Hanoi, Towers of, 128–31
HANOI (program), 130–31
Hardware, 3–7
HASHFILE (program), 262–69
HASH (function), 259, 267–69
Hashing, 258–69
Header
    function, 110
    procedure, 115
    program, 21–22
Higher-level languages, 8–9
Host type, 138

I

Identifiers, 20–21
    scopes of, 118–23
IF statement, 91–92
    in multiway selection, 99–102
    in one-way selection, 91
    in two-way selection, 92
    nested, 97–99
Indentation
    of compound statements, 23
    of FOR statements, 67–69
    of nested IF statements, 98–99
Indexed variables, 146
    compared with field designators,
        208–9
Index type, 146
    ordinal types as, 148
Index values, 145ff
Information processing, 1–2
INITIALIZE (program), 260–62
Input devices, 5–6
INPUT (standard file), 22, 243–44
IN (relational operator), 276–77

INSERT
    in binary-tree program, 228–31
    in hash-file program, 265–67
    standard procedure, 162
INTEGER (standard data type),
        11–12, 31, 135
Integer variable, 30
Interactive files, 244–45
Interactive programs, 39–40
    reading data for, 79–84
Internal sorting, 183
Interpreters, 9
Intersection, of sets, 275–76
Inventor-of-chess problem, 73–75
INVESTMENT (program), 70–71
INVESTMENTS (program), 85–87
Item counts, 79–80

K

Key, 247
KEYBOARD (standard file), 281

L

LABEL (reserved word), 289-90
Language processors, 9
Lazy evaluation, 244–45
Left child, of node, 221
LENGTH (standard function), 162
Line printers, 6
Line separator, 241
Linked list, 231–32
Linker, 10
LISP, 8–9
List, linked, 231–32
LISTMASTER (program), 251
Loading factor, 260
Local files, 245
Local variables, 114, 123
LOCK, in CLOSE procedure, 247
Logo, 8–9

M

Machine language, 7–8
Magnetic disks, 1–2, 6–7
Magnetic tape, 6–7
MAKECHANGE (program), 44–46
MAKENODE (function), 230–31
Mask, 279
Master file, 247
MASTER (record), 249
MAXINT (integer constant), 12

Memory
auxiliary, 4, 6–7
main, 1, 4–5
MESSAGE (program), 21–23
Microcomputer, 6
Microprocessor, 5
MILLIONAIRE (program), 78-79
MOD (operator), 24–25, 50–52
in change-making (program),
45–46
MONTH (data type), 136
MOVE (procedure), 130–31
Multidimensional arrays, 165–71
Multiplication operator, 24, 50–52
Multiway selection, 97–105

N

Named memory locations, 29–30
Nesting
of FOR statements, 75–76, 168–71
of function and procedure
declarations, 120–23
of parentheses, 52
of records, 210–12
NEW (standard procedure), 219
NEXT (function), 259, 267–69
NIL (pointer constant), 220
Node, of binary tree, 220
NODE (record), 222
Noninteractive programs, 40–41
reading data for, 79–84
NOT (operator), 61-63
Null string, 159–60

O

OF (reserved word)
in array declarations, 145ff
in CASE statement, 102
in record with variant parts,
214–16
One-dimensional arrays, 145–53
One-way selection, 91–92
OPENFILES (procedure), 253–54
Operand, 24
Operating system, 9–10
Operations, on sets, 275–77
Operator priorities, 50–52, 61–62
Operators
arithmetic, 24
Boolean, 61–63
on ordinal types, 139
relational, 59–61, 139, 157, 161,
276–77

on sets, 275–77
Order
of definitions and declarations,
136, 290
of values of ordinal types, 149
Ordinal numbers, 140
Ordinal types, 135–43
as index types, 148
ORD (standard function), 140–42
OR (operator), 61–63
Output devices, 5–6
OUTPUT (standard file), 22, 243–44
Overhead, 190

P

Packed arrays, 153–54
PACKED (reserved word), 153–54
PACK (standard procedure), 154
Padding, 158
PAGE (procedure), 241, 243
Parallel arrays, 157
Parameters
actual, 54, 110
field-width, 17–19
formal, 110ff
value, 116
variable, 116–18
Parentheses
for enclosing record variant,
214–16
in expressions, 51–52
nested, 52
PASSENGER (record), 210
PATTERN (program), 75–76
PAY (program), 82–83
PAYROLL (program), 83-84
Period,
at end of program, 23
in field designator, 208
Personal computer, 6
Personal investment, 70–71
PERSON (record), 211
Pointer types, 218–31
Political poll, example of array
processing, 166–71
POS (standard function), 161–62
Post-office box analogy, 4
PRED (standard function), 140
PRICERECORD (record), 261
PRICES (program), 177–79
Printers, 5–6
PRINTFACTORIALS (program), 114,
118–19
PRINTVOL (procedure), 115–16

Procedure header, 115
PROCEDURE (reserved word), 115
Procedures, 109, 115–18
Procedure statement, 115–16
PROCESSTRANSACTIONS
        (procedure), 255–56
Program, 2–4
Program header, 21–22
PROGRAM (reserved word), 21–22
Programming, 2–4
Programming languages, 7–9
Prompts, 39–40
Pseudorandom numbers, 124–26
PURGE, in CLOSE procedure, 247
PUT (standard procedure), 240

Q

Quicksort, 192–203
QUICKSORT (procedure), 197–98
QUICKSRT (procedure), 198–99
QUIKSORT (procedure), 201–2
Quotient-remainder division, 25

R

RAM (random-access memory), 4
Random access
    for auxiliary memory, 7
    for files, 256–69
    for main memory, 4
RANDOM (function), 124–26
READ
    as standard procedure, 116
    statement, 37–38, 241–44
Reading data, 79–84
READLN
    as standard procedure, 116
    statement, 37–38, 241–44
Read-only memory, 4
Read-write head, 7
REAL (standard data type), 31, 135
Real variable, 30
Record definitions, 207–10
    nested, 210–12
RECORD (reserved word), 207
Records, 207–31
Record variables, 208–9
Record variants, 213–16
RECTANGLE (program), 57–58
Recursion, 127–31
    in Quicksort, 192–203
    removal of, 198–203
    tail, 198–99
REFERENCE (record), 214–16

Relational operators, 59–61
    for ordinal types, 139, 276–77
    priorities of, 61, 277
    for strings, 157, 161
REPEAT statement, 84–87
    contrasted with WHILE
        statement, 85
Repetition, 67–87
Reserved words, 20
    list of, 287
RESET (procedure), 238–39
    in UCSD Pascal, 246
REWRITE (procedure), 239
    in UCSD Pascal, 246–47
Right child, of node, 221
ROM (read-only memory), 4
Root, of binary tree, 220
ROUND (standard function), 55–56
Rows, of two-dimensional arrays,
        165–66

S

SALESCOMMISSION (program),
        104–5
Scanner, 280–82
SCAN (program), 280–82
Scopes
    of field identifiers, 216–18
    of identifiers, 118–23
Search, 175–83
    binary, 179–83
    binary-tree, 220–31
    sequential, 175–79
SEARCH procedure
    using binary search, 180–82
    using sequential search, 177–78
Seed, for pseudorandom number
        generator, 124–26
SEEK (standard procedure), 256–58
Selection, 91–105
    multiway, 97–105
    one-way, 91–92
    two-way, 92–96
Selector expression, 103
Sentinel, 80–81
    in sequential search, 176–77
Separator, line, 241
Sequential access, for files, 237–56
Sequential search, 175–79
Set constructor, 275
Set declarations, 273–74
SET (reserved word), 273
Sets, 273–82
Shell sort, 190–92

SHELLSORT (procedure), 191–92
Simple data types, 135–43
Software, 3, 7–10
Sorting, 183-203
    external, 183
    internal, 183
SORTTEST (program), 185–88
SQR (standard function), 54–55
SQRT (standard function), 55
Stack, 200–201
    array representation of, 200–201
    linked list representation of, 233
STACK (data type), 232–33
Standard data types, 135
Standard functions, 54–56
Statement part, 23
Static variables, 218
Stepwise refinement, 75–76
String assignment
    for fixed-length strings, 155–56
    for variable-length strings, 160
String constants, 15–16, 155ff
String input
    for fixed-length strings, 156–57
    for variable-length strings, 160–61
String output
    for fixed-length strings, 156
    for variable-length strings, 160–61
STRING (standard data type), 159–65
Strings, 155–65
    fixed-length, 155–59
    variable-length, 159–65
Structured types
    arrays, 145–71
    records, 207–31
    files, 237–69
    sets, 273–82
Subrange types, 138ff
Subset, 277
Subtraction operator, 24, 50–52
SUCC (standard function), 140
Superset, 277
Symbol, 280
System software, 7–10

T

Tables
    translation, 152–53
    two-dimensional arrays as, 165–66
Tag field, 214–16
Tail recursion, 198–99
TAX (program), 41–43
    noninteractive version of, 43
Temperature conversion, 52–53

TEMPERATURES (program), 149–51
Text files (also called textfiles),
    240–44
THEN (reserved word), 91
TO (reserved word), 67–68
Top, of stack, 200
Towers of Hanoi, 128–31
Transaction file, 247
TRANSACTION (record), 251
Translation tables, 152–53
Translator, 9–10
TRIANGLES (program), 101–2
TRUE (Boolean constant), 15
TRUNC (standard function), 55–56
Two-way selection, 92–96
TYPE (reserved word), 136

U

UCSD Pascal, 11–12, 17, 39–40,
    154–55, 159–65, 225
    external files, 245–47
    interactive files, 244–45
    KEYBOARD file, 281
    limitations on sets, 274
    random access, 256ff
    program header, 22
    STRING type, 159–65
Union, 275–76
UNPACK (standard procedure), 154
UNTIL, in REPEAT statement, 84
UPDATERECORD (procedure),
    255–57

V

Value, 11
    dividing-line, 192–97
    returned by function, 110, 114–15
    returned via variable parameter,
        116–18
    of variable, 30
Value parameters, 116
Variable declarations, 30–32
Variable-length strings, 159–65
Variable name, 30
Variable parameters, 116–18
Variables, 29ff
    array, 146
    buffer, 238
    dynamic, 218
    in expressions, 34–37
    global, 123–26
    indexed, 146
    local, 114, 123

record, 208–9
    static, 218
Variant part, 213–16
Variants, record, 213–16
VAR (reserved word), 31
Video games, 2
VOLUME (function), 112–13

W

WHEAT (program), 73–75
WHILE statement, 76–79
    contrasted with REPEAT, 85

Window, file, 237
WITH statement, 212–13
Word processing, 1–2
WRITE, as predefined procedure,
    116
WRITELN, as predefined procedure,
    116
WRITELN statement, 16–20, 241–44
WRITE statement, 19–20, 241–44

†